First World War
and Army of Occupation
War Diary
France, Belgium and Germany

21 DIVISION
Divisional Troops
Royal Army Medical Corps
65 Field Ambulance
28 August 1915 - 5 June 1919

WO95/2148/1

The Naval & Military Press Ltd
www.nmarchive.com
Published in association with The National Archives

Published by

The Naval & Military Press Ltd

Unit 10 Ridgewood Industrial Park,

Uckfield, East Sussex,

TN22 5QE England

Tel: +44 (0) 1825 749494

www.naval-military-press.com

www.nmarchive.com

This diary has been reprinted in facsimile from the original. Any imperfections are inevitably reproduced and the quality may fall short of modern type and cartographic standards.

© **Crown Copyright**
Images reproduced by permission of The National Archives, London, England, 2015.

Contents

Document type	Place/Title	Date From	Date To
Heading	WO95/2148/1 65 Field Ambulance		
Heading	21st Division 65th Field Ambulance Aug 1915-1919 Jun		
Heading	21st Division 65th Field Ambulance Vol I August & Sept 15		
War Diary	Willy Camp	28/08/1915	10/09/1915
War Diary	Southampton	10/09/1915	10/09/1915
War Diary	Havre	11/09/1915	12/09/1915
War Diary	Audruicq	13/09/1915	13/09/1915
War Diary	Lostrat	13/09/1915	20/09/1915
War Diary	Nordasques	20/09/1915	20/09/1915
War Diary	Arques	21/09/1915	21/09/1915
War Diary	Mazinghem	22/09/1915	22/09/1915
War Diary	Bellery	22/09/1915	24/09/1915
War Diary	Four A Chaux	25/09/1915	25/09/1915
War Diary	Mazingarbe	25/09/1915	28/09/1915
Heading	21st Division 65th Field Ambulance Vol 2 Oct 15		
Heading	War Diary Of No. 65 Field Ambulance From 24.9.15 To 31.10.15		
War Diary	Bethune	29/09/1915	29/09/1915
War Diary	Auchy Au Bois	30/09/1915	01/10/1915
War Diary	Boeseghem	01/10/1915	02/10/1915
War Diary	Caestre	02/10/1915	31/10/1915
Heading	21st Division 65th Field Ambulance Vol 3 Nov 15		
War Diary	Caestre	01/11/1915	30/11/1915
Heading	21st Div. 65th F.a. Vol 4		
War Diary	Caestre	01/12/1915	31/12/1915
Heading	21st Division F/165/2 65 F.A Jan 1916 65th F.A. Vol 5		
War Diary	Caestre	01/01/1916	31/01/1916
Heading	Feb 1916 65th Field Ambulance		
Heading	65 F.A. 21st Div. Vol 6		
Miscellaneous	Herewith A.Fs C2118		
Heading	War Diary Of 65th Field Ambulance (West Lancs T.F.) From 1st February To 29th February (Volume VI)		
War Diary	Caestre Field Ambulance Hill Admg As Regt Station For 21st Division	01/02/1916	10/02/1916
War Diary	Caestre	11/02/1916	29/02/1916
Heading	21st Division March 1916 No 65 F. Amb		
Heading	65 Field Amb Vol 7		
War Diary	Caestre	01/03/1916	31/03/1916
Heading	April 1916 No. 65 F.A.		
War Diary	La Neuville	01/04/1916	06/04/1916
War Diary	Ville	08/04/1916	30/04/1916
Heading	War Diary Of 65 Field Ambulance From May 1st 1916 To May 31st 1916 Vol VIII		
War Diary	Ville	01/05/1916	31/05/1916
Miscellaneous	D.A.G. 3rd Echelon		
Heading	War Diary Of 65 Field Ambulance Volume IX June 1916		
War Diary	Ville	01/06/1916	04/06/1916

War Diary	Ville-Mill	04/06/1916	05/06/1916
War Diary	Ville	06/06/1916	20/06/1916
War Diary	Ville Mill	20/06/1916	28/06/1916
War Diary	Chateau E 26a64 Map Albert	28/06/1916	30/06/1916
Heading	21st Division 65th Field Ambulance July 1916		
War Diary	Meaulte (Chateau E22 A 64	01/07/1916	02/07/1916
War Diary	Meaulte	03/07/1916	04/07/1916
War Diary		03/07/1916	03/07/1916
War Diary	Le Mesge	08/07/1916	10/07/1916
War Diary	Ville Mill	04/07/1916	05/07/1916
War Diary	Picquigny	05/07/1916	07/07/1916
War Diary	Chateau	12/07/1916	13/07/1916
War Diary		10/07/1916	10/07/1916
War Diary	Ville Mill	11/07/1916	11/07/1916
War Diary	Chateau	11/07/1916	19/07/1916
War Diary	Allonville	20/07/1916	20/07/1916
War Diary	Argoeuves	21/07/1916	22/07/1916
War Diary	Langue St Pol	22/07/1916	22/07/1916
War Diary	Sars-Lez-Bois	23/07/1916	31/07/1916
Miscellaneous	Appendix No 1		
Miscellaneous	Appendix No 2		
Miscellaneous	Appendix No. 3		
Heading	War Diary Of 65th Field Ambulance From Aug 1st 1916 To Aug 31st 1916 Volume XI		
War Diary	Liencourt	01/08/1916	31/08/1916
Heading	21st Div 65th Field Ambulance Sept 1916		
Heading	War Diary Of 65th Field Ambulance September 1916 Volume XII		
War Diary	Liencourt	01/09/1916	11/09/1916
War Diary	On March	12/09/1916	14/09/1916
War Diary	Dernancourt	15/09/1916	15/09/1916
War Diary	Pommiers	16/09/1916	16/09/1916
War Diary	Divl Coll Stn	17/09/1916	24/09/1916
War Diary	Divl Rest Stn	24/09/1916	27/09/1916
War Diary	Divl Coll Stn	27/09/1916	30/09/1916
Heading	War Diary Of 65th Field Ambulance 21st Div From 1st October 1916 To 31st October 1916 Volume XIII		
War Diary	Ribemont	01/10/1916	02/10/1916
War Diary	Bulgny L'Abbe	03/10/1916	07/10/1916
War Diary	Haut Rieux	08/10/1916	10/10/1916
War Diary	Labourse	11/10/1916	31/10/1916
Heading	21st Div War Diary Of The 65th Field Ambulance From November 1st 1916 To November 30th 1916 Volume 15		
War Diary	Labourse	01/11/1916	30/11/1916
Heading	21st Div. 65th Field Ambulance Dec 1916		
War Diary	Labourse	01/12/1916	31/12/1916
Heading	21st Div 65th Field Ambulance		
War Diary	Allovagne	01/01/1917	26/01/1917
War Diary	Poperinghe	27/01/1917	31/01/1917
Heading	21st Div. 65th Field Ambulance		
War Diary	Poperinghe	01/02/1917	11/02/1917
War Diary	On The March	12/02/1917	13/02/1917
War Diary	Bethune	14/02/1917	28/02/1917
Heading	21st Div. 65th Field Ambulance March 1917		
War Diary	Bethune	01/03/1917	02/03/1917

War Diary	Hamen Artois	03/03/1917	08/03/1917
War Diary	Lignylez Aire	09/03/1917	09/03/1917
War Diary	Valhuon	10/03/1917	10/03/1917
War Diary	Honval	11/03/1917	11/03/1917
War Diary	Halloy	12/03/1917	25/03/1917
War Diary	Lacauchie	26/03/1917	28/03/1917
War Diary	Humbercamp	29/03/1917	29/03/1917
War Diary	Boiry Ste Rictrude	31/03/1917	31/03/1917
Heading	21st Div. War Diary Of The 65th Field Ambulance (3rd W. Lancs T.F) From April 1st 1917 To April 30th 1917 Volume (Pages)		
Miscellaneous	B.E.F. Summary Of Medical War Diaries For 65th F.A. 21st Divn. 7th Corps. 3rd Army Western Front. April-May 17		
Miscellaneous	65th F.A. 21st Divn. 7th Corps. O.C. Lt. Col/Thompson 3rd Army	17/04/1917	17/04/1917
War Diary	Boiry St Rictrude	01/04/1917	13/04/1917
War Diary	S12 D.7.4 Boyelles	14/04/1917	15/04/1917
War Diary	Boiry Ste Rictrude	15/04/1917	26/04/1917
War Diary	Boyelles	27/04/1917	30/04/1917
Heading	War Diary Of The 65th Field Ambulance (3rd W. Lancs T.F) From 1/5/1917 To 31/5/1917 Volume (Pages)		
Miscellaneous	Summary Of Medical War Diaries For 65th F.A. 21st Divn. 7th Corps 3rd Army Western Front April-May 17		
Miscellaneous	65th F.A. 21st Divn. 7th Corps. O.C. Lt. Col/Thompson 3rd Army	17/05/1917	17/05/1917
War Diary	Boyelles 518f.7.5	01/05/1917	04/05/1917
War Diary	Boyelles	05/05/1917	11/05/1917
War Diary	Basseux	12/05/1917	31/05/1917
Heading	War Diary Of The 65th Field Ambulance (3rd W. Lancs. T.F) From 1st June 1917 To 30th June 1917 Volume XXI (5 Page)		
War Diary	St Leger	01/06/1917	19/06/1917
War Diary	Basseux	20/06/1917	24/06/1917
War Diary	La Cauchie	15/06/1917	30/06/1917
Heading	No. 65. F.A. July 1917		
War Diary	La Cauchie	01/07/1917	31/07/1917
Heading	War Diary Of The 65th Field Ambulance (3rd W. Lancs T.F) From 1st August 1917 To 31st August 1917 Volume XXIII		
War Diary	La Cauchie	01/08/1917	25/08/1917
War Diary	Avesnes Le Comte	26/08/1917	31/08/1917
Heading	War Diary Of The 65th Field Ambulance (3rd W. Lancs. T.F) From 1/9/17 To 30/9/17 Volume XXIV		
War Diary	Avesnes Le-Comte	01/09/1917	16/09/1917
War Diary	Pradelles	17/09/1917	24/09/1917
War Diary	Boeschepe	25/09/1917	30/09/1917
Heading	War Diary Of The 65th Field Ambulance (3rd W. Lancs. T.F.) From 1/10/1917 To 31/10/1917 Volume XXV		
War Diary	Boeschepe (R10.A. 2.8 Sheet 27)	01/10/1917	09/10/1917
War Diary	La Belle Hotesse	10/10/1917	19/10/1917
War Diary	Dickebusch A 34 A. 08	20/10/1917	31/10/1917
Heading	War Diary Of The 65th Field Ambulance (3rd W. Lancs T.F) From 1/11/1917 To 30/11/1917 Volume XXVI		
War Diary	Dickebusch	01/11/1917	14/11/1917

War Diary	G 21. C. 6.7		15/11/1917	17/11/1917
War Diary	Doulieu		18/11/1917	18/11/1917
War Diary	La Couronne		19/11/1917	19/11/1917
War Diary	Annezin		20/11/1917	20/11/1917
War Diary	Barlin		21/11/1917	24/11/1917
War Diary	Mingoval		25/11/1917	30/11/1917
Heading	War Diary Of The 65th Field Ambulance (3rd W. Lancs T.F.) From 1/12/1917 To 31/12/1917 Volume 28			
War Diary	Hamel		01/12/1917	02/12/1917
War Diary	Tincourt		03/12/1917	31/12/1917
Heading	War Diary Of The 65th Field Ambulance (3rd W. Lancs T.F) From 1/1/18 To 31/1/18 Volume XXVIII			
War Diary	Tincourt		01/01/1918	03/01/1918
War Diary	Hamel		04/01/1918	25/01/1918
War Diary	Lieramont		26/01/1918	26/01/1918
War Diary	Lieramont D18.b.8.6		27/01/1918	31/01/1918
Heading	War Diary Of The 65th Field Ambulance (3rd W. Lancs T.F) From 1/2/1918 To 28/2/1918 Volume XXIX			
War Diary	Lieramont (D 18.f 8.6 Sheet 62.c)		01/02/1918	04/02/1918
War Diary	Lieramont Covercoat Camp		05/02/1918	28/02/1918
Heading	War Diary Of The 65th Field Ambulance (3rd W. Lancs. T.F) From 1/3/1918 To 31/3/1918 Volume XXX			
War Diary	Lieramont		01/03/1918	22/03/1918
War Diary	Bussu		23/03/1918	23/03/1918
War Diary	Maricourt		24/03/1918	24/03/1918
War Diary	Bray		25/03/1918	25/03/1918
War Diary	Sailly Le Sec		26/03/1918	26/03/1918
War Diary	Contay		27/03/1918	28/03/1918
War Diary	Molliens Aux Bois		29/03/1918	30/03/1918
War Diary	Hangest Sur-Somme		31/03/1918	31/03/1918
Heading	War Diary Of The 65th Field Ambulance (3rd W Lancs TF) From 1/4/1918 To 30/4/1918 Volume XXXI			
War Diary	Hangest S. Somme		01/04/1918	02/04/1918
War Diary	Mont. Des Cats		03/04/1918	09/04/1918
War Diary	Wippenhoek		10/04/1918	29/04/1918
War Diary	27/Kid.C.44		29/04/1918	30/04/1918
Heading	No. 65 F.A. May 1918			
Heading	War Diary Of The 65th Field Ambulance (3rd W. Lancs T.F) From 1/5/18 To 31/5/18 Volume XXXII			
War Diary	Lederzeele		01/05/1918	05/05/1918
War Diary	Jonquery		06/05/1918	12/05/1918
War Diary	Pevy		12/05/1918	12/05/1918
War Diary	Vaux Varennes (Chateau)		13/05/1918	27/05/1918
War Diary	Pevy & Ville En Tardendis		28/05/1918	28/05/1918
War Diary	Mareuil Le Porte		29/05/1918	29/05/1918
War Diary	Vauciennes		30/05/1918	30/05/1918
War Diary	Chaltrait		31/05/1918	31/05/1918
Heading	War Diary Of The 65th Field Ambulance (3rd W. Lancs T.F) From 1/6/18 To 30/6/18 Volume XXXIV			
War Diary	Chaltrait		01/06/1918	02/06/1918
War Diary	Congy		03/06/1918	08/06/1918
War Diary	Les Essarts		09/06/1918	15/06/1918
War Diary	Pont Remy		16/06/1918	16/06/1918
War Diary	Lambercourt		16/06/1918	17/06/1918
War Diary	Neuville Coppegueule		18/06/1918	21/06/1918
War Diary	Flocques		22/06/1918	30/06/1918

Heading	War Diary Of The 65th Field Ambulance (3rd W. Lancs T.F) From 1/7/18 To 31/7/18 Volume XXXIV		
War Diary	Talmas	01/07/1918	31/07/1918
Heading	War Diary Of The 65th Field Ambulance (3rd W. Lancs T.F) From 1/8/18 To 31/8/18 Volume XXXV		
War Diary	Talmas	01/08/1918	25/08/1918
War Diary	Mailly-Maillet	25/08/1918	25/08/1918
War Diary	In The Line (Mish 09) Sheet 57c	26/08/1918	28/08/1918
War Diary	M 23.a.93 Sheet 57c	28/08/1918	31/08/1918
Heading	War Diary Of The 65th Field Ambulance (3rd W. Lancs. T.F) From 1/9/18 To 30/9/18 Volume XXXVI		
War Diary	In The Field	01/09/1918	08/09/1918
War Diary	In The Field W 14 F 33	09/09/1918	19/09/1918
War Diary	W22 F.8)	20/09/1918	20/09/1918
War Diary	T3d Central	21/09/1918	23/09/1918
War Diary	V 2d 3.8	24/09/1918	30/09/1918
Heading	War Diary Of The 65th Field Ambulance (3rd W. Lancs T.F) From 1/10/18 To 31/10/18 Volume XXXVII		
War Diary	V 2d 3.8	01/10/1918	04/10/1918
War Diary	W 4 6.6.8	06/10/1918	07/10/1918
War Diary	R 36a 5.9	08/10/1918	08/10/1918
War Diary	M 28. C. 30	09/10/1918	10/10/1918
War Diary	O.15.a.5.6	11/10/1918	11/10/1918
War Diary	Caullery	12/10/1918	22/10/1918
War Diary	Inchy	23/10/1918	23/10/1918
War Diary	Neuvilly	24/10/1918	24/10/1918
War Diary	Vendegies	24/10/1918	25/10/1918
War Diary	Ovillers	26/10/1918	28/10/1918
War Diary	Vendegies F7d.73	29/10/1918	31/10/1918
Heading	War Diary Of The 65th Field Ambulance (3rd W. Lancs T.F) From 1/11/18 To 30/11/18 Volume XXXVIII		
War Diary	Vendegies	01/11/1918	08/11/1918
War Diary	T24 D 6.4	09/11/1918	10/11/1918
War Diary	V 23 b.3.7.	11/11/1918	26/11/1918
War Diary	Limont Fontaine	27/11/1918	30/11/1918
Heading	War Diary Of The 65th Field Ambulance (3rd W. Lancs T.F) From 1/12/18 To 31/12/18 Volume XXXIX		
War Diary	Limont Fontaine	01/12/1918	17/12/1918
War Diary	On The March	18/12/1918	31/12/1918
Heading	21 Div Box 1876 War Diary Of The 65th Field Ambulance (3rd W. Lancs T.F) From 1/1/19 To 31/1/19 Volume XL		
War Diary	Saveuse	01/01/1919	31/01/1919
Heading	Feb 1919 No. 65 F.A.		
War Diary	Saveuse	01/02/1919	28/02/1919
Heading	War Diary Of The 65th Field Ambulance (3rd W. Lancs T.F) From 1/3/19 To 31/3/19 Volume XLII		
War Diary	Saveuse	01/03/1919	11/03/1919
War Diary	Ailly S. Somme	12/03/1919	31/03/1919
Heading	War Diary Of The 65th Field Ambulance (West Lancs T.F.) From 1st April 1919 To 30th April 1919 Volume XLIII		
War Diary	Ailly S. Somme	01/04/1919	04/04/1919
War Diary	Condie Folie	05/04/1919	30/04/1919
Heading	War Diary Of The 65th Field Ambulance (3rd W. Lancs T.F.) From 1/5/19 To 31/5/19 Volume XLIV		

War Diary	Condie Folie	01/05/1919	31/05/1919
Heading	June 1919 65th F.A.		
War Diary	Condie Folie	01/06/1919	05/06/1919

WO95
2148/1

65 Field Ambulance

21ST DIVISION

65TH FIELD AMBULANCE
AUG 1915 - ~~DEC 1918~~
1919 JUN

21ST DIVISION

21st Division

12/6907

summaries

65th Field Ambulance
Vol: I
August 1 a Sep! 15.

Dec '18

August 1915 S
Sept.

Army Form C. 2118.

WAR DIARY
or
INTELLIGENCE SUMMARY.
(Erase heading not required.)

Instructions regarding War Diaries and Intelligence Summaries are contained in F.S. Regs., Part II. and the Staff Manual respectively. Title pages will be prepared in manuscript.

Place	Date	Hour	Summary of Events and Information	Remarks and references to Appendices
Aldershot Camp	28.8.15		Arrived with unit — 182 men & 10 officers from Cow Gap Camp Eastbourne.	Nil.
"	29.8.15		Reported arrival to A.D.M.S. 21st Division. Separated portion of ordnance equipment from that of the 63rd & 64th Field Ambulances.	Nil.
"	30.8.15		Completed separation of ordnance equipment, and checked the following equipment. Items were deficient.	
			(a) Water carts ... 3	
			(b) G.S. wagons ... 6 new	
			(c) Medical Belfast panniers unfitted & unfilled	
			(d) Driving reins, whips and N.C.Os saddle	
			(e) Ambulance wagons were without equipment	
			(f) Operating tents	
			(g) Ground sheets (Section 2.A)	
			(h) Shovels (Section No 2.B)	
			(i) Nose bags, brushes horse (Section 5.A)	
			(j) Bags Winchester tins	
			(k) Felt large shields, felt, jointed drainers & anvil (Section No 7)	
			Nudler. pincers iron, screwdrivers & saw sets	
			(l) Yokes wearing (Section No 9.A)	
			(m) See where of section No 9.A.	
			(n) " " " No 9.B.	

Army Form C. 2118.

WAR DIARY
or
INTELLIGENCE SUMMARY.
(Erase heading not required.)

Instructions regarding War Diaries and Intelligence
Summaries are contained in F. S. Regs., Part II.
and the Staff Manual respectively. Title pages
will be prepared in manuscript.

Place	Date	Hour	Summary of Events and Information	Remarks and references to Appendices
Netley Camp	30.8.15		(o) The work of Section No 10 A.	
			(P) Stores @ Premises @ Portable (lecture No 12)	
			(Q) Water Supply (lecture No 14)	
			(R) Jacks & lifting (lecture 20)	
			(S) Poles whips for Ambulance wagons. (lecture No 21 &	
			(t) Packing jackets (lecture 23)	
			(u) Check detainment outfit	
			(v) Distinguen[?] boxes are refilled	
			Full Parade As it so far as possible.	
	31.8.15		15 Riding horses drawn from Remounts. All but three appear in bad condition. Instruction given in conduct use of ordnance [?] to [?] made that stock ordnance equipment SADSs unable to give any information.	
	1.9.15		Medical Equipment taken over detailed from Au Connach A.l.C [?] Personnel attached from 1/3 Coy Coach Names overleaf and working. 4 Section of Field Ambulance began	

2353   Wt. W2544/1454 700,000 5/15 D. D. & L.   A.D.S.S./Forms/C. 2118.

Army Form C. 2118.

WAR DIARY
or
INTELLIGENCE SUMMARY.
(Erase heading not required.)

Place	Date	Hour	Summary of Events and Information	Remarks and references to Appendices
Wellingborough	1.9.15		Two hundred thirty eight O.A. blankets returned to Ordnance Store Aldershot. Fitting of harness continues. Further enquiries elicited the fact that we would have to draw Ordnance equipment from Aldershot (distance 44 miles) no transport available.	Ind.
"	2.9.15		Draught Animals drawn from Remounts Aldershot — 18 mules — 2 horses. Animals watered & commenced fitting of harness. Includes Indent Slow Cart (only vehicle available)	Ind.
"	3.9.15		Continues fitting of harness — O.S. Wagons Water Carts drawn. Water carts arrived absolutely unfitted — it is necessary to which send for each item of equipment — considerable delay in seeing from Ordnance Stores. An officer at Aldershot all day trying to complete equipment.	
"	5.9.15		Instruction in packing of Wagons.	Ind.
"	6.9.15		Instruction as above continued. Issue O.S. Wagons at Aldershot drawing equipment. I.E.P. Checking of equipment drawn yesterday & distribution to Sections.	Ind.

WAR DIARY
or
INTELLIGENCE SUMMARY.

(Erase heading not required.)

Army Form C. 2118.

Place	Date	Hour	Summary of Events and Information	Remarks and references to Appendices
Nolay Camp	7.9.15		Mules horses inspected by Superior of Remounts. One mule – one horse Cast. He found out that animals were in poor condition. Sent officer to attempt to replace these animals. Obtained parties in packing wagons. Part of equipment of Water Carts received also, part of equipment of Ambulance wagons. Unable to obtain paraffin or kerosene from Ord Supplies indents sent in some days ago.	
~ ~	8.9.15		Complete work on the road for the first time. Covered about 6 miles – under the circumstances did fairly well. Some animals good, some too weak harness (new) has been unable to obtain different dubbing after repeated indents and application at Advance Ordnance. Received orders to purchase Primus Stove – Portable Stove locally. Orders received to entrain on 10.9.15.	and
	9.9.15		Cleaning up of Camp – packing of wagons for entrainment etc	and
	10.9.15	2.35am	first train load entrained at Le Nolay Gondo Station.	
		4.05am	Second train ~	

Army Form C. 2118.

WAR DIARY
or
INTELLIGENCE SUMMARY.
(Erase heading not required.)

Instructions regarding War Diaries and Intelligence Summaries are contained in F. S. Regs., Part II. and the Staff Manual respectively. Title pages will be prepared in manuscript.

Place	Date	Hour	Summary of Events and Information	Remarks and references to Appendices
Southampton	10.9.15		Entrainment carried out satisfactorily	
	10.9.15	6 am	First train load arrived	
	" "	7 am	Second train load arrived. One horse (riding) Staff Major left Rawl. Staff Major left his horse behind in Willan Camp. Wired OC Details Willan Camp to recover and hand to Remounts. Veterinary Inspection of animals. One horse drawn from Remounts to complete establishment	
	" "	9 am	Transport horses embarked on Inn S. Inventor, with OC Personnel + officio Rank + 9 Rawl	
	" "	4 pm	Remainder of unit (Batteries - 158 R+9 Rawl) embarked on Inn S. Empress Queen (No 1806)	
	" "	8.35 pm	Left Southampton	
Havre	11.9.15	9.15 am	Disembarked at Havre - Journey without incident	fuel
	" "	10.30 am	Inn S. Inventor arrived with transport personnel. Disembarkation carried out.	
	" "	5 pm	Arrived at No 5 Rest Camp at 5 pm. One mule sick handed in + another replaced from Remounts	
	12.9.15	9 am	Left Rest Camp for entrainment (Route 3 Gare d'Marchandises)	Ful

Army Form C. 2118.

WAR DIARY
or
INTELLIGENCE SUMMARY.
(Erase heading not required.)

Instructions regarding War Diaries and Intelligence Summaries are contained in F. S. Regs., Part II. and the Staff Manual respectively. Title pages will be prepared in manuscript.

Place	Date	Hour	Summary of Events and Information	Remarks and references to Appendices
HAVRE	12.9.15	11.30am	Entrainment completed	
—	—	1.19 pm	Departure from Havre	
AUDRUICQ	13.9.15	6.30 am	Arrived at tent at DeBatament – Journey without incident. No trouble in watering or feeding horses. O/c Detrnment	nil
LOSTRAT	13.9.15	11 am	Arrived in billets ac. Arrangements made for billets, unit nearly at farm in village. Searching round – no suitable position for Receiving Station for sick	
—	—	2 pm	Receiving Station opened for reception of casualties from our Bgde.	nil
—	14.9.15		No information as to when Mechanical Transport will join. etc.	
—		10 am	Received wire from A.M.O. 2nd Div. that Casualties were to be evacuated to No. 20 Casualty Clearing Station ST. OMER. Transport to be requested from that helium Convoy. Eight cases evacuated to St OMER.	
—	15.9.15		Evening of personnel in accordance with Para 304 Route Marching, cavalcant. Training continued as above. O.I.C. personnel cleaning harness. Annals short.	
—	16.9.15		Four cases evacuated to St OMER. Water Ambulance – horses – Water Bottles – one and seventeen men of M.T. arrived	fill

2353 Wt. W2544/1454 700,000 5/15 D. D. & L. A.D.S.S./Forms/C. 2118.

WAR DIARY
or
INTELLIGENCE SUMMARY

Army Form C. 2118.

Place	Date	Hour	Summary of Events and Information	Remarks and references to Appendices
LOSTRAT	16.9.15		Training of personnel in morning. Route march in afternoon with complete transport. Sick cases evacuated to St OMER. Interviewed Requested Medical Officers of Brigade and instructed them in procedure of sending cases to Field Ambulance.	
LOSTRAT	17.9.15		Training continued in morning. Route march in afternoon. Sick cases evacuated to St OMER. Inspection of Mechanical Transport perfected water Ambulance wagons. Detailed for different Relieve and Brig hosp of hosps opened for each. One riding horse sick today – seen by A.D.V.O. 31st Div. (Pneumonia). Indented for a horse in Remounts at Head qrs of 2 Dn. Supplies of food, fodder etc arrived in good time. Indented on No 3 Advanced Depôt of Medical Stores for various extra dressings.	last
LOSTRAT	18.9.15		Usual training in morning. Route march in afternoon. Two reports on sick yesterday died at A.g.y.s hospital St OMER and ARQUES today. Motor Ambulances now running a regular Service. Some difficulty experienced by W.O.s of Regiments sending men for evacuation without return for the day – without rifles or equipment.	Fever R+B

Army Form C. 2118.

WAR DIARY
or
INTELLIGENCE SUMMARY.
(Erase heading not required.)

Instructions regarding War Diaries and Intelligence Summaries are contained in F. S. Regs., Part II. and the Staff Manual respectively. Title pages will be prepared in manuscript.

Place	Date	Hour	Summary of Events and Information	Remarks and references to Appendices
LOST RAT.	18.9.15		Water refused to Brigade scouts who appear met in Brigade Orders.	
			Drawings intended for yesterday received today, also a listing of ambulance Servau- refugees.	
			Some trouble with water carts. They had been sent out absolutely unfilled and over-	
			Some of the morning fresh could be obtained before departure. Being Also a —	
			chloride of lime in cleansing tank.	Sent
LOST RAT.	19.9.15		Sunday. Church Parade in morning. Route march west of Arneke in afternoon.	
			Men & transport went well. Warned 2 cases to Casualty Clearing Station at ONER.	
		10 pm	Received Preliminary Orders from Head Qrs. 2nd Div. "W. Division (less Art. except	
			Div Amm Column will move back tomorrow morning 20" inst.	feet.
	20.9.15	1 am	Received O.O. No 1 2nd Div. Scadge bent to be a starting point at 4.5 pm.	
NORDAUSQUES		7.5 pm	Left starting point marching in rear of 4026 field Coy RE.	
ARQUES	21.9.15	1.30 am	Arrived ARQUES and went into billets. Opened Dressing Station for Brigade sick	

WAR DIARY
or
INTELLIGENCE SUMMARY.

(Erase heading not required.)

Army Form C. 2118.

Place	Date	Hour	Summary of Events and Information	Remarks and references to Appendices
ARQUES	21.9.18	11 a.m.	Evacuated McCann (1 officer + 13 men) to No 20 CCS ST OMER.	
"	"	1 pm	Received preliminary orders for tonight's march	
"	"	3 pm	Received Div. O.O. No 4. march route to be continued tonight. Order of march :-	
			8th Brigade Inf.	
			New Field Amg R4.	
			65" Field ambulance	
"	"	8.45 pm	Starting point: crossroads south of ARQUES church.	
			Route: ARQUES – WARDRECQUES – WITTES – AIRE – MALINGHEM	
			During the night unit evacuated	
			During the march a considerable number of men fell out and on completion of march Ambulance wagons were almost full.	
MALINGHEM	22.9.18	1.30 am	Halted at MALINGHEM & billeted	
		2 am	Dressing station opened for Brigade sick in school house	
		6 am	Notified 8 Div S. got Div + Brigade to use portion of dressing station	

Army Form C. 2118.

WAR DIARY
or
INTELLIGENCE SUMMARY.
(Erase heading not required.)

Instructions regarding War Diaries and Intelligence Summaries are contained in F. S. Regs., Part II. and the Staff Manual respectively. Title pages will be prepared in manuscript.

Place	Date	Hour	Summary of Events and Information	Remarks and references to Appendices
MATLINGHEM	22.9.15	3 pm	Received Div. O.O. No 5. March will be commenced tonight, in same order as last night.	
"	"	5.30 pm	Received Orders Lt. Regt. O.O. No 5. Starting point for Field Ambulance road fork ½ mile west of foot of	
"	"	7 pm	of LA COULEE at 8.15 pm. Closed Evening Station and evacuated last of Cases to No 22 C.C.S. at AIRE. Total Cases evacuated during	
"	"	8.15 pm	the day 11. Passed Starting Point	
BELLERI	23 " "	10.30 pm	Arrived at billeting area. Went into billets without any delay. Officers and men supplied September water carts detailed to billets.	
"	28.9.15	6 am	Commenced portion to Agn I. & Agn II. O.O.	
"	"	8 am	Opened Dressing Station in billets. in field on left hand side at AMES-AMETTE road.	
"	"	12.30 am	Received following message from Bde. Sectge - "Two Zeppelins ared a beche passed over ESQUELBECQ 6.55 am this morning travelling N.W. direction." Evacuated 10 cases to West Riding C.C.S at LILLERS. Large numbers of men treated for abrasions of feet. Sgd.
BELLERI	24.9.15	11 am	Received Preliminary Orders of Movement tonight. Sgd.	

2353 Wt. W2544/1454 700,000 5/15 D. D. & L. A.D.S.S./Forms/C. 2118.

No 65 Field Ambulance

WAR DIARY
or
INTELLIGENCE SUMMARY.
(Erase heading not required.)

Army Form C. 2118.

Page 11

Place	Date	Hour	Summary of Events and Information	Remarks and references to Appendices
BELLERY	24.9.15	7.30pm	Left BELLERY Orders of March – 64th Inf Brigade. 136th Field Cas Hz. 65th Field Ambulance. 106th Cos Div Train. Route - BELLERY - FEREMY - MAZLES LES MINES - BRUAY - HOUCHIN - FOUR à CHAUX	Ref Sheet 37A MAZEBROUCK Sheet 11 LENS
FOUR A CHAUX	25.9.15	2.30 am	Arrived FOUR à CHAUX. Bivouacs for the night. Heavy bombardment in progress in direction of LOOS.	Lead
"	25.9.15	10.30 am	Received Divisional Orders to proceed. The 21st Division will now proceed to the area south and west of MAZINGARBE	
"	25.9.15	11.30 am	Left FOUR A CHAUX Route FOUR A CHAUX – NOEUX LES MINES – MAZINGARBE	
MAZINGARBE	25.9.15	4 pm	Arrived outside village of MAZINGARBE. Attend conference of Inf. Brigade. The Brigade the Brigade is to go into action tonight at the village of LOOS.	
"	25.9.15	4.30 pm	Received following orders from A.D.M.S. 21st Division – "Stand fast at MAZINGARBE. Have Water Ambulances and Bearers should be ready at short notice"	
"	25.9.15	5.30 pm	Field Ambulance in position at church in MAZINGARBE. Bearers sent to A.D.M.S. saying unit now in required position.	
"	25.9.15	10.10 pm	Ambulance in same position. Received orders from A.D.M.S. to give one spare pellenl to No 63 & Ambulance. Complied with.	

Army Form C. 2118

WAR DIARY
or
INTELLIGENCE SUMMARY.
(Erase heading not required.)

Page 12.

Instructions regarding War Diaries and Intelligence Summaries are contained in F. S. Regs., Part II. and the Staff Manual respectively. Title pages will be prepared in manuscript.

Place	Date	Hour	Summary of Events and Information	Remarks and references to Appendices
MAZINGARBE	25/9/15	11.48 PM	Received following message from A.D.M.S. and got in touch with Regimental units 63 & 64 Brigades. "Open one Section dressing Station at M+3 in Sq A-R B E and line G 27 and to line G 21 and a."	Ref. 82744642 trench mat 25A+B.
—	26.9.15	12.15 am	Sent following message to A.D.M.S. "Dressing Station opened in release in village of MAZINGARBE. Bearer Ambulances have been sent to get in touch with 63rd & 64th Lt. Brigades. Two bearer officers reconnaissance of area have hitherto sent up as Motor Ambulances to front indicated"	
—	26.9.15	2 am	Received following message from Senior Officer "Area reached. Harassed in this area. No advance has progressed and we are following."	
—	—	3.30 am	First Casualties arrived in Motor Ambulances. These Casualties had been brought in from LOOS.	
—	—	8 am	Telegram sent Motor Ambulance Convoy at LILLERS giving position of Dressing Station and asking them to evacuate.	

Army Form C. 2118

WAR DIARY
or
INTELLIGENCE SUMMARY.
(Erase heading not required.)

Page 13.

Instructions regarding War Diaries and Intelligence Summaries are contained in F.S. Regs., Part II and the Staff Manual respectively. Title pages will be prepared in manuscript.

Place	Date	Hour	Summary of Events and Information	Remarks and references to Appendices
MALINGARBE	26/9/15	noon	Casualties coming in in large numbers. Motor Ambulance Convoy has not arrived. Sent following message to A.D.M.S. "Large numbers of Casualties coming in. Motor Ambulance Convoy not yet arrived."	
"	"	2 pm	Casualties still coming in and personnel at work very great. To evacuation possible. M.A.C. not arrived	
"	"	3.45 pm	Two hundred & fifty Cases have now arrived and hurried bulk Dressing Station crowded and no evacuation yet possible. Hurryed evacuating in four horse Ambulance Wagons – empty GS Wagons but D.D.M.S. 1st Corps who has visited the Dressing Station decided from this method	
"	"	6 pm	Crowded with wounded. Have obtained another large room at one end of village which holds about fifty Cases. Now numbering three hundred, which include one hundred fifty lying down Cases and one Case unfit for transport. Decided to evacuate Cases to nearest hospital in two four horse ambulance wagons but following message to A.D.M.S. "Three hundred cases now in urgent need Motor Ambulance Convoy has not yet turned up. Several urgent Cases which need immediate hospital treatment. Ahead of Shelter. Wounded still coming in large numbers"	
"	"	7 pm	Sent fourteen of the most urgent Cases in Motor Ambulances of MAC to SIOEUX	
"	"	9 pm	Work continuing in both Dressing Stations.	

Army Form C. 2118.

WAR DIARY
or
INTELLIGENCE SUMMARY.
(Erase heading not required)

Page 14

Instructions regarding War Diaries and Intelligence Summaries are contained in F. S. Regs., Part II. and the Staff Manual respectively. Title pages will be prepared in manuscript.

Place	Date	Hour	Summary of Events and Information	Remarks and references to Appendices
MAZINGARBE	26.9.15	11 pm	No 8 Motor Ambulance Convoy arrived and evacuated sick & some cases	Init.
"	26.9.15	—	Opened 2 Second Dressing Stations in 2 Barracks sheds at entrance to village	
"	27.9.15	12.30 am	Work proceeding in both Dressing Stations	
"	"	10 am	Received following message from Head qr 2d Div. "All supply lorries are placed at your disposal after refilling supply stations."	
"	"	10.30 am	Empty supply lorries arrived. Removed all the sitting up cases	
"	"	11 am	Motor Ambulance Convoy arrived and removed all lying down cases. Both Dressing Stations was empty and ready to receive further casualties.	
"	"	3 pm	About 100 sit Casualties have come in to this Dressing Station & that it is advisable to work in daylight. Orders have been withdrawn and will be sent up tonight.	
"	"	6.30 pm	Brown & Ambulances sent up. All cars got into village of LOOS. Barro's Brigade have been in action today most of casualties occurring as belong to them	Init.
"	28.9.15	10.30 am	Work continuing. Most serious cases have to be evacuated by own Motor Ambulances to LAPUGNOY.	

WAR DIARY or INTELLIGENCE SUMMARY.

(Erase heading not required.)

Army Form C. 2118.

Page 131

Place	Date	Hour	Summary of Events and Information	Remarks and references to Appendices
MAZINGARBE	28.9.15	9.30am	Sent us that loaned ambulances along have gone to LOOS they brought back successful cases suffering from gas poisoning, had to be withdrawn owing to the heavy shell fire which was then in progress.	
"	"	2pm	Have made arrangements to send up all available vehicles under cover of darkness to remove casualties which have been treated by the bearer division.	
"	"	6pm	Received Divisional operation orders noted as follows :- 2/0.O. was noted tonight to area BEUVRY - BETHUNE. Route LA BOURSE - VERQUIGNEUL	
"	"	"	Sent following message to agent :- Reported for your information that considerable numbers of wounded are reported in relays of 200 and westwards of HILL 70. Have made arrangements to clear area to urged by any field ambulances. Could still clear position by walker ambulances which could report at BETHUNE at 7pm. Consider numerous Bearers stretch until dawn today when further clearance became impossible.	
"	"	9.30pm	Received no further orders. Ready to move to area BETHUNE - BEUVRY. Remarks on the methods of the Field Ambulance during the operations extending from Sept 25 to Sept 28.	
			(1) The chance of billeting for housing the casualties in MAZINGARBE was practically nil. The most suitable buildings for the purpose had previously been taken over as Headquarters for Divisional Staff &c. The wealth was reported but apparently no action could be taken.	

Army Form C. 2118

Page 16

WAR DIARY
or
INTELLIGENCE SUMMARY.
(Erase heading not required.)

Place	Date	Hour	Summary of Events and Information	Remarks and references to Appendices

(2) The working of twenty 8 wheeler Ambulance Convoy in obtaining touch with the Divisions & Posts was unsatisfactory and three hundred cases awaited for evacuation for more than twenty four hours.

(3) The replenishing of Medical Stores was satisfactory. They were supplied from the Boulogne Medical Store Depot at LILLERS.

(4) A request for a further supply of the cases sent by Motor Ambulance Convoy went round no response.

(5) Our Use hundred Patients were habitual for twenty four hours have been too difficult was experienced in obtaining supplies.

Considering that it was the first time the First Ambulance had worked as a unit the organisation was successful. There were some Hours at the Clearing Station, who being unaccustomed to the work, failed to take all cases seasonally.

Over four hundred cases including fifteen Officers was attended to & Evacuated in the forty eight hours.

The following message was received from Don hastings - the Corps Commander wishes to express his appreciation of the good work carried out by the Field Ambulances of the Division.

The G.O.C. 2nd Division visited the Unit on 29/10/15. and congratulated the unit on the work done.

121/7430.

65th Field Ambulance
Vol: 2
Sept & Oct 15

Vol II

War Diary of No. 65 Field Ambulance

From ... 24. 9. 15"

To ... 31. 10. 15.

WARDIARY
or
INTELLIGENCE SUMMARY.
(Erase heading not required.)

Army Form C. 2118

Page 17

Place	Date	Hour	Summary of Events and Information	Remarks and references to Appendices
			The names of the following officers men have been returned to the 2nd Gen. Depôt for the service they had rendered :-	
			Lieutenant George Rolph	
			" Walter Macfarlane	
			Serjeant Clifford Nash	
			No M2/079154 Corporal James Wanhart - Mechanical Transport Section	cont.
BETHUNE	29.9.15	3.30am	Arrived BETHUNE went into Billets.	
"	"	11am	Received operation orders 2nd Div - for 1st Bgde move tonight	cont.
"	"	11.30pm	Left BETHUNE	cont.
Auchy au Bois	30.9.15	3.30am	Arrived AUCHY-au-BOIS went into Billets.	cont.
"	1.10.15	8.30pm	Left AUCHY au BOIS.	cont.
BOESEGHEM	1.10.15	12.30pm	Arrived BOESEGHEM went into Billets	cont.

Army Form C. 2118

WAR DIARY
or
INTELLIGENCE SUMMARY.

(Erase heading not required.)

Page 18

Place	Date	Hour	Summary of Events and Information	Remarks and references to Appendices
BOESEGHEM	2.10.15	6 am	Received Divisional Operation Order. Aug. 9th will be brought in the area North-North East of HAZEBROUCK	
~	2.10.15	9.15 am	Left BOESEGHEM	
CAESTRE	2.10.15	2.15 pm	Arrived CAESTRE went into Billets	
~	3.10.15		at CAESTRE.	

Army Form C. 2118.

WAR DIARY
or
INTELLIGENCE SUMMARY.
(Erase heading not required.)

Page 19

Instructions regarding War Diaries and Intelligence Summaries are contained in F. S. Regs., Part II and the Staff Manual respectively. Title pages will be prepared in manuscript.

Place	Date	Hour	Summary of Events and Information	Remarks and references to Appendices
CAESTRE	4.10.15		Refitting. Evacuated Group to C.C.S. HAZEBROUCK this a.m.	init
"	5.10.15		Evacuated Group to HAZEBROUCK this a.m.	init
"	6.10.15		Evacuated officers — men sick	init
"	7.10.15		Visit from D.A.D.M.S. 2nd Division. Proposed to offer allowances for sanctioned at CAESTRE	init
"	8.10.15		Arrangements being made to obtain authority to take over a suitable building for Div. Rest Station	init
"	9.10.15		Evacuated four sick	init
"	10.10.15		Evacuated sick. Sick to HAZEBROUCK	init
"	11.10.15		Our officer and our men evacuated sick	init
"	12.10.15		Sick evacuated. Church were built ub. Gone suitable quarters. Evacuated sick one officer —	init
"	13.10.15		Inspection by D.D.M.S. 2nd Corps & A.D.M.S. 2nd Division. Authority has yet obtained to take over building as Rest Station. Men were of 100 Coy R.E. put to ARMENTIERES to refuse then Wet.	init
"	14.10.15		Sick evacuated sick.	init
"	15-10-15		Evacuated three sick to HAZEBROUCK	init
"	16-10-15		Evacuated men sick to HAZEBROUCK. Received following wire from D.H.S. 2nd Army "Chateau near Garde Station has been afternoon as a Rest Station for 21st Division please Arrange to take over as soon as possible." Chateau taken over and work of cleaning and preparing commenced.	init
"	17-10-15		Work at Chateau continued. Report to A.D.M.S. 21st Division that the Rest Station will be ready for reception of patients the 19 inst. Evacuated two men sick to HAZEBROUCK	init

2353 Wt. W2544/1454 700,000 5/15 D. D. & L. A.D.S.S./Forms/C. 2118.

Army Form C. 2118

WAR DIARY
or
INTELLIGENCE SUMMARY.
(Erase heading not required.)

Page 20.

Instructions regarding War Diaries and Intelligence Summaries are contained in F. S. Regs., Part II. and the Staff Manual respectively. Title pages will be prepared in manuscript.

Place	Date	Hour	Summary of Events and Information	Remarks and references to Appendices
CAESTRE	18-10-15		Divisional Rest Station opened. "A" Sec., Medical wards. "B" Sec., Surgical wards "C" Sec, bathing, washing, latrines, cooking and general fatigues.	AD
"	19-10-15		Nine patients admitted or evacuated.	
"	20-10-15		Sick evacuated nil.	BD
"	21-10-15		Sick evacuated, one.	bd
"	22-10-15		Sick evacuated, one officer, one man.	bd
"	23-10-15		Sick wounded wounded one, sick three.	bd
"	24-10-15		Sick evacuated, two.	bd
"	25-10-15		Sick evacuated, one.	bd
"	26-10-15		Sick evacuated, ten. 33 born in Hospital	
"	27-10-15		Sick evacuated four - wounded one.	bd
"	28-10-15		Sick evacuated, five	bd bd
"	29-10-15		Sick evacuated, seven.	bd
"	30-10-15		Sick evacuated five. 58 born in Hospital.	bd
"	31-10-15		Sick evacuated, one officer, six other ranks.	bd

2353 Wt. W2544/1454 700,000 5/15 D.D. & L. A.D.S.S./Forms/C. 2118.

Nov 14/15

21st Hussain 131/7621

131/7621

65th Field Ambulance
Vol: 3

Nov 15

Ans

Army Form C. 2118.

WAR DIARY
or
INTELLIGENCE SUMMARY.
(Erase heading not required.)

1/5 C^y 1^m Page 21.

Place	Date	Hour	Summary of Events and Information	Remarks and references to Appendices
CAESTRE	1-11-15		Evacuated 8 sick. Field Ambulance still acting as Div. Rest Station for 21st Div. 1 Officer and 141 other Ranks of 98 Field Coy. R.E. attached to Unit for purpose of assisting in work of improving the area and Billets. This work was undertaken in accordance with circular letter of 21st Division (AA 515, dated 22-10-15). The present Billeting Area of the Unit is part of the Rest Area occupied in turn by the Brigades composing the 2nd Corps, and the object of the General Officer Commanding, is to initiate a scheme of permanent improvements in the area. Reports on water supply, billets, amptic schemes and repairs necessary to convert the Schestaen into a suitable Divisional Rest Station have already been submitted to the A.D.M.S.	
"	2-11-15		Evacuated 8 sick	ful.
"	3-11-15		" 1 wounded 13 sick	
"	4-11-15		" 5 sick	
"	5-11-15		" 4 sick	
"	6-11-15		" 4 sick	
"	7-11-15			ful.

Army Form C. 2118

WAR DIARY
or
INTELLIGENCE SUMMARY.
(Erase heading not required.)

Page No.

Place	Date	Hour	Summary of Events and Information	Remarks and references to Appendices
CHESTRES	8-11-15		Evacuated 1 wounded 3 sick. Ind	
"	10-11-15		3 sick. Ind	
"	11-11-15		1 sick Ind	
"	12-11-15		2 wounded. Ind	
"	13-11-15		3 sick. Ind	
"	14-11-15		4 sick Ind	
"	15-11-15		2 sick. 1 N.C.O. and 19 men detached temporarily to 21 St. Sanitain Section. Officers and men of 98 Field Coy. R.E. complete work at Chateau. Upwards of well constructed permanent shelter, latrines, baths and reservoir constructed. Permanent shelter erected for horses and mules. Divining rough, emplacement and supplied by pumping from adjacent pond. Incinerator for burning of excreta completed and found to be effective. Ind	
"	16-11-15		Evacuated 5 sick	
"	17-11-15		1 sick Ind	

Army Form C. 2118.

WAR DIARY
or
INTELLIGENCE SUMMARY.
(Erase heading not required.)

Page 23

Place	Date	Hour	Summary of Events and Information	Remarks and references to Appendices
CHESTRE	18-11-15		November 3 sick hd	
"	19-11-15		1 sick hd	
"	20-11-15		sick hd	
"	21-11-15		" wounded 3-3-etc hd	
"	22-11-15		" 3 sick hd	
"	23-11-15		" five sick hd	
"	24-11-15		" two sick hd	
"	25-11-15		" two sick hd	
"	26-11-15		" six sick hd	
"	27-11-15		" three sick hd	
"	28-11-15		" one wounded three sick hd	
"	29-11-15		" one sick hd	
"	30-11-15		" four sick Inspection Any 20, D.M.S. 2nd Corps. hd	

65th F.A.
Vol: 4

D/
7909

2d Div.

F11651"

Div. hos. rgts.

Army Form C. 2118

WAR DIARY
or
INTELLIGENCE SUMMARY.
(Erase heading not required.)

Vol IV   Page 2 +

Instructions regarding War Diaries and Intelligence Summaries are contained in F. S. Regs., Part II. and the Staff Manual respectively. Title pages will be prepared in manuscript.

Place	Date	Hour	Summary of Events and Information	Remarks and references to Appendices
CAESTRE	1-12-15		Evacuated five sick.	
	2-12-15		Evacuated two sick.	
	3-12-15		Evacuated five sick.	
	4-12-15		Evacuated two sick. Admitted during week 189 cases. Returned to duty, 61 cases. Evacuated French Hospital 89 cases. Remaining two cases.	
	5-12-15		Evacuated three sick.	
	6-12-15		nil	
	7-12-15		two sick	
	8-12-15		nil	
	9-12-15		one wounded, four over sick	
	10-12-15		nil	
	11-12-15		two sick. Admitted during week, 99 cases. Returned to duty, 95 cases. Evacuated 11 cases. Remaining in Hospital 95 cases	
	12-12-15		Evacuated nineteen, one sick	

2353 Wt. W2544/1454 700,000 5/15 D.D.& L.   A.D.S.S./Forms/C 2128.

Army Form C. 2118

Page 73

WAR DIARY
or
INTELLIGENCE SUMMARY.
(Erase heading not required.)

Instructions regarding War Diaries and Intelligence Summaries are contained in F. S. Regs., Part II. and the Staff Manual respectively. Title pages will be prepared in manuscript.

Place	Date	Hour	Summary of Events and Information	Remarks and references to Appendices
CAESTRE	13-12-15		Evacuated one wounded, two sick.	
"	14/12/15		One sick. One case of "measles" evacuated to Isolation Hospital	
"	15/12/15		One wounded, two sick	
"	16/12/15		Three sick	
"	17/12/15		Two sick	
"	18/12/15		Two sick. Admitted during week 98 cases. Returned to duty 77 cases. Evacuated 16 cases. Remaining in Hospital 90 cases.	
"	19/12/15		Evacuated sick vie.	
"	20/12/15		One wounded, five sick	
"	21/12/15		Three sick	

WAR DIARY
or
INTELLIGENCE SUMMARY
(Erase heading not required.)

Army Form C. 2118

Page 76

Place	Date	Hour	Summary of Events and Information	Remarks and references to Appendices
CAESTRE	22/12/15		Evacuated one sick.	
"	23/12/15		" one sick	
"	24/12/15		" one sick	
"	25/12/15		100 cases in Hospital.	
"			During week 43 cases. One sick admitted during week, 8 cases returned duty. Evacuated, 13 cases. Remaining 158 cases	
"	26/12/15		Evacuated one sick. Inspection by D.M.S. U.S.A. Q.M.G. 2nd Army and	
"	27/12/15		" four sick Lieut. J. Horner Cochran 65th	
"			Field Ambulance RAMC vacancy died.	
"	28/12/15		Evacuated sick nil	
"	29/12/15		" three "	
"	30/12/15		" two "	
"	31/12/15		" two "	

Lindsay
Captain RAMC
O.C. 65th Field Ambulance

21st Division

F/1165/2.

65 F.A

65

Jan 1916

65th F.a.
Vol 5

WAR DIARY
INTELLIGENCE SUMMARY

65 Field Ambulance
January 1916.
Page N° 1

Army Form C. 2118.

Vol V

Place	Date	Hour	Summary of Events and Information	Remarks and references to Appendices
CAESTRE	1/1/16		No Evacuations. Admitted Annyances, 98. Evacuated, 1. Returned to duty	
"	2/1/16		Two sick evacuated. Remaining, 98. duty	
"	3/1/16		Lieut Jn.º Crulee returned Unit from 17 C.C.S duty	
"	4/1/16		Four sick evacuated duty	
"	5/1/16		Three " " duty	
"	6/1/16		Sick evacuation nil duty	
"	7/1/16		Evacuated two wounded duty	
"	8/1/16		" two wounded, one sick duty	
"	"		one wounded eleven sick. Sight of knee sent Eye cases sent to No 4 Stationary Hospital for examination duty	
"	9/1/16		Three sick evacuated. Weekly summary: Admn. 113, Evac 30, Died 79, Rem'g 90. duty	
"	10/1/16		No sick evacuated. Lieut J.M. Schist attached for temporary duty with 10th Yorkshire Rgt in Lieu in Lieu & O/rr 15. N. Snetzler proceeded to England on duty leave of absence dated 18/1/16	

R.L.S

WAR DIARY
or
INTELLIGENCE SUMMARY.

Army Form C. 2118.

65 Field Ambulance
January - 1916.

Page 7.

Place	Date	Hour	Summary of Events and Information	Remarks and references to Appendices
CAESTRE	11/1/16		Evacuated one sick lad	
"	12/1/16		Evacuated three sick lad	
"	13/1/16		Three sick. Lieut A.D. Sharp detached for temporary duty to 96 Bde R.F.A. lad	
"	14/1/16		No evacuations lad	
"	15/1/16		Evacuated one wounded, two sick lad	
"	16/1/16		Evacuated two wounded, three sick. Weekly summary admitted 113, Discharged 81, Evacuated 17, remaining 93 lad	
"	17/1/16		Evacuated one wounded, two sick lad	
"	18/1/16		Evacuated six sick lad	
"	19/1/16		Captain H.M.J. Perry relinquished command of the Unit in accordance with A.D.M.S. 2nd Army No M6/294/5. The command was handed over temporarily to Lieut-R. Stowers R.A.M.C Ret-cd subsequently once	

WAR DIARY
or
INTELLIGENCE SUMMARY.
(Erase heading not required.)

65th Field Am Army Form C. 2118.
January - 1916
Page No 3

Place	Date	Hour	Summary of Events and Information	Remarks and references to Appendices
CAESTRE	20/1/16		Evacuated two sick. RS	
"	21/1/16		Evacuated one sick RS	
"	22/1/16		Evacuated eight sick. Weekly Summary Admitted 175, Discharged 71, RS	
"	23/1/16		Evacuated one sick. Evacuated 25, Remaining 108 RS	
"	24/1/16		Evacuated two wounded, five sick RS	
"	25/1/16		Evacuated one sick. Lieut J.W. Elliot proceeded to England RS on leave to assume under 3½ RS	
"	26/1/16		Evacuated two sick RS	
"	27/1/16		Evacuated four sick. RS	
"	28/1/16		Evacuated two sick RS	
"	29/1/16		Evacuated three sick. Weekly Summary Admitted 177, Discharged to duty 118, Evacuated 18, Remaining 109 RS	

Army Form C. 2118.

65th Field Ambulance
Date January /16
Page No 4.

WAR DIARY
or
INTELLIGENCE SUMMARY
(Erase heading not required.)

Place	Date	Hour	Summary of Events and Information	Remarks and references to Appendices
CAESTRE	29/1/16 (cont.)		MAJOR R.J.C. THOMPSON, D.S.O., R.A.M.C. assumed command of the Unit.	
"	30/1/16		Evacuated three wounded, three sick.	
"	31/1/16		Admitted one sick three. 390 patients discharged duty during the month.	

R J Thompson
Major R.A.M.C.

Feb 1916.
S
65th Field Ambulance.

65. F. A.
21st Div.
Vol. 6.

Officer i/c
A.G.'s Office
　　　Base

Herewith A.F.ᵈ C2118
being the War Diary for
Feb. 1916.

R A C Thompson
Major RAMC.
OC 65 Field Ambulance

Army Form C. 2118.

WAR DIARY
or
INTELLIGENCE SUMMARY.
(Erase heading not required.)

CONFIDENTIAL.

WAR DIARY
of
65th FIELD AMBULANCE (WEST LANCS. T.F.)

From 1st February To 29th February.

(Volume vi.)

Army Form C. 2118.

WAR DIARY
INTELLIGENCE SUMMARY
(Erase heading not required.)

65 Field Ambulance
February 1916   Page 1.
Vol VI

Place	Date	Hour	Summary of Events and Information	Remarks and references to Appendices
CAESTRE Field Ambulance HQ acting as Regt. Station for 21st Division.	1-2-16		Two Sick evacuated. Lieut R.O. EADES R.A.M.C. (S.R.) examined medical charge of the 15th Durham Light Infantry and was struck off the strength of this unit. Captain F. GARRATT R.A.M.C. (T.C.) taken on the strength of the unit. Lieut E.N.H. Gray attended a course of lectures and demonstrations on Preventive measures against gas attacks at OXELAIRE.	
	2-2-16		3 Field and 1 wounded evacuated. Lieut Gray attended two lectures.	
	3-2-16		Two Sick evacuated	
	4-2-16		Three Sick evacuated	
	5-2-16		Two Sick evacuated. Weekly summary of Cases: Admitted 128, Discharged 92, Evacuated 25, Transferred 2nd Army Rest Station 9, Remaining 99	
	6-2-16		Four Sick Evacuated	
	7-2-16		Capt. E.N.H. GRAY appointed for temporary duty at 2nd Division Headquarters as Instructor in Preventive measures against gas attacks.	
	8-2-16		Two Sick Evacuated. Lieut J.M. ELLIOT assumed temporary Medical charge of the 10th Kings Own Yorks Light Inf.	
	9-2-16		Two Sick evacuated	
	10-2-16		Five Sick evacuated	

R.A. Thompson
Major

Army Form C. 2118.

WAR DIARY
or
INTELLIGENCE SUMMARY.
(Erase heading not required.)

65th Field Ambulance
February 1916
Vol VI   Page III

Place	Date	Hour	Summary of Events and Information	Remarks and references to Appendices
CAESTRE	11-2-16		Five Sick evacuated.	
	12-2-16		Weekly Summary of cases. Admitted 134, Discharged 94, Evacuated 28. Transferred to 2nd Army Rest Station, 18. Remaining 90. Eleven of the evacuations were men of Divisions other than the 21st. The 1st, 2nd and 3rd Brigades of the Canadian Field Artillery, also the 113th A/c R.F.A and the 118th Howitzer Bde R.F.A. were acting in this area. As these Units were not in touch with the Field Ambulances of their Division in all Sick for Hospital treatment passed through the 65th Field Ambulance.	
	13-2-16		Two Sick evacuated.	
	14-2-16		One Sick evacuated. (21st Div.)	
	15-2-16		Three Sick evacuated (21st Div.). 11 Sick (other Divisions) went evacuated. Seven of these were cases of "SCABIES" from the 118th How Bde R.F.A.	
	16-2-16		One Sick evacuated (21st Div.). 28 cases, other Divisions, in Hospital.	

R.A.C. Thompson
...

WAR DIARY or INTELLIGENCE SUMMARY

65 Field Ambulance
February 1916
Vol VI
Page III

Place	Date	Hour	Summary of Events and Information	Remarks and references to Appendices
CAESTRE	17-2-16		3 Sick evacuated (71st Div) Capt E.N.H. GRAY finished his turn of duty at 21st Divisional Headquarters.	
	18-2-16		Two Sick evacuated (71st Bw)	
	19-2-16		Three Sick evacuated (71st Bw) 40 cases admitted to this Rest Hospital. Two Hospital Marquees, which had been drawn from No 8 C.C.S. on the 10th inst. in accordance with the instructions of D.M.S. 2nd Army, were pitched in the field adjoining the Hospital grounds. 147 patients slept in the Hospital during the night of 19th & 20th inst. Lieut J.M. ELLIOT reported back from temporary duty with the 10th Kings Own (Malahive Irish Infantry). Summary of Cases Admitted 147, Discharged 100, Evacuated 38 (including 30 of the Bris (?)) Transferred to 3rd Army Rest Station 19. Lieut H.C. WERT evacuated (71st Bw) details for temporary duty with 96 Bde R.F.A.	(?) Shenfin
	20-2-16			

Army Form C. 2118.

WAR DIARY
or
INTELLIGENCE SUMMARY.
(Erase heading not required) Page iv

65th Field Ambulance
February 1916
Vol VI

Place	Date	Hour	Summary of Events and Information	Remarks and references to Appendices

CAESTRE 2-2-16

Sgt in Sick evacuated (21st Div.)
Lieut. A.D. SHARP R.A.M.C. (T.C.) having assumed medical charge of the 4th Battn. Middlesex Regt. was struck off the strength of this Unit.
Lieut. P.J. MURPHY R.A.M.E. (T.C.) was taken on the strength vice Lieut. Sharp.

The erection of two huts, each 30 ft × 15 ft, was completed. One of these was fitted up as an office. The front room of the Chateau on the ground floor, which had been previously used as an office, was converted into a Dining Room, the intervening being to me this room and the adjoining room as a Dining Room — the two rooms together having an area of about 1350 sq. feet. Similar for the convenience (for of tables) indented for on the 14th inst., had not yet been received. Lack of sufficient Dining Room accommodation had always been a great disturbance to the smooth working of the Rest Hospital, from the attempt having to be arranged for even meal.

R.H. Shufhaye

Army Form C. 2118.

WAR DIARY
or
INTELLIGENCE SUMMARY.

(Erase heading not required.)

65 Field Ambulance
February 1916.
Page 7

Vol VI

Instructions regarding War Diaries and Intelligence Summaries are contained in F. S. Regs., Part II. and the Staff Manual respectively. Title pages will be prepared in manuscript.

Place	Date	Hour	Summary of Events and Information	Remarks and references to Appendices
CAESTRE	22-2-16		Two Sick evacuated (71st Div)	
	23-2-16		Three Sick evacuated. (71st Div)	
	24-2-16		Two Sick, one wounded evacuated.	
	25-2-16		Three Sick evacuated.	
			Capt. R. STOWERS detailed to visit the following units daily for morning sick parade in accordance with D.M.S. 2nd ARMY No 408 dated 23-2-16	
			1st Bde Amm Col, C.F.A. 118th Bde. R.F.A.	
			3rd Do Do 118th Bde Amm. Col. R.F.A.	
	26-2-16		One Sick, one wounded evacuated.	
			Lieut H. E. WERT returned from temporary increase charge of 96 Bde R.F.A.	
	27-2-16		One Sick evacuated.	
	28-2-16		Three Sick evacuated.	
	29-2-16		Three Sick one wounded evacuated.	
			676 Cases admitted, 429 discharged during month. Average length of time under treatment 5.8 days.	

R.L.C. Thompson
Major

21st Division

No. 65 F. Amb.

March 1916

S

65 Field Amb
Vol 7

Army Form C. 2118.

WAR DIARY
INTELLIGENCE SUMMARY.
(Erase heading not required.)

65 Field Ambulance
March 1916
Vol VII Page 1.

Instructions regarding War Diaries and Intelligence Summaries are contained in F. S. Regs., Part II and the Staff Manual respectively. Title pages will be prepared in manuscript.

Place	Date	Hour	Summary of Events and Information	Remarks and references to Appendices
CAESTRE	1-III-16		Three Sick evacuated – Unit still acting as 21st Division Rest Station	
"	2-III-16		Two Sick evacuated	
"	3-III-16		One Sick evacuated	
"	4-III-16		Two Sick evacuated. Weekly Summary of Cases Admitted 201, Discharged to duty 131, Evacuated to C.C.S. 24, Transferred to Second Army Rest Station 51, Remaining 105.	
"	5-III-16		Five Sick evacuated	
"	6-III-16		Two Sick evacuated.	
"	7-III-16		One Sick evacuated.	
"	8-III-16		Six Sick evacuated.	
"	9-III-16		Two Sick evacuated	
"	10-III-16		Two Sick evacuated	
"	11-III-16		Three Sick evacuated. Weekly Summary of Cases. Admitted 230, Discharged to duty 177, Evacuated to C.C.S. 21, Transferred to Second Army Rest Station 43, Remaining 114.	
"	12-III-16		Three Sick evacuated.	
"	13-III-16		One Sick evacuated.	
"	14-III-16		Three Sick evacuated.	
"	15-III-16		Two Sick evacuated.	
"	16-III-16		One Sick evacuated.	
"	17-III-16		Four Sick evacuated	

R.J. Sharpin

Army Form C. 2118.

65 Field Ambulance
March 1916   Page 2.

WAR DIARY
INTELLIGENCE SUMMARY.
(Erase heading not required.)

Vol VII

Place	Date	Hour	Summary of Events and Information	Remarks and references to Appendices
CAESTRE	8.iii.16		Three Sick evacuated. Weekly Summary of cases admitted 136	
"	19.iii.16		Discharged to duty 103. Evacuated to C.C.S. 27. Transferred Second Army Rest Station 59. Remaining 109.	
"	20.iii.16		Two Sick evacuated	
"	21.iii.16		No Evacuations. Lieut. J.W. COURTER reported to O.C. 11.30 KINCOLNSHIRE REGT. for temporary duty	
"	22.iii.16		No Evacuations.	
"	23.iii.16		Three Sick evacuated	
"	24.iii.16		Three Sick evacuated.	
"	25.iii.16		Three Sick evacuated	
"	"		No evacuation. Weekly Summary of cases admitted 146. Discharged to duty 91. Evacuated to C.C.S. 20. Transferred Second Army Rest Station 49. Remaining 71.	
"	26.iii.16		Six Sick Evacuated	
"	27.iii.16		Four Sick Evacuated.	
"	28.iii.16		Three, four Sick Evacuated. This in consequence of orders having been received to close the Rest Station	

R.A. Trumpeter

Army Form C. 2118.

WAR DIARY
or
INTELLIGENCE SUMMARY.

(Erase heading not required.)

15th Field Ambulance
March 1916. Page 3

Place	Date	Hour	Summary of Events and Information	Remarks and references to Appendices
CAESTRE			Our wounded and thirty-six first line transport. The Field Ambulance was acting on the part shown for the 31st Divn. in form 19 October 1915 to date. Cases were received from the two field ambulances of the Division, which was occupying the ARMENTIÈRES sector of the line. Also a large number of such were treated at field ambulance cases from the various units who were stationed in the neighbourhood of CAESTRE. The following is a summary of the total cases dealt with during the period 19 Oct. 1915 to 29 Feb. 1916. Admitted — 3000. Evacuated — 645. [98 of these were located and Eye cases which were sent to the B.R.S. (which acted as a centre for such cases). Also included are 156 cases from the feet ambulance as obtained from the B.R.S.] Transferred to Second A.R.S. — 430 Discharged to duty — 1805. 60.2% of Total Admissions Rd to Duty Months	

WAR DIARY

INTELLIGENCE SUMMARY.

(Erase heading not required.)

Army Form C. 2118.

65th Field Ambulance
Arrived 1916 Part 4

Place	Date	Hour	Summary of Events and Information	Remarks and references to Appendices
CAESTRE	31/7		The unit marched to GODSWAERSVELDE and entrained by 6 a.m. The horses marching 1 hour & 20 minutes. Arrived at LONGUEAU at 5.10 h.m. after an uneventful journey via BOULOGNE, ETAPLES. Detrained by 6 h.m. and marched to la NEUVILLE via CORBIE - billeting in a barn 800 metres west of the village. The Chateau at CAESTRE and the D.R.S. Equipment taken to Field Ambulance Equipment was handed over to the 53rd Field Ambulance head by T. Kaye. All motorised details were sent to him and Bustede Post was kept to date. But the culprits having to go to the hand during the month were mostly, an epidemic of Influenza, and a small one of Enteric sprue, but sent onwards. R. E Humphries [?]	

2353 Wt. W2544/1454 700,000 5/15 D.D. & L. A.D.S.S./Forms/C. 2118.

Vol 2

65th Field Ambulance
APRIL - 1916
Page 1.

WAR DIARY
INTELLIGENCE SUMMARY.
(Erase heading not required.)

Army Form C. 2118.

Instructions regarding War Diaries and Intelligence Summaries are contained in F.S. Regs., Part II. and the Staff Manual respectively. Title pages will be prepared in manuscript.

Place	Date	Hour	Summary of Events and Information	Remarks and references to Appendices
La Neuville	1st		Carried on in the Farm of M. Maret. The baths in the village were from the 32nd Div.	
	5th		Handed over to the 63rd Field Ambulance	
	6th		Moved to Ville-sur-Corbie and took over the hill where the 18th Divn Laundry was found to be in order also Baths which had been under 7th Divn'l control	
Ville	8th		Advanced Dressing Station installed at MEAULTE taken over from 23rd Field Ambulance on 6th	
Ville	11th		Heavy bombardment at night. 20 wounded admitted the number of Rifle grenade wounds being very noticeable. Casualty Clearing Station at CORBIE did not carry evacuates, while the 22nd Field Ambulance at DAOURS acts as Corps (XIII) Rest Station	

2353 Wt. W2544/1454 700,000 5/15 D. D. & L. A.D.S.S./Forms/C. 2118.

Army Form C. 2118.

WAR DIARY
or
INTELLIGENCE SUMMARY.
(Erase heading not required.)

65th Field Ambulance
APRIL - 1916
Page 2

Place	Date	Hour	Summary of Events and Information	Remarks and references to Appendices
VILLE	12th		The Frenchies held by the two battalions of the Queen's have good Regimental Aid Posts - The Field Ambulance cars being able to go up as far as the Queen's Relaters of empty cars back to the A.D.S. A post is also established in BECORDEL where cars unloading & waiting cases.	
"	15th		MÉAULTE mainly shelled - 3 men admitted, 2 of whom died of wounds - 10-4+2 chiefly affected - Rifle female wounds still turning over 90% of all battle casualties admitted.	
"	16th		In addition to Anti-Tetanic Serum, the wounded passing through this Field Ambulance receives ½ c.c. doses of Morpho Anti-Gangrene Vaccine. Case of Enteric - Spinal Meningitis suspected - another passed through to the 10	

Army Form C. 2118.

65th Field Ambulance
APRIL 3rd 1916
Page III

WAR DIARY

INTELLIGENCE SUMMARY.

(Erase heading not required.)

Place	Date	Hour	Summary of Events and Information	Remarks and references to Appendices
VILLE	20th		Working party employed on a large dug out between Bearth and Querriu Road it to be used as a undressing Advanced Dressing Station during an action	
"	24th		The Caro was has between Meaulte and Querriu Retreat on ALBERT	
"	30th		BECOURT WOOD and BECORDEL Curler opened M. Carnet isolated from 178 Tunnelling Co. R.E. and Becordetel Very severe bombardment of Becordel by Gas shells. 35 Officers and men admitted "gases" and 35 wounded. The Field Ambulance in addition to the Batts has charge of the Laundry was taken over from the 18 Division 9 cases of Scarlet fever have been admitted during the month.	

R.A.C. Thompson, Major
O.C. 65th F.A. Ambk

Army Form C. 2118.

65 FA mb

Vol 9

WAR DIARY
or
INTELLIGENCE SUMMARY
(Erase heading not required.)

CONFIDENTIAL

WAR DIARY
of
65 Field Ambulance

from 1st May 1st 1916 to May 31st 1916

Vol VIII

COMMITTEE FOR THE
MEDICAL HISTORY OF THE WAR
Date 26 JUN. 1915

1 JUN 1916

Army Form C. 2118.

65 Field Ambulance
May - 1916
Page 1.

WAR DIARY
INTELLIGENCE SUMMARY.
(Erase heading not required)

Instructions regarding War Diaries and Intelligence Summaries are contained in F.S. Regs., Part II. and the Staff Manual respectively. Title pages will be prepared in manuscript.

Place	Date	Hour	Summary of Events and Information	Remarks and references to Appendices
VILLE	MAY 1st		Evacuated 5 Officers wounded (including three "gassed") and 3 sick, 75 wounded and "gassed" other ranks. These being the casualties admitted on the night of 30th April 1st May as a result of Bombardment of Becordel by Gas shells. The majority of the "gassed" cases were slight.	
VILLE	3rd		The 63rd Field Ambulance having established a Divn'al Rest Station at ALLONVILLE sick are now sent there from this Ambulance in the cars of the 64th Field Ambulance who are at BOIRE. Slightly wounded cases are detained and "heater" here. No x M.A.C. collects cases for evacuation to 5 CCS and 3 CCS once daily. All urgent cases are evacuated as soon as admitted in the cars of this Ambulance. Bombardment of MÉAULTE (Huge 51.) at 8p.m. three wounded admitted and one civilian (female) who died of wounds.	R. Hamilton

Army Form C. 2118.

65 Field Ambulance
May - 1916
Page 2.

WAR DIARY
INTELLIGENCE SUMMARY.
(Erase heading not required.)

Instructions regarding War Diaries and Intelligence Summaries are contained in F.S. Regs., Part II. and the Staff Manual respectively. Title pages will be prepared in manuscript.

Place	Date	Hour	Summary of Events and Information	Remarks and references to Appendices
VILLE	11th	12.30 pm	High Shell, MEAULTE again bombarded. Thirteen other ranks admitted wounded.	
VILLE	7th		Evacuations for previous seven days. Officers 2 sick, 8 wounded. Other ranks 42 sick, 120 wounded (including three officers and 35 O.R. "gassed".	
VILLE	14th		CAPTAIN R. STOWERS R.A.M.C. (S.R.) and 3 O.R. R.A.M.C. transferred to newly formed XV Corps Cyclist Battn. Evacuations for previous seven days. Officers wounded two sick two. Other Ranks wounded 144 sick 19. The number of Rifle Grenade wounds is not so great in during last month, the majority of the casualties having occurred during the shelling of BECORDEL and MEAULTE.	
VILLE	21st		Unit inspected by General Officer commanding XV Corps.	[signature]

2353 Wt. W2544/1454 700,000 5/15 D.D. & L. A.D.S.S./Forms/C. 2118.

Army Form C. 2118.

WAR DIARY
of
INTELLIGENCE SUMMARY.

65 Field Ambulance.
3 May – 1916.
Page 3.

(Erase heading not required.)

Place	Date	Hour	Summary of Events and Information	Remarks and references to Appendices
VILLE	21st		Evacuations for previous seven days Officers two sick one wounded. Other Ranks, 25 sick, 18 wounded.	
VILLE VILLE	25 28th		Major R.J.C. Thompson R.A.M.C. (Then commanding) evacuated sick. Evacuations for previous seven days Officers sick two. Other Ranks wounded 26, sick 25.	
VILLE	29th		Evacuated O.R. Hope sick, 14 wounded. One of these were sent in diagnosed "Shell Shock". None of the cases were serious.	
VILLE	31st		MAJOR T.D. RICHMOND assumed command of the Unit. In addition to the ordinary work of a Field Ambulance the Unit has entertained 150 m. in the Baths and Laundry taken over from the 18th Division. Here an average of 1500 men are bathed daily and 500 sets of clothing washed. Four cases of German Measles and 18 cases of scabies during month. No other infectious cases.	

D.A.G.
3rd Echelon.

Herewith AF³ C2118, Being Vol II of the War Diary of this unit — month of June 1916 please.

J S Richmond
Major RAMC
O.C. 65 Field Ambce

10/76.

Army Form C. 2118.

65 J Fmb
Vol 10
June

WAR DIARY
or
INTELLIGENCE SUMMARY.
(Erase heading not required.)

CONFIDENTIAL

War Diary of 65 Field Ambulance
Volume IX
June 1916.

5 AUG. 1916

WAR DIARY or INTELLIGENCE SUMMARY

Army Form C. 2118.

O.C. 65 "F" Fd. Ambulance

Place	Date 1916	Hour	Summary of Events and Information	Remarks and references to Appendices
VILLE	June 1		Evacuations — 4 sick & 7 wounded. Captain STOWERS R.A.M.C. rejoined from XV Corps Cyclist Historian.	
	2		Evacuations — 4 sick & 7 wounded. 23rd & XV Corps & others 21st Divs inspected main dressing station & advanced dressing station today. Was inspected by 23rd & that next medical officer intents made to be emptied and in full as possible given the precaution so as not to attract too also unto a large number of dropping & when to be kept in more during station & used advanced dressing station R.A.M.C. dugouts were investigated in battery	
	3		& QUEENS REDOUBT UNITS. Regimental aid posts at QUEENS REDOUBT & BUNTS REDOUBT examined — 3 sets & 40 units WELLINGTONS RIDGE. G.O.S. at HÉBUTERNE, QUEENS REDOUBT two Regimental aid posts having conversations in the trenches. (fair amount of hostile shelling)	
		9 a.m.	Received Boards 22 men for classification (3 — for observation post 4 TCCS, 2 for Div Rest Station, 6 "D1" 9 "light the service at front") Enemy continues over paid him & hands found in trenches.	
	4	10 a.m.	33 wounded & 5 sick admits. 30 wounds evacuated at	
		10.30 a.m.	Have altered arrangements at Buvk him by this that ambulance is not now do not mention after training to the men in which they inclined. a lot has been impressed to out help report breakdown of the working after being made in wards in cases & values to left & ambulance district not the later immediately. By the Ambulance dressing stt can be brought forward to the infection & also can brought forward to the infection & can disease stuck to the infection & been obstructed. Received message from Capt Dorris that a field "is to be attempts kingfor on hostile Ts matter of Carpets units near at 3 KINGS AVENUE & RECIP by 1 ME YORKS	

WAR DIARY
or
INTELLIGENCE SUMMARY

(Erase heading not required.)

O.C. 65 Field Ambulance

Army Form C. 2118.

Place	Date 1916	Hour	Summary of Events and Information	Remarks and references to Appendices
VILLE-MLL	June 4 contd		Returned by A/Sgts to 6 & 6 Stretcher Squads & 1 N.C.O. to Report. Stretcher Officer 1st E. YORKS. at QUEENS REDOUBT at midnight 4-5. Party left at 10 P.M. Sgt JACKSON in charge. Two motor Ambulances will assist.	
		10 PM	BECORDEL & 2 am Brown sent to Enemy. BECORDEL & 2 am Brown walking cases to be managed together there. All personnel arrived safely. Attempts to run owned an enemy dummy from stores. Bang convoys to return at midnight hits ADS. & fresh arrangements made. Bepaints kept not obvious, with brigade on enemy planes. It was indicated that exposed rumors & no orders that it has been under fire previously.	
	5		By 10.30 am 1 WO 4 officer wounded admitted. 58 OR & 4 WC arrived at 11 am by X MAC works by adding informs us that Grps in front of the horse line capable of office use to be evacuated at from + Ambulance . Orders that 7.A. forwards X.Y.A. himself to walk remain. On asks if acts become empty which will improve at much. It is Lt. Col. ads viewed 23 OR at MERICOURT to be the arrangement those men apparently obtained more from their instruction Gums & accommodation Replies by laundry. Laundry at eve cases but mostly four separate ten owner has 3 large huts	

WAR DIARY
INTELLIGENCE SUMMARY

of 65th Field Ambulance

Army Form C. 2118.

Place	Date 1916	Hour	Summary of Events and Information	Remarks and references to Appendices
VILLE	June 6		Evacuations 1 sick, 7 wounded. Visited ADS. Rearrangements and modifications ADS's mules & transports in that ADS's have been moved so that the ammunition (4 horses) in the horse lines used by this ambulance can be maintained & transport moved obtained. 3 bell tents & a marquee in which to keep tents got a small advance fate. Evacuations 2 sick & 3 wounded.	
	7		Captain E.V.H. GRAY R.A.M.C. (SR) attached to 2nd van Malone turned to struck off strength of 65 Fd Ambulance. Captain W/H. S. MOORE R.A.M.C. (T.C) reports arrived spoken on strength. Lieut MACLACHLAN up for duty ENGLAND on expiration of 1 year contract & struck off strength of Unit. Von Maclaren full address needs in RAB von twenty for 20 weeks be for tonsilitis. New arrangements for handling the bearers of elementary out there stalls that are made important 3 girls then A.F. B.117 was not being received in this unit is coming there it applies steps taken to ensure this being done in future. Owner of home interviewed regarding proposed rearrangement of the stables re von milling offices & on duties.	
	8		Capt. ELLIOT RAMC proceeds on 8 days leave on expiry of 1st year contract. Owner of home now stable made arrangement for family unseen Home refuses them to hire 5 & asks for instruction money for family. Inquiry re money Fd Ambulance regiment & tel von wings.	

Army Form C. 2118.

WAR DIARY
or
INTELLIGENCE SUMMARY.

(Erase heading not required.) OT 65 Fuel Ambulance

Instructions regarding War Diaries and Intelligence Summaries are contained in F.S. Regs., Part II. and the Staff Manual respectively. Title pages will be prepared in manuscript.

Place	Date 1916	Hour	Summary of Events and Information	Remarks and references to Appendices
VILLE	June 8	1.30 am	Guns kept up same shrapnel burst over our army station throughout & manage [illegible] observed in trench.	
			Guns throughout have been comparatively quiet, in getting intermittent outbursts of rapid & probably shelled 2 officers staff went into action. Sentry having been to stretcher & orderly much of the fullness and stretches until communicating the walk of the water. Sever fires started. Some room down, many strikes – no advantage to [illegible].	
	9			
	10		5 beef cutter drawn from Ordnance.	
	11		Various advances & laundry Station. Attention began being paid to drainage ventilation etc. of our buildings. At last have not received position to live & cannot from to [illegible] in laundry 1 room & lime washes to [illegible] & [illegible] of a saltpeter.	
			Showering took place nothing of any special importance. Lieut Macrae Lieut Mason & other interviews ME & will give definite answer tomorrow.	
	12		Capt. GARRATT left unit to another Ambulance today. 15th Corps Sergt [illegible] Artillery Park.	

Army Form C. 2118.

WAR DIARY
or
INTELLIGENCE SUMMARY. 5 C.S. Jul & Aug
(Erase heading not required.)

Instructions regarding War Diaries and Intelligence Summaries are contained in F. S. Regs., Part II. and the Staff Manual respectively. Title pages will be prepared in manuscript.

Place	Date 1916	Hour	Summary of Events and Information	Remarks and references to Appendices
VILLE	June 8		Find that there has been considerable difficulty in getting tech returns. Range which is to compete promptly. In office work we still want 4 forms toilets lock of coordination between various departments from has. Standing orders topped which make self matters separately.	
	9		Report situation in regards Known & Known objects to adms than dump station struck by small fire. Stamped Army no pushing one	
	10		5 additional Bell tents drawn from Ordnance works & slaves & Dressing Stn & Commences attention in arrange	
	11		from laundry & baths. Visits by advns & Jadns & Jadns Divisions. Emptying of new advance dressing stn. Prepared approximate liaison. For interviews over & from re. Prepare approx. & for needs & expenditure from medical augents.	
	12		Capt. GARRATT R.A.M.C. left with 15 Corps Seige artillery Park. For temporary duty with 51 Div. Train.	
	13	4 pm	Transport inspected by Ot. Div. Train. Visited by adms 5/6 Dns. Visits advanced dressing station at QUEENS REDOUBT & SUBWAY. At Queens Redoubt nothing done out completed yet. At Lens store there is 1 much work in progress & much debris to clear away for & westrall hours is no more for striches but will be MIDDLESEX trench. Officers present	

2353 Wt. W3514/1454 700,000 5/15 D. D. & L. A.D.S.S./(Forms)/C. 2118.

6

Army Form C. 2118.

WAR DIARY

INTELLIGENCE SUMMARY.

(Erase heading not required.)

O.C. C6 Fld Ambulance

Instructions regarding War Diaries and Intelligence Summaries are contained in F.S. Regs., Part II. and the Staff Manual respectively. Title Pages will be prepared in manuscript.

Place	Date	Hour	Summary of Events and Information	Remarks and references to Appendices
VILLE-	1916 June 13 contnd		Sent Adjm [Adjutant] party to assist in work on dug-out ordinary duties by Regiments. Who vacated by him. I was this afd [afternoon] of view & leaving Range. Owner of house refuses to let us in there. Horses required for ADMS visits asked him to get Subway depot vacates for us. Dr. Cns [?] asked him arrangements to obtain Chaplain.	
	14		Ht Fields Medical Card (W.3118) Ran and have intvd by the unit was for 5,000 cards & envelops & arranges scheme to be adopted for the issuing of trolleys & trolley patients at the drying station. Returned the horses & Ht Harveys stores & to en [?] incidents for (Noble Quartermaster) to put in to dugouts. Drew up report to Received instructions from ADMS that from today our Survey Station is to be kept as empty of stretcher as possible, are not likely to be got full when in a march are to be sent to 1.C.C.S.	
	15		Sent up some stores to Subway dugout, began arranges tarenues to be at various stations during advance & of positions stores alongway up at names Ale factory asked orders to be ? in a St [?] railway station — visits A.D.S.	

A.D.S.S./Forms/C.2118.

Army Form C. 2118.

WAR DIARY
or
INTELLIGENCE SUMMARY.
(Erase heading not required.) O.C. 65- Fd Ambulance

Place	Date 1916	Hour	Summary of Events and Information	Remarks and references to Appendices
VILLE	June 16		Most of remaining 85th interviewed for Loans Reservist & Subway taken up tonight. Trenny hours 20 laid steads to be from Rev am surrey. Knewes Trophouse in hours & dugouts an in trenches. Turnover for Officers & their hours new Jugouts an organisation room. Lieut S. POOL Rauc Sergeant Lees assistance for rum company along with infantry infermen.	
	18		Issued Rums in project as all contents (7 men) Classified as "T.U" & to ment to CCS as trundus. W.C ADMS. visits Surgeon Sherry Reserve Small Regimental aid posts attached and 'le relieves by 65 Fd A. Took up Captain STOWERS Ranc & 2 NCO's who will be in charge of Bearers. Gradually all 85th interviews on dugouts and new installs they had been course of all ambulance wagons or rigin.	
	19		Three Dressing Staton & Advanced Dressing Station inspected by Surgeon General MACPHERSON as the accompanied by DDN's XV Corps & ADMS 21st Div	
	20		Work proceeding Subway at fd Station. A great and has had to be in use in cleaning up & disinfectly, also by man. So an Ken in cleaning up & disinfectly, also by man. So an Inspection & Officiers previous handled Summer of civil struck in VILLE village during Station on few days & through or under the hospital form and fresh day when men but in VILLE by Trunks Jus Ronges	

A.D.S.S./Forms/C. 2118.

Army Form C. 2118.

WAR DIARY
or
INTELLIGENCE SUMMARY.
(Erase heading not required.)

O.C. 65-7 Fd. Ambulance

Place	Date 1916	Hour	Summary of Events and Information	Remarks and references to Appendices
VILLE MILL	Jan 20th		Visits tile factory at adms & noted how preparations were made at MEAULTE & in WILLOW avenue in regards their probability for wheeled stretchers. Received from adms plans & material arrangements in the event of action. Yesterday the 65th Fd. Ambulance endeavours to transfer to grounds. Reviewed points at Railway station at Queens Redoubt, Gateway to MEAULTE. Removed Sheep but will be taken to a main dressing station from these ADS's formed by 64th F.A. The 65th will establish also an Dr'g in some collecting station set up — Chateau (made a rumour field factory) from when the wounded will be conveyed by wagons & pontoon from 1 to 36 CCS at HEILLY. Separate medical arrangements, to all in absence, were made. Transport arrangements (green) Ambulance were: Fd Factory of ADS — nil transport speed, & No 2 ? MT. Captain STOWERS visits QUEENS REDOUBT with adms.	
	21			
	22		visits 64th F.A. at BOIRE.	
	23		arranged to make tour of two Regimental aid posts Capt STOWERS who will be in charge. From Petaw leaving here at 10 am tomorrow with NCO's	
	24	10—	adms visits the advanced dressing station & Regimental aid posts at MEAULTE shown to Queen Redoubt & returns to cooperate. Saw Capt visits ADS at MEAULTE SUBWAY & QUEENS REDOUBT with adms. Wanted to watch D.D. & L. D.A.D.S.S. Ford/C.2118 & men who are already at places when they are attacked when during new operations	

WAR DIARY or INTELLIGENCE SUMMARY

Army Form C. 2118.

(Erase heading not required.) OC 65th Field Ambulance

Place	Date 1916	Hour	Summary of Events and Information	Remarks and references to Appendices
VILLE MILL	June 24 cont.	6.30 PM	Visits the history of ADS MEAULTE & Reviews situation that gas mask was not the gas trays at 10 PM.	
			The enemy all morning action jammed as complete at Queen Redoubt showing 9 ADS MEAULTE is temporary station the "working party" intended for subway.	
		6.45	Received message from ADMS that all ambulances from Army Group in ADS should in consequence send to 64th Field ambulance MERICOURT from the 25th inclusive. Enemys at ADS that the wounds came into force at 9 am. However that is probable would be relieved "ADS 65th & 6 " & that they would not be admitted on as APD took with OC 64 FA & that effect then is the provisional arrangement.	
		9 PM	ADMS visits however. OC 64 FA visits proposes from from Hq. Headquarters however the grass not there note at OC 64 FA	
	25		He however sent 6 intended stretchers to Queen's Redoubt, 6 to twenty, & reminders for the training army lorries giving entrances all night.	
	26	10.30 AM	Receives instructions from ADMS to send an officer up to SUBWAY during action. Capt MOORE details it and relieves stage still.	
		3 PM	Visits SUBWAY & QUEENS REDOUBT ADSs. Took up 1 officer (Lieut McKAY) & NCO's & to Beavers, numerary to make two of trenches from Redoubt to RAPs	OC 65 FA

WAR DIARY or INTELLIGENCE SUMMARY

Army Form C. 2118.

Unit: 1/1 65th Field Ambulance

Place	Date	Hour	Summary of Events and Information	Remarks and references to Appendices
VILLE SOUS MILL	June 26 1916 continued		in 3 factors Active retaliation was going on against our trenches & gas has been replied to all about mid day. Many trenches were shelled. I arrived not complete until 2 officers given to Capt STOWERS (Mc QUEENS REDOUBT A.D.S.) Sketch maps of trenches & bearer posts, also nominal roll of bearers but of "Y" & "Sun" Division & Regiments known to be in the various R.A.P.s. One Serjeant at Queens Redoubt is being used temporarily by a medical officer in a R.A.P. & has hopes to be able to do so at a later date. Bearers today will get all haven up to Queens Redoubt & in position & any before the amount but firs will not be able to do so. 7 stretcher and up in mby in tumber before that reminder will be wounded at MEAULTE [next to a] she dug outs at Pollat the 3 Queens entertainments (the Factory) For regiments painfully tired at Pollat. they are now A.D.M.S. expects alone where no others had applied. Mr. COTTERALL and arrangements) one team of 65 Fld Amb & 100 stretcher has arrived here afternoon in Quine in front of A.D.S. Heavy rain fell the afternoon.	[signatures]

| | | | | |
Place: | VILLE SOUS MILL A.D.S at MEAULTE | | | |

WAR DIARY
INTELLIGENCE SUMMARY of 65 Field Ambulance

Army Form C. 2118.

Place	Date 1916	Hour	Summary of Events and Information	Remarks and references to Appendices
VILLE SUR MILL	June 27		Numerous efforts made for medical stores from various officers and regimental units have been very urgent. There has been conflict with our own M.O.s to admit to a depot of Famine stores. Unit M.O.s reported what we kept then - we did not seem to have up to the supplies apparently in that right to do - but seen then mentioned to now run low and we work up to the fact on the eve of battle. Remaining patients (8 in number) discharged to duty today, are patients from A.D.S. now being taken down to MERICOURT (64 Fd) Forty six (46) patients passed through NEAVILTE A.D.S. from 5.30 pm yesterday to 5.30 am today. Twenty beds to casualty men bearers are taken in strength of ambulance Lieut. S.C. SHANKS R.A.M.C. (T.C.) arrived & taken in strength of unit	
	28	9 am	Lieut HUMPHREYS & Lieut McKAY proceeded to take up positions in SUBWAY + QUEENS REDOUBT advanced dressing stations respectively	
		9.30	R.A.M.C. of section order no 15 received. Received of personnel & medical stores to CHATEAU ("the Factory") in readiness to open a divisional collecting station E.2.a.6.4. Received change cancelling instructions in orders no. 15 . Unit will stand by full packet orders. Departures 16 Bearers to Queen Redoubt - if these two are to be attached to each	E.22.a.3.4. [?]
		2.30		
		5 PM		

Army Form C. 2118.

WAR DIARY
or
INTELLIGENCE SUMMARY.

(Erase heading not required.) Of 65th Field ambulance

Place	Date 1916	Hour	Summary of Events and Information	Remarks and references to Appendices
CHATEAU E26 a 64 nr. ALBERT	June 28		Regimental medical officer Recces. A.D.S's M.144 Scout movement of stretchers.	
	29		50 men stretcher relands received. Quiet day. Got much useful work done in repairing huts & roads at Bush used subway Operation (CHATEAU). Vendu faily good, received shows of operation order no 16 received	
	30	7.15 am		
		11.30 am	Visits A.D.S's at MEAULTE SUBWAY & QUEENS REDOUBT, & gave instructions re st:ours no 76 to officers stretcher pats Zones brought in order & trauma.	
		2.30	1 officer & 50 o.r's from C of 64th Fuses Ambulance reported at CHATEAU. (reported of moviment & 2 bun ambulance 65 f.A) arranges sent forward. will leave than at 3:30 am	
		10.30 pm	moved to Queens Redoubt. A.D.S. Weather very good. Troops going up to trenches appear in excellent splints.	

J.D. [signature]
Lt Col
O.C. 65 F.Amb.

21st Division

65th Field Ambulance

July 1916.

VOL II
MEDICAL

WAR DIARY or INTELLIGENCE SUMMARY.
Army Form C. 2118.

JULY 1916
OC 65 Field Ambulance

Place	Date 1916	Hour	Summary of Events and Information	Remarks and references to Appendices
MEAULTE (CHATEAU ETANG)	July 1	AM	Attack on FRICOURT fixed to begin at 7.30 am today.	
		4.45	First mortuary cars arrived (2 wounded)	
		6.30	Two bearer sub-divisions of 65 Fd Amb and left CHATEAU (Divisional Collecting Stn) to proceed to Queens Redoubt where they were to form up by 7 am. Also two squads on horse ambcars of 64 F.A. On leaving CHATEAU (64 F.A.) were also in reserve.	
		6.30	Under orders of Divn dispatched 5 stretcher squads of bearers (as a reserve) to Queens Redoubt.	
		7.15	4 wounded men arrived. Have just orders for bearer sub-division & 6 horse ambulance wagons & CCS at HEILLY, in house & large numbers of wounded & wagons & 6.15 patients have been admitted & evacuated to CCS from the divisional collecting station.	
	PM 3.		Have had a large number of wounded & wagons & 6.15 patients have been admitted & evacuated to CCS from the divisional collecting station.	
		9.40	1707 patients have been evacuated, by means of horse wagons, empty lorries char-a-bancs to the MAC. The MAC were two vacs, & cleared 110 lying & 51 sitting at 6.30, which patients were brought down by various farm wagons & vehicles, temp. brought in by various farm carts through to MAC the patients who had marched down, have been fed & rested early, and every evidence of the patients was made apparent. All the patients have been patiently attended to, emptying the carts, demand & further applications for more supplies was made, some in great demand. The carts nevertheless still toil together and eager to be served as empty wagons	
			total personnel (38 in all) were busily engaged.	

WAR DIARY
INTELLIGENCE SUMMARY. of 65th Field Ambulance

Army Form C. 2118.

Place	Date 1916	Hour	Summary of Events and Information	Remarks and references to Appendices
MEAULTE (CHATEAU) E.22.a.6.4	July 1		+ was attrbn. to watch the large numbers of cases. Genie & ventures (chiefly military potion) are enemy put in the evacuating station were large numbers are being dealt with. Approximately about 1800 patients last seen numbers (see appendices I of Summary of numbers treated)	E.22.a.6.4 Appendix I
	2	10 a	Lieuts XV Corps & 2 ARMQ X3 Corps inspects Div adv: recg. station.	
		10.30	Visit Advanced aid station at MEAULTE, SUBWAY & QUEEN'S REDOUBT. Personnel are there. Great strain of wounded arriving. Seven generally are stoning up of patients are very complete owing in the roads. Such are brought back from aid. medical. Composting far patients running into thousands evacuating station was	
		6.30 PM	Capt MENZIES 64 Fd Ambulance reports from that the roads from Sunken road through FRICOURT were very difficult by the Engineers to that it would not be possible to take ambulances up to SUNKEN ROAD. Ambce. got away many wounded who had not been well to get out before. Proceeded with him & many 5 horse ambulance wagons, picking up four men of the divisional Energy Company to act as train: wagon men got up to a point opposite LOZENGE WOOD about the two teams then was impossible for wagons to reach it. mention from right few were taken with it	about X.27 & 3.2
	12 mdngt			

Army Form C. 2118.

WAR DIARY
or
INTELLIGENCE SUMMARY. OF 63- Field Ambulance
(Erase heading not required.)

Place	Date 1916	Hour	Summary of Events and Information	Remarks and references to Appendices
MEAULTE	JULY 3 contd		engines with lying cases, so stopped retaining motor ambulances after MEAULTE. Owing the more severe cases to C.C.S.	
		8 PM	Sent Capt ELLIOT to FRICOURT to meet Capt MENZIES who has established a dressing station there.	
		6 PM	Received orders to take heavy to move at short notice as the Division was being withdrawn. We use stands over to 51st Field Ambulance (17th Division) all personnel in motor from A.D.S. on relief by 51st Field Ambulance	Afternoon 26th (Summary July) see noted
		8.30	All running cases & lances are to some dressing Station 51st Field Ambulance	
		11 PM	A.D.S. parties arrives	
		11.30	Capt ELLIOT Party arrives from FRICOURT with rifle wounds right forearm. He was eventually removed by 51st Field Ambulance	
	4	1 am	Received orders that personal moves entrain at DERNANCOURT siding at 10 am. Transport proceeding by road.	
		8.30 am	Left CHATEAU for VILLE MILL	
		11.20	Transport left for AILLY-SUR-SOMME in charge of Captain ADDIS.	
		11.45	Motor ambulances left under LIEUTENANT EMBLEM.	

Army Form C. 2118.

WAR DIARY
or
INTELLIGENCE SUMMARY.
(Erase heading not required.)

Oc 65 Field Ambulance

Place	Date 1916 July	Hour	Summary of Events and Information	Remarks and references to Appendices
	3rd		About 40 wounded were found in a large German dugout near the Sunken Road. Some of them had been put into the Sunken Road since the North advance and were to have been sent back after dressing. Other cases were sent down to the Motor Waggon which took them on to the enemy advanced dressing station. Much contest in our advance to the German dugouts to bearers up to the Capture margin [or] point. Returns to Fricourt at dawn great many [by] the Withdrew capture [?] of gas bombs from shell turns to our waggons. STONES from Queens Redoubt A.D.S. to meet at the enemy where moving the waggons were [?] removed into new [?] the FRICOURT road is practicable.	
		12 noon	a waggon loads of sitting cases arrived at the Queens attending station from the troops engaged in the morning attack (master 8:46 am). During the afternoon many patients arrived walking & many Sealily wounded were brought in cars from evacuation post at FRICOURT, or the A.D.S. at the enemy was congested. About 50 German wounded were redirected also lying cases amongst German wounded were transferred to Cavalry field ambulance at MORLANCOURT. Very busy all afternoon. Became	

Army Form C. 2118.

WAR DIARY
or
INTELLIGENCE SUMMARY.
(Erase heading not required.)

OC 65 Field Ambulance

Place	Date 1916	Hour	Summary of Events and Information	Remarks and references to Appendices
LE MESGE	JULY 8		Details Officer to Section & appointed Transport Officer (Capt ADDIS) & Adjutant (Capt STOWERS). Starts to check & sort equipment which less serviceable owing to burious moves.	
	9		Receive orders from 64th Infantry Brigade to prepare to move — transport protected by red mourn, personal System in following day. Instructs men regarding move. Leaving, packing of equipment continues. C Section renders open to field during tobrum.	
		11:15 am	Receive orders for move. Transport under 3 hour removals.	
		2:30 pm	Transport moves out & marches to QUERRIEU, rests there & march to VILLE in following day.	
		10:00	R.A.M.C. further order No 19 received. Personnel entrains at HILLY not 62. Bayonne in train leaving 10:15 am onward march to-day. Move at 7 am	
	10	1:30 am	Receive 64 Bde. Operation order No 59 which states 65th Fd. Amb moves at 6 am. that in view of ADDIS's own orders to entrain to move at 7 am.	
		7 am	Personnel starts by electric works.	
		9 am	Left LE MESGE after arranging for collection & disposal of sick of units in Brigade area. BILLY. Winnow Capt STOWERS.	

Army Form C. 2118.

WAR DIARY
or
INTELLIGENCE SUMMARY.
(Erase heading not required.)

Oc 65 Yeus Amentaine

Instructions regarding War Diaries and Intelligence Summaries are contained in F. S. Regs., Part II. and the Staff Manual respectively. Title pages will be prepared in manuscript.

Place	Date 1916	Hour	Summary of Events and Information	Remarks and references to Appendices
VILLE- MILL	JULY 4th	9.40 AM	Left with transport to entrain at DERNANCOURT up 10 AM trains. Was not entrain before 2 PM, but where for be at DERNANCOURT at	
		12 noon	arrived at DERNANCOURT & reported to MAYOMC.	
			about 1 PM a very thunderstorm accompanied by heavy rain which continues all afternoon. Some rendering very trying to the unwary.	
			Troops.	
		7 PM	Tents then were running up.	
		8 PM	Train left at AILLY-SUR-SOMME	
	5th	1 AM	arrives quarters at AILLY. & marches its billets	
PICQUIGNY		2.30	arrives at billets in PICQUIGNY. billets in large house in main road. Excellent accommodation but sanitation not good.	
			Capt. RICHARDSON. & lads report today	
	6	9 PM	Received message that unit will move to LE MESGE, time to march to be Notifies later	
		11 (PM)	Rane Op. order. received. ordering unit will move before 3 PM tomorrow	
	7	3.30 PM	Left PICQUIGNY grounds via SOVES to LE MESGE	
		6 PM	arrives at LE MESGE. Billets in same in main road EAST of church accommodation very limited put one section into tents.	

Army Form C. 2118.

WAR DIARY
or
INTELLIGENCE SUMMARY.
(Erase heading not required.)

OC 65 Field Ambulance

Instructions regarding War Diaries and Intelligence Summaries are contained in F.S. Regs., Part II. and the Staff Manual respectively. Title pages will be prepared in manuscript.

Place	Date	Hour	Summary of Events and Information	Remarks and references to Appendices
CHATEAU	JULY 1916 12	8.30 am	Received message from OC 63 Fd Amb to take over of all above here station tents & operated sites to 80 bearers.	
		10 am	Visited Sidings (new dressing station of 63 Fd Ambulance) to inspect part of 63 as in charge of evacuation.	
		2 pm	Received Route Orders No 20. Sent in to addrs. list of names of Officers, NCOs & men acting as worthy mention for gd'ts & similar purposes.	
		9 pm	Arrange relays Stand prepared 24 hours	
	13	10 am	Visited MERICOURT (64 Fd Amb emergency) to arrange next to OC 64 Fd Amb about transfer of patients to our front.	
		4 pm	With 8 cars units of 63 Fd Amb ambulance at sidings and proceeded through MAMETZ to arrange movements receiving parts of our line of evacuation.	
		7 pm 7.45 pm 9.14 pm	Previous message as to time of attack. Sent up 3 ford cars to go up to 50 yards dist to be reached by motor Chan a-bancs arriving in evacuation for hrs to CCS. Stored vehicles with living wounded down. Slept.	
		7 pm	Sent 6 ... vehicles to 65 Fd ambulance wounded expected from 12 noon gathering 12 noon today = 100	

Army Form C. 2118.

WAR DIARY
or
INTELLIGENCE SUMMARY.
(Erase heading not required.) O.C. 65 Field Ambulance

Instructions regarding War Diaries and Intelligence Summaries are contained in F. S. Regs., Part II. and the Staff Manual respectively. Title pages will be prepared in manuscript.

Place	Date 1916	Hour	Summary of Events and Information	Remarks and references to Appendices
	JULY 10th contd		Proceeded by cars through AMIENS & ALBERT to CHATEAU (1E 22 a 6 4) to make arrangements for taking over from 57th Field Ambulance. Found Chateau very congested with transport & personnel to & chiens to have transport & personnel at VILLE MILL of possible. Made arrangements accordingly. Learnt that present detachment entrenches at AILLY at 6 P.M. may arrange for men to billet for night at VILLE MILL to delay in relieving.	
VILLE-MILL	11	1.15 am	Received message from OC 57th Field Ambulance that to may entrench at 7 am at MEAULTE.	
		2.30	Personnel arrived towing wounded from CORBIE	
		5.30	Dressing Station opened at CHATEAU by C Section.	
CHATEAU		10 am	Instructed by Adms to send patients to 64th Field Ambulance at MERICOURT and those dying of dressing Station must be examined for wounds.	
		2 pm	Supports Lieuts SHANKS, McCRAY & MOL to report to OC 63 FA at Sydney.	
		2.30	Notes Subway recorded. unit was of relieving parties etc for ___ relieving Station thence , should no more patients of ___ room at MEAULTE as a manner despatched from there in a long number of troops there apparently entrenched ___ officers	

Army Form C. 2118.

WAR DIARY
or
INTELLIGENCE SUMMARY.

(Erase heading not required.)

Lt. 65th Yorks Ammunce

Place	Date 1916	Hour	Summary of Events and Information	Remarks and references to Appendices
CHATEAU	JULY 15	12 NOON	Numbers admitted & wounded from noon yesterday till noon today = 956. Reinforcements 15 cavalry 2 infantry. All three patrols have been advanced & driving dug-outs, wounded sent entertainers fed and recovered. Artillery efforts. Twelve lorries as now in use especially waggons to evacuate to Vigneumont & 4 cross field from subway to ruins. Louvely, the Lorries much supplies by running that all pair through our farming hut and an important rest to the removed rolls of each between lots are made three to the new of "Agripa" accordingly. A given as numbers getten too. All the arrival of all the van itr in front in cases up convoys in relays at other pennants at hours. Kept eight running from the vicinity as far as possible thing at house strangling from other party message to divn. The vigilance of the cooks that guards from the relieved well higher than efforts other arrived rich and sent to CdB. The dispatch rider rescued two of a different copy kept. All convoys etc on the way to or from VIOQUEMONT no transport was allowed out without ORDS. Relays have been running in fact all trains on almost a day & night for empty lorries.	Relieved Lt. 65 Yd annuluar
		6 PM		

Army Form C. 2118.

WAR DIARY
or
INTELLIGENCE SUMMARY.

O.C. 65·4 Field Ambulance

(Erase heading not required.)

Instructions regarding War Diaries and Intelligence Summaries are contained in F. S. Regs., Part II and the Staff Manual respectively. Title pages will be prepared in manuscript.

Place	Date 1916	Hour	Summary of Events and Information	Remarks and references to Appendices
CHATEAU	JULY 14	10.30 am	240 cars leaves our 3rd corn.	
		11 am	D.D.M.S. XV corps orders strained dressing station & improvised our sends all sitting cases to C.C.S. at VECQUEMONT and only lying cases to HÉRICOURT (64th Field Ambulance) from 12 noon onwards. Thirteen empty lorries arrived for 374 patients evacuation.	
		12 noon 12.30		
		4 pm	286 cases evacuated since 12 noon, 570 remaining.	
		5.10	Rest very heavy. Left for C.C.S. since 12 midnight, 232 ... 64th F.A.	C.C.S.
		5.55 pm	328 ... C.C.S. 7 German wounded	
		8.45 pm	Since 5.55 pm 177 patients (including 2 officers & 3 Germans) have been evacuated to C.C.S.	
		9.40	The lorries departed to VECQUEMONT at 5.15 PM have not returned. The journey from here to C.C.S. is long (15 miles) and by roads encumbered with traffic. The difficulty in removal from here to C.C.S. is insuperable. Taking this into consideration the train up of 12 supply lorries to ars. as one journey serious inconvenience has been experienced by C.C.S. the train now available for mere numerous trips to the evacuation of sitting cases & transport of lying cases.	
		10.45 pm	Subsequent reports clear of sitting cases	

Army Form C. 2118.

WAR DIARY
or
INTELLIGENCE SUMMARY.

Of 65th Field Ambulance

(Erase heading not required)

Place	Date 1916	Hour	Summary of Events and Information	Remarks and references to Appendices
CHATEAU	JULY 15	6.30	Receive instructions that 3rd CCS at HEILLY is now at the CCS & only half an hour emergency in VECQUEMONT, to maintain out be kept in touch with	
		6.30 pm	Two supply columns form under...	
		7.25	Supply column left with 223 patients for HEILLY	
		10 pm	Three (3) supply convoys reports from our supply column & with 66 patients	
	16		Quiet night but night staff attended a most welcome rest. Received damage that 7th Sur 33rd Div, next 64th Infantry Bde as support with reserve and attack HIGH WOOD at 5 pm	
		11 am	Number of patients evacuated from 12 noon yesterday to 12 midd today = 935. So that the two evacuations	
		12 noon	...about one thousand patients passed through each day. Weather continues inconveniently hot....	
		2 pm	A large convoy...	
		6 pm	...by orders XV Corps to return all ... to C.C.S. met up our transport...	

Army Form C. 2118.

WAR DIARY
or
INTELLIGENCE SUMMARY.
(Erase heading not required.)

Of 65 Fld Ambulance

Instructions regarding War Diaries and Intelligence Summaries are contained in F. S. Regs., Part II and the Staff Manual respectively. Title pages will be prepared in manuscript.

Place	Date 1916	Hour	Summary of Events and Information	Remarks and references to Appendices
CATTEAU	JULY 16	7.30 p.m.	Horse Transport returned from Herrin in [?] good condition considering the strenuous work they had had. The mules [?] have of two mules have been destroyed of [?] the [?] type of [?] ambulance two bar animals by [?] on staff our horses ambulances wagons [?]. One shrapneled car ambulance returned, notwithstanding [?] to [?] our stud car (with 4 lying patients) has its cover pierced by [?] pieces of steel, fortunately none of the patients were injured.	
			Another quiet night.	
	17.	12 noon	Patients have been evacuating in steadily throughout in small numbers. 156 have been admitted & evacuated since 12 noon yesterday.	
		7.45	Capt MENZIES returned from OT 63 Fd. ambulance, OT ask that all transport of spare [?] trans be sent to 15 Stationary tonight, in an attempt on our [?] tonight in the morning.	
		8.30	Ran[?] of motor men No 21 arrived. 33rd Div relieved 21st Div [?] motor transport between two [?] divisions. 65 Fd ambulance with remainder of [?] & motor [?] took over as of J.C. Station [?]	
	18	3.30 pm	Provins & Officer have all returned.	
		12 noon	195 patients admitted evacuated from noon yesterday to noon today.	

Army Form C. 2118.

WAR DIARY
or
INTELLIGENCE SUMMARY.
(Erase heading not required.)

Of 4.5th Fd Ambulance

Place	Date 1916	Hour	Summary of Events and Information	Remarks and references to Appendices
CHATEAU CORBIE	JULY 18th contd	am 2.30	Staff Officer (Capt. MOORE, Lieut. HUMPHREYS & Lieut McKAY) have proceeded to 2nd 64th Field Ambulance at MERICOURT, (more instructions from ADMS)	
		on 6.30	Bearer Officers doing duty with 63rd Field Ambulance returns to Headquarters. Message received that officers & footprints await further orders.	
			195 patients admitted & evacuated from 12 noon yesterday to 12 noon today	
	19	11 am	Received message from ADMS to have an all stretchers equipments to 33rd Bde Field Ambulance & various parks at the CHATEAU. Patients admitted in last 24 hours = 579	Appendix 2 (enclosed) amended 24 enclosed. Total (11-19 July)
		12 no.		
		12.45	Received verbal order from ADMS to move to ALLONVILLE this afternoon via QUERRIEU.	
		3.30	55 (Lieuts in Mac. L5 not needed to date. Sent message to 27 MAC asking if he can to clear 27 & starts to CCS	
		4 pm	Of 99th Fd Amb Ambulance arrives to take over marks out tent sub for marching out 3 MAC cars arrives to take all patients that are waiting of 16 admins & everyone put in convoy not today	
		10.15 pm	Arrives ALLONVILLE	

Army Form C. 2118.

WAR DIARY
or
INTELLIGENCE SUMMARY. O.C. 65 Fld Ambulance
(Erase heading not required.)

Place	Date 1916 JULY	Hour	Summary of Events and Information	Remarks and references to Appendices
ALLONVILLE	20	1 PM	Receives orders to move to ARGOEUVES. It in afternoon. To 64th Fd. Amb.	
		3 PM	Marches out.	
		6 PM	arrives ARGOEUVES.	
ARGOEUVES	21	6.30 PM	Receives orders to entrain at LONGEAU tomorrow at 6.48 to be at entraining station at 5.48 am transport at 3.48 am. Lieut HUMPHRYS arrives for duty on temporary exchange charge 15-9-9 × 9 Transport left for LONGEAU marching via DREUIL of AMIENS	
	22	12.15 am	R.A.M.C personnel left at 2.15 am & arrives at LONGEAU at 5.40 am motor ambulances waggons left at 7am as a convoy under Lieut POOL	
		2.15 am		
		7 am	Train left	
		11.45	arrives & began to detrain. Detraining facilities very good.	
			Reported to D.A.D.M.S who informed me full move to HOUVIN HOUVIGNEUL 64 Fd Amb was not to take place today or tomorrow, yet in fact no staff Captain into town to see, or ascertain. Sent Officer (mounted) officers.	
		12.41 PM	Left St POL.	
		4.15	Whilst horses Sans 1 HOUVAIN not D.A.D.M.S who informed us on WM 15 in at SARS-LEZ-BOIS, sent 1 empty lorry in front of, battery R.E.	
		5.15	arrives SARS-LEZ-BOIS. Transport/wagons Accommodation very limited indeed. Men very tired after long march.	
SARS-LEZ-BOIS	23		Lieut McKAY evacuates this evening to C.C.S. FREVENT suffering from tenosynovitis right wrist	
	24		Motor ambulances giving much trouble in consequence of broken trains - 3 fare now in workshop.	

Army Form C. 2118.

WAR DIARY
or
INTELLIGENCE SUMMARY. Of 65 Field Ambulance

(Erase heading not required.)

Instructions regarding War Diaries and Intelligence Summaries are contained in F.S. Regs., Part II and the Staff Manual respectively. Title pages will be prepared in manuscript.

Place	Date 1916	Hour	Summary of Events and Information	Remarks and references to Appendices
SARS-LEZ BOIS	25 JULY	4 PM	Went into formation of NCO's. Received preliminary name of taking over from 44th Fd Amb (14th Div) their 4 stretcher cases in charge of the Rail Station at LIENCOURT and Advanced dressing station at ARRAS.	
		5.30	Visits 44th Fd Amb at LIENCOURT	
	26	3 PM	Sent up advance party to ADS at ECOLE NORMALE. ARRAS. Two Officers (Capt RICHARDSON & Lieut POOL), 1 NCO, 11 Bearers, 1 Clerk, 1 Nursing Orderly, 1 cook.	
		3.15	Received RAMC OO No 23. 65th Fd Ambulance taken over ADS & 2 collecting posts (St NICHOLAS & St CATHERINE) on 27th, also D.R.S. on 29th.	
	27	10.30 AM	Visited ADS. Took up 20 Bearers of C Section.	
		5 PM	Set up advance of C Section with Capt WELCH RAMC who will act right aid at ADS till Lt-Colonel FETCHIN his battalion, Lieut SHANKS attached for temporary duty with 1st EAST YORKS & and at battalion. The evening arranged to take over at 2 am tomorrow. Delivery rations.	JR 25.7.16 JR 26.7.16
	28	2 AM		

Army Form C. 2118.

WAR DIARY
or
INTELLIGENCE SUMMARY. OC 65 F.dS Ambulance
(Erase heading not required.)

Place	Date 1916	Hour	Summary of Events and Information	Remarks and references to Appendices
SARS-LEZ-BOIS	JULY 28 cont'd	AM 12.45	Visited ADS. There is much improvement in same and in the basement of ECOLE NORMALE men are supplied stores as furniture is available at RAP.s. Arranged to send up Brown Sprechenen (3 sets) to the Memou types ADR.s to arrange for us to obtain telephone between ADS & DR.S. enemy but the distance (1½ miles) between them is keeping one set of very great use.	
		5 PM	Capt STOWERS left to attend gas demonstrations at 3rd Army Headquarters.	
	29	11.45 1.15	Motor amb SARS-LEZ-BOIS arrived LIENCOURT proceeded to take our Divisional Rest Station, returning 116 patients.	
	31		Number of patients in DR.S. today – 121 of whom 9 for discharge ADR.S notified.	

J.B. Richmond
O.C. 65 F.dS Amb...

APPENDIX 201

Army Form C. 2118.

65th Field Ambulance
May 1916

WAR DIARY
or
INTELLIGENCE SUMMARY.
(Erase heading not required.)

Summary of Events and Information

SUMMARY OF CASES ADMITTED & EVACUATED — July 1st/4th n. 15 July 4k. (795.m.)

DATE.		ADMISSIONS						EVACUATIONS						TRANSFERS					Remarks
---	---	2 Div	7th Div	14th Div	34th Div	Other Divs.	Total.	21 Div	7th Div	14th Div	34th Div	Other Divs	Total.	21 Div	7th Div	14th Div	34th Div	Other Divs	Total.
Sat. 1/7/16	W	86				10	96	77				8	85							
	S	3					3	3					3							
Sun. 2/7/16	W	1505	1	282	50		1838	1379		293	43		1696	75	— Nil —	9	4	88	
	S	2			—		2	2					2	—	— Nil —				
Mon 3/7/16	W	107		23	10	1	141	127	1	18	10		156	32	—	5		34	
	S	16		10			27			3		1	5	12		7		19	
Tues 4/7/16	W	169		172	5	3	349	166		172	5	3	346	3		2		5	
	S	5		9			14	2		4		3	9						
Grand Totals	Wounded	1867	1	477	65	14	2424	1449	1	463	58	12	2283	117	—	14	4	135	
	Sick	26		19	1		46	8		10		1	19	15		9		24	

3 men (S) and 5 men (W) were returned to duty
34 officers were admitted and evacuated
200 wounded German Prisoners were admitted & transferred to 2nd Can. Fd. Amb.

APPENDIX W 2

Army Form C. 2118.

65th Field Ambulance
July 1914

WAR DIARY or INTELLIGENCE SUMMARY.

(Erase heading not required.)

SUMMARY OF CASES ADMITTED & EVACUATED July 11th (6 a.m.) to July 19th (4 p.m.)

DATE	OFFICERS ADMISSIONS Sick W'DD		OFFICERS EVACUATIONS S	W	OTHER RANK ADMISSIONS S	W	OTHER RANK EVACUATIONS S	W	RET'D DUTY S	W	MAIN D.S.(64TH) S	W	GERMAN W.	Remarks
July 11th					14	41								
" 12th		1	1		9	40					13	38		
" 13th	1			1	25	92		24	2	20	9	39		
" 14th		9		9	27	929	29	920	4	1	18	61	Approx 100	
" 15th		3		3	11	970	21	969		4			50	
" 16th		3		3	20	19	20	14						
" 17th		3		3	38	229	30	220	6	10				
" 18th		4		4	22	11	18	62		1		8		
" 19th	1		1		30	14	19	49						
GRAND TOTALS	2	23	2	23	194	2443	135	2257	12	36	38	144	150	

Of the above 1386 (W) and 93 (S) belonged to Divisions other than R.3rd Division

WAR DIARY or INTELLIGENCE SUMMARY

Army Form C. 2118.

68th Field Amb.
July 1916.

Place	Date	Hour	Summary of Events and Information	Remarks and references to Appendices

System of Recording Casualties at 21st Div Collecting Station.

July 1st to July 3rd and July 11th to July 19th 1916.

1. ADMISSION

(A) All Patients "tallied" with A.F. W 3118 "FIELD MEDICAL CARD" in waterproof envelope, and entered in A&D's.R. (Correspondence Book). Twelve of these had been ruled in columns beforehand, and the designs of the Field Ambulance had been entered in the Cover.

(b) Two clerks worked together, one entering the Patient's particulars on the Card, the other in the Book.

(C) A N.C.O. was made, on the basis of the Card, that anti tetanic Serum had been given when given, time and dose of MORPHIA were also entered.

(d) Sixteen Patients were entered on each page of the "Correspondence Book" and cover page was closed and sent for further reference.

(e) At 6 a.m., Noon and 9 p.m., when returns had to be rendered to A.D.M.S., the books in use were taken to the Orderly Room, and other books substituted.

(f) Returns were compiled from these books, which were handed to the Clerks in charge of the "A and D" Book Proper, who first made out A.F. A36 in triplicate, the originals A.F.A 36 were duplicated to the Base in convenient batches, and later the two, been copied from the carbon copies.

Note :— This Attenda is a resume of the System adopted for Recording casualties at a Divisional Collecting Station, following the share the early morning of July 1st.

The given remarks in A.D.S. from this system now used dead end.

Largely due to the unobtrusive work of No. 1831 Staff Sgt. PARRY R.E., who worked the desk, keeping thought his work entirely & inspiring their work.

J.R. Livingston Major.
O.C. 68 Field Ambulance.

System of Decoding, Canadian (cont'd)

Army Form C. 2118.

WAR DIARY
or
INTELLIGENCE SUMMARY.
(Erase heading not required.)

Instructions regarding War Diaries and Intelligence Summaries are contained in F. S. Regs., Part II. and the Staff Manual respectively. Title pages will be prepared in manuscript.

Place	Date	Hour	Summary of Events and Information	Remarks and references to Appendices

Remarks. The men apparently experienced more in the typing in of the envelopes containing the cards — this took up far more time than the actual reading of the cases. Also, a large number of the envelopes were found to be adherent on the inner surface. These had to be separated before the card could be inserted.

At one period, when the pressure was at its highest, 280 cases were recorded in one hour. Normally four clerks were employed (two outside each dressing room), but when there became another four clerks was employed.

2. EVACUATION. After seeing pen, patients were assisted to a special resting area pending the arrival of the evacuating vehicle. The duplicate nominal Rolls were prepared, each Roll containing 23 names – this representing the normal load to a motor lorry or char-a-banc. All the patients were examined to see whether their respectively "killed" and marked on the mid-rift the "T" showing that A.T.S. had been given in the dressing room. The nominal roll was sent with the patients, the duplicate was sent to the office for returns and "A.D." Hook.

3. DISCHARGE TO DUTY. Nominal Rolls of Sick & Cases, treated & returned to duty, were sent with the men. Duplicates being sent to the office for returns and "A.D." Book.

Army Form C. 2118.

WAR DIARY
or
INTELLIGENCE SUMMARY.
(Erase heading not required.)

21st Div.
Vol 12.

CONFIDENTIAL

WAR DIARY.
of
65th FIELD AMBULANCE.

From Aug 1st 1916. To Aug 31st 1916.

Volume XI

W. Thompson
Capt RAMC
O.C. 65th Field Ambulance

MEDICAL

Army Form C. 2118.

Page 1.

WAR DIARY
or
INTELLIGENCE SUMMARY. OC 65 Fd Ambulance

(Erase heading not required.)

Instructions regarding War Diaries and Intelligence Summaries are contained in F.S. Regs. Part II and the Staff Manual respectively. Title pages will be prepared in manuscript.

Place	Date 1916	Hour	Summary of Events and Information	Remarks and references to Appendices
LIENCOURT	August 1		Visited Advanced Dressing Station at ECOLE NORMALE, ARRAS, not at ST NICHOLAS & regimental aid posts in Caurié trenches. Walked as 14 becomes Fm Regimental aid posts to receive party at ADS, where walks & regts in great activity up. Bearer carry no sent up to R.A.P's find the evacuation from other regiments known of patients in Divisional Rest Station today = 110	Atk LENS II 1/8/1916
	2	10 am	DMS 3rd Army, DDMS VI Corps & ADMS 21st Div inspected the Rest Station.	
		8 PM	C.R.E. II Div visits Rest station & reputated huts & met request to march Governments & them be for repairs. Improvements in Rest Station = 1056 Visited Advanced Dressing Station. Reports stored stores they there is given acknowledgment for personnel stores they have to be kept than a very large number of them flew have never been attendance at the aneaness Dressing Station. Seaches for treating gummen and lying down as they that to be immediately the accumulation of rifles at the Town necessary which are in carry of Staff & into camino the gamins to ECOLE NORMALE. Fewer than 1790 known of patients in chase of Army in other to Anghal ony 121.	
	3			

Page 7

WAR DIARY
or
INTELLIGENCE SUMMARY.   of 65 Field Ambulance

Army Form C. 2118.

Place	Date 1916	Hour	Summary of Events and Information	Remarks and references to Appendices
LIENCOURT	August 3rd contd		The cinematograph document operator to different Reports & ADMS & Surgeons took some pictures of cases outside ARR & turned to "leapers of groups". Number of patients in Res Stn station = 103	
	4		Pack out (Ronny) Reserves cheque (£30) from ADMS for advance to field Ambulance Band. Number of patients in Rest Station = 98. Paid	
	5		visit to 49 CCS receiving pro. Rest Station = 147 (50 hospital) number of patients in (yesterday) from 63" Field Ambulance. Patients received were that feel Retrain not put	
	6		Visit 37 C.C.S. to see that Retrain into (water) = 150 to enemy next Retrain	
	7		Number of patients today. Captain W. A. COATS (RAMC TC) arrived & taken on strength & posts to "C" Section. Number of patients = 169 visited ADS, collecting post & RAPs in March & august respectively	JSD changes pts 68-89 20

Army Form C. 2118.

Page 3

WAR DIARY
or
INTELLIGENCE SUMMARY.
(Erase heading not required.)

of 65th Field Ambulance

Instructions regarding War Diaries and Intelligence
Summaries are contained in F.S. Regs., Part II.
and the Staff Manual respectively. Title pages
will be prepared in manuscript.

Place	Date 1916	Hour	Summary of Events and Information	Remarks and references to Appendices
LIENCOURT	August 8		Number of patients in Rest Station = 163	
	9		Started forwarding 1 mine field every morning attended return by country begins 3 armoury (Col GRAY) on spirits — at 164th field amb (VI corps before 7 inst.morn) number of patients = 142	
	10		Visited A.D.S. number of patients in Rest Station = 107. new field over mint water note chemin prepal roary number of patients = 90.	
	11		number of patients = 86	
	12	12 n	Received return from adv.ing. instructing me to hand over command of 65th field ambulance to Capt ADDIS and proceed to	
		4.30 pm	CROVEN to division's visits A.D.S.	
	13		number of patients = 113. Handed over to Capt ADDIS Ramc.	

J.D. Richmond
Major Ramc

Army Form C. 2118.

Page 41
63rd (2nd N.) Field Ambulance

WAR DIARY
or
INTELLIGENCE SUMMARY.
(Erase heading not required.)

Instructions regarding War Diaries and Intelligence Summaries are contained in F.S. Regs., Part II. and the Staff Manual respectively. Title pages will be prepared in manuscript.

Place	Date 1916	Hour	Summary of Events and Information	Remarks and references to Appendices
Linghem	August 14.		Took on command of the Ambulance from Major J.D. Richmond. 4 cases were Evacuated from the DRS & 2 from the M.D.T. at Station.	
	15.		4 cases evacuated from DRS & 2 from the ADS. Remaining in DRS 144. DDMS VIIth Corps visited ADS. OOMS VIIth Corps visited DRS & hospital personnel - horses & went round the huts.	
	16.		9 cases evacuated from DRS & 2 from ADS.	
	17.		1 evacuated from DRS & 6 wounded & 4 sick from ADS (included 3 minor (San Cesaro) wounds on removal of field ambulance. 15 Capt. 16th Thompson to Hume 1st Lieut. Ross Capt. Rollings 2 cases evacuated	
	18.		Took on command from Capt. W.R. Riddle Rome (T.C.) 8 cases evacuated to DRS. Cold running 144. from DRS. nil from ADS. W. Thompson Capt in charge	
	19.		Visited ADS Ecole Normale & collecting Post St Nicholas 14 cases evacuated to DRS. 121 Remaining. 20 evacuated to ADS.	
	20		GOC VIIth Corps accompanied by DDMS VIIth Corps visited DRS & went round huts & horse lines. 13 cases evacuated. Capt. Coats & 2 NCOs proceeded to VII. Corps School of Instruction LIGNEREUIL for 6 days course there.	

WAR DIARY or INTELLIGENCE SUMMARY

Page 5
by Lt Col Wanless-Hume

Place	Date 1916	Hour	Summary of Events and Information	Remarks and references to Appendices
LIENCOURT	21/8/	—	DRS. 14 CCS evacuated. 31 admitted. Remaining 111. 36 admitted to ADS.	
"	22"		Visited ADSt + RAPs in Isel-lès (Rue de Cambrai + Rue de Douai) also ADMS 21st Divn; AA+QMG + DADOS 21st Divn + DDMS VIth Corps.	
"	23"		6 cases evacuated from DRS. 31 admitted. Remaining 126. Admns 21st Divn visited DRS also Capt Kelly RE (Staff Officer to CE VIth Corps) to advise re erection of Cork hm shelter; lying down of Horse Standings etc.	
"	24"		4 evacuations from DRS. 111 Remaining. Visited ADS returning the high Nt.	
"	25"		Met ADMS in ARRAS who was going round RAid Posts in I Sector. Accompanied by Lieut Pool visited collecting Post St Nicholas + RA Post in March, August, Sunday, + R.A. Aid Post at St Catherines. I, J, + K, sectors. INCD + 6 other wounds detailed for duty at 21st Divl Baths. Returned in evening to DRS.	
"	26"		Evacuations. 146. Remaining. Visited 64 Field Ambulance.	
"	27"		11 evacuations 158 Remaining. Capt WR Addis proceeded to England on short of the strength of the Unit. Visited DDMS VIth Corps.	

Army Form C. 2118.

WAR DIARY
or
INTELLIGENCE SUMMARY.
(Erase heading not required.)

Page 6
1st Division
65th Field Ambulance

Instructions regarding War Diaries and Intelligence Summaries are contained in F.S. Regs., Part II. and the Staff Manual respectively. Title pages will be prepared in manuscript.

Place	Date 1916	Hour	Summary of Events and Information	Remarks and references to Appendices
LIENCOURT	28/8/	–	8 evacuations. 2.6 Discharged, 193 Remaining. Visited A.D.S. The Rev. P.L.E. FOXALL (C of E) reported his arrival for short temporary duty with the Field Ambulance	
"	29/8/		2 evacuations. 7 Discharged. 188 Remaining	
"	30/8/		4 Evacuations. 7 Discharged. 196 Remaining. Capt OWD Steel RAMC (T.F.) reported his arrival for duty was taken on the strength.	
"	31/8/		2 Evacuations. 19 Discharged. 191. Remaining. Lieut. S. Pool R.A.M.C. proceeded to tachment duty with 97th Brig. R.F.A. Visited A.D.S	

W. Thompson
Capt RAMC
O.C. 65 Field Ambulance

140/1734

21st 10ns

65th Field Ambulance

COMMITTEE FOR THE
MEDICAL HISTORY OF THE WAR
Date 30 OCT. 1915

Army Form C. 2118.

WAR DIARY
or
INTELLIGENCE SUMMARY.

(Erase heading not required.)

CONFIDENTIAL

War Diary
of
68th Field Ambulance

SEPTEMBER 1916.

Volume XII

65 Field Ambulance
SEPTEMBER 1916
Page 1

WAR DIARY or INTELLIGENCE SUMMARY
(Erase heading not required.)

Army Form C. 2118.

Instructions regarding War Diaries and Intelligence Summaries are contained in F.S. Regs., Part II and the Staff Manual respectively. Title pages will be prepared in manuscript.

Place	Date	Hour	Summary of Events and Information	Remarks and references to Appendices
LIENCOURT	1/9/16		107th Field Ambulance arrived & we evacuated just north of the village. Visited 64th Field Ambulance. 24 Cases admitted. 2 Evacuated. 19 Discharged. 191 Remaining.	
"	2/9/16		O.C. 107th Field Ambulance visits. 16 D.R.S. evacuated. 1 & 2 Main & 20 O.R. from 107 F.A. went up to A.D.S. ECOLENORMALE. 8 & 9 ADS personnel returned here. 4 Cases evacuated. 14 Discharged. 207 Remaining.	
	3/9/16		33 Cases admitted. 9 Evacuated. 27 Discharged. 196 Remaining. 14 O.R. from ADS returned.	
	4/9/16		At 24 Cases admitted. 10 Evacuated. 14 Discharged. 176 Remaining. Capt. Richardson & 2 N.C.O's went to VIth Corps School of Instruction. Relief of ADS completed at 8 pm.	
	5/9/16		6 Cases admitted. 5 Evacuated. 19 Discharged. 183 Remaining. Sitting 2 " Sit wards I.C.D.R.S. Two men employed by Grave Commission returned from ARRAS.	
	6/9/16		The D.D.M.S. VIth Corps & Sir A. Wright visited 1st D.R.S. 41 Cases admitted. 4 Evacuated. 11 Discharged. 176 Remaining.	
	7/9/16		7 Cases admitted. 14 Evacuated. 17 Discharged. 157 Remaining.	

W. Humphreys
Capt. R.A.M.C.
O.C. 65th Field Amb.

65 Field Ambulance
SEPTEMBER
page 2

WAR DIARY
or
INTELLIGENCE SUMMARY
Army Form C. 2118.

(Erase heading not required.)

Place	Date	Hour	Summary of Events and Information	Remarks and references to Appendices
LIENCOURT	8/9/16		12 Cases admitted. 4 evacuated. 14 discharged. 120 Remainry. Half the Unit went on a Route march in Full marching order.	
"	9/9/16		57 Cases admitted. 10 evacuated. 12 discharged. 193 Remaining. Rest of unit went on Route march. Visited 64th Field Ambulance. Horses & strained mules.	
"	10/9/16		31 Cases admitted. 12 evacuated. 31 discharged. 195. Remaining	
"	11/9/16		Handed over Adv. Res Station to 107, 2nd Aus. F. (35th Div.) - 2 Ambulance (15/?) Handed over 16½ sick	
			10 Horses with 62nd Brig. on Movement. "March orders" for 12/9/16 Received.	
On March 12/9			Left LIENCOURT 9.30 a.m. & joined Brig Transport at Starting Point at 10.30. a.m. Arrived AUTHIE 6 p.m. Rained & unit strength A.S.C. 2.	Ref 2 F.As + Divisions Maps 1-100,000
"	13/9		Left AUTHIE at 9.30 a.m. & took the road via MARIEUX - RAINCHEVAL - TOUTENCOURT - CONTAY - FRANVILLERS to DERNANCOURT arriving there 7 p.m. distance 20 miles. 1 Horse (sick) + 1 Mule evacuated to M.G.V.S Sec at COUIN (handed over to O.C No 3 Field Amb.) at AUTHIE.	
"	14/9		Marched with 64th Brig. on this day. Billets not good. Horses & personnel all well. 19 Sick from Dist transferred to Corps Rest Sta.	

65 Field Ambulance

Army Form C. 2118.

SEPTEMBER
Part 3

WAR DIARY
or
INTELLIGENCE SUMMARY.
(Erase heading not required.)

Place	Date	Hour	Summary of Events and Information	Remarks and references to Appendices
DERNANCOURT	15/9/		Left DERNANCOURT at 6 am & joined Brig. Transport according to orders at March table at 7 A.M. Orders were to proceed to TRICOURT CAMP (no Map Ref given). 2nd Mule arrived at point on ALBERT-MEAULTE - TRICOURT road S. of last named, but failed to get into touch with this Sub in advance to meet Staff Captain. Halted eventually at RED COTTAGE at 10 p.m. Received order to march eventually to POMMIERS on MAMETZ - MONTAUBAN Rd. & arrived there 6 p.m. bivouacked just N. of Rd. At 12 midnight received orders from Authors K and 3. Officers & Tuns Subdivisions of B & C sections to reinforce 14th Div. Collecting Stn. A2 b 80. — 2 Officers (Lts Humphreys & Penn) with Bearer Sub Div. O.C. & A section Rent to reinforce 41st Div. ADS at QUARRIES S21 g 25 T — as possible. 1 Mule evacuated to 32 Mot. Vol. Rec. Meaulte — At 11.30 p.m. Received RAMC. O.O. 27. Sent in shine tres to LSTR from 14th Div. Coll. 9 Stn. at A2.8.80.	Ref sheet ALBERT (corrected March) 1:40,000
POMMIERS	16/9/		Capt Skill with bearer Subdisa, of BASSFORD to form an A.D.S. (after breaking a reconnaissance) on the LONGUEVAL - FLERS Rd no close to FLERS Finished taking over at 2 a.m. 17-9-16.	

65 Field Ambulance
SEPTEMBER
page 4

Army Form C. 2118.

WAR DIARY
INTELLIGENCE SUMMARY
(Erase heading not required.)

Place	Date	Hour	Summary of Events and Information	Remarks and references to Appendices
Dist CLIP SM	17.9.16 to 12 midnight		ADMS visited at 10 a.m. DOMS 10th Corps & Colonel BLENKINSOP also Lt Col A SLOGGETT visited ADMS 41st & NEW 25th & ND Divisions. Evacuated/wounded 25 Lying 109 Sitting. Sick 25 (including 2 officers) wounds lying sent to Corps Main Dressing Stn, & Sitting 15 Corps Coll Stn). The sick to Corps Rest Stn. The OC P.R.C.S Southern then called. I saved various stores & comforts. Visited ADS furnished by personnel of 6th Field Ambce Much at NW corner of BERNAFAY WOOD. Heavy rain during night 17th–18th. On morning 18th Lieut Humphreys find 15th Durham L.I. & Reg't. his KOE was reported previous. one killed (Cpl Irish name) wounded 65 (including 20 guns) & 46 sick been evacuated to Corps Collecting Stn. 1 Capt RAMC 5th respectively. Raining heavily all through the night. The 21 section of A Camp tent by 141st/22nd Cavalry Field Amb have returned 1 section 1 officers at 11 pm.	
	18/9			
	19/9/		Rain continued throughout day. Rel Stn visits MDS (in? 2nd Australian) that OMDS & OC 27 MAC also is ambiguous he calls "La Chaussée" (all carrying 25 sitting casu) All my trained bearers are at defeat 2 OR'S except & Std'bakers for lying cases Patrick - 5 cases in each day. Wounded 62 Lifework Lost Sick 164 (includes 4 officers)	Wholemeans diphteria 25 admt

1819

65 Field Ambulance
SEPTEMBER
Page 5

WAR DIARY or INTELLIGENCE SUMMARY
Army Form C. 2118.

Place	Date	Hour	Summary of Events and Information	Remarks and references to Appendices
Divl Collecting Stn	20/9/16	12 mn to midnight 20/9	From midnight 19th to midnight 20th 79 wounded were evacuated & 105 sick. Rained theoretically during the day (20th) & road very difficult for transport. O.C. 27 M.A.C. visited & has promised to lend us 2 G.S. wagons temporarily. A/D.M.S. 37th Divn visits & lunches. Visits A.D.S. accompanied by Lt. R.A.M. Emslem. They are getting rations & forage satisfactorily.	MAP ALBERT (Cambrai Sheet) A2.6.4.0
"	21.9.16	12mn 20/9 to 12mn 21/9	51 wounded evacuated & 112 sick (including 10 officers). Capt & Crown Ranne from 64 Field Ambulance returned with R.Y.D. Physis. Lieut W.E.C. EASTON reports for duty. Brigr there works to C.C. ReelOn (via Lt. Humphreys to 16th D.L.I.) Yorkshire Pt.S from the Base three hours Collecting Stn, weather fine but dull. A/D.M.S. O.C. 27 M.A.C. visits. Rev. W.M. FALLOON (chaplain) 16" D.L.I. in afternoon.	
"	22/9/16	12mn 21/9 to 12mn 22/9	101 wounded evacuated + 66 sick. Visited A.D.S. arrived & is attached temporarily to this unit.	
"	23/9/16	12mn 22/9 to 12mn 23/9	22 wounded evacuated & 81 sick (including 1 officer). O.C. Capt Gallashey 5th 1 O.C. 27 M.A.C. visits. Visits A.D.S. & attached Bearer party S.R. DELVILLE WOOD. Orders arrived from A/D.M.S. to send 1 med officer to 10th Yorkshire Regt to replace Lieut Purcell Roberts sick.	
"	24/9/16	12mn 23/9 to 12mn 24/9	Lieut EASTON proceeded at 6.30 am in Med Officer to 10th Yorkshire Rgt. Rev. W.M. Fallon A.C.C. visited & in evening we 3 mules to replace 3 mules 22 wounded evacuated & 35 sick evacuated. 3 mules arrived. Yorkshire A.D.S.	

W. Thompson
Capt RAMC
OC 65 Fd Amb

WAR DIARY
INTELLIGENCE SUMMARY
Army Form C. 2118.

SEPTEMBER
Page 6

Place	Date	Hour	Summary of Events and Information	Remarks and references to Appendices
Dis. Rest Stn.	12 noon 24/9/15 to 12 noon 25/9/15		Received orders from DDMS 6th Corps Capt Craig as hostilities to J. LEICESTERS to replace Bushby (who wounded). (Lieut COCHRANE R.A.M.C.) and DDMS Cavalry inf'ty. Captain Ross Rowie from D.A.I. attached to Brit Bleechey Stn for duty. Today, Sir A. Sloggett, Major Burton Blake, Two war correspondents (Mr Gibbs & Mr Phillips) & Mr Effard Mackintosh. Arrived with the above visited many wounded in Dis Collecting Stn. Interviewing the wounded & sketching from pictures. Col Straker from Army. OC 27 MAC & DDMS XV Corps visited during the afternoon. 784 cases evacuated (includes 57 sick).	
	12 noon 25/9/15 to 12 noon 26/9/15		Captain A. G. M. FARLANE R.A.M.C reported his arrival for duty - was attached to 9th LEICESTERS to Capt Coats (who has not got to the regt). There was no news & hrs at 7 pm yesterday the ADS with a paint [illegible] on day 25/9/. L'Colonel C.K. MORGAN R.A.M.C & Major Barclay Black visited this collecting Stn from G.H.Q. Also DDMS XV Corps - 422 cases evacuated (including 3 Officers, & 31 German wounded).	
	12 noon 26/9/ to 12 noon 27/9/		174 Cases evacuated (including 3 Officers). Visited ADS & the Advanced Dsng there Captain McFarlane returned 16th hours & was posted to C. section Capt Coates having eventually turned up with the 9th LEICESTERS an enemy Aeroplane dropped bombs close to the Encampment about 10-30pm Several Casualties were brought in. Capt Keith Conn R.A.M.C 64th Fld Amb returned to that unit.	

W Murphy Capt RAMC OC Dis Rest Stn

65th Ambulance

Army Form C. 2118.

SEPTEMBER

WAR DIARY
or
INTELLIGENCE SUMMARY.
(Erase heading not required.)

Instructions regarding War Diaries and Intelligence Summaries are contained in F. S. Regs., Part II. and the Staff Manual respectively. Title pages will be prepared in manuscript.

Place	Date	Hour	Summary of Events and Information	Remarks and references to Appendices
Divl Coll Stn	27/9/16	12 mn	151. Cases evacuated (including 10 men sick) PDMS + DADMS XIV Corps	Ref MAP ALBERT (Trenches Sheet) A.2.6.9.0
	28/9/16	12 mn	Visited. Lieut E Purcell RAMC attached temporarily for duty (recovering from gunshot wound)	
	28/9/16	12 mn	136 Cases evacuated (75 sick + 61 wounded) – ADMS visited. Moved bell tent.	
	29/9/16	12 mn		
	30/9/16	12 mn	106. Cases evacuated (including 10 officers wounded). Received R.A.M.C. O.O. no 2.B. 12th Divn. when 2.1st Brig. in night op. 1/2 sect Bn Contracting St moved to 5.22. at 4.4. + 1 Sect of Tent Divn. were posted there + handed over to 38th Field Ambulance on 1/10/16.	

W Brownson
Capt H Field Amb
OC 65
1/15/16

Confidential.

WAR DIARY
OF
65TH FIELD AMBULANCE 21st Divn.

FROM 1ST OCTOBER 1916 TO 31ST OCTOBER 1916

VOLUME XIII

COMMITTEE FOR THE
MEDICAL HISTORY OF THE WAR
Date 9 DEC. 1916

MEDICAL

65th Field Ambulance
OCTOBER 1916.
Vol XIII
page 1.

WAR DIARY

Army Form C. 2118.

Instructions regarding War Diaries and Intelligence Summaries are contained in F.S. Regs., Part II. and the Staff Manual respectively. Title pages will be prepared in manuscript.

INTELLIGENCE SUMMARY.

(Erase heading not required.)

Place	Date	Hour	Summary of Events and Information	Remarks and references to Appendices
RIBEMONT	1/10/16	12 nn	The Field Ambulance marched from 3rd Collecting Stn (A2,B,9,O) at 5.45 pm & arrived RIBEMONT at 10.30 pm. Transport arrived 12.30 am 2/10/16. 49 Wounded + 40 Sick evacuated.	MAPS. ALBERT (trench sheet) 1-40,000 AMIENS 1-100,000 ABBEVILLE 1-112,000
"	2/10/16		Remains in Hutts at RIBEMONT. Lieut EASTON rejoined from 10th Yorks Regt. Have Transport ready. Captain McFARLANE marched with 64th Brig. Transport to Sᵗ SAUVEUR starting at 11.45 am & arrived with him. Unit to Sᵗ SAUVEUR starting at 11.45 am.	
"	3/10/16		The Unit Entrains at 5 pm & detrains at LONGPRÉ Les-CORPS-SAINTS at 12-15 am. Transport arrived from Sᵗ SAUVEUR at 8 pm. Three arriving there 5-15 am 3/10/16. At 1-30 am started on march to BUIGNY-l'ABBÉ.	
BUIGNY l'ABBÉ	"		Unit rested in billets. ADMS & BADMS 21ˢᵗ Divn. visited. Dvt H.Q. at AILLY	
"	4/10/16	"	AFˢ W3121 forwarded to ADMS. Feet, Boot, inspection of personnel.	
"	5/10/16	"	Kit inspection by section in morning. Route march in afternoon. Bathing visited. 12 cases from 64th Brigade evacuated to ÉTAPLES & ABBEVILLE	
"	6/10/16	"	Route march by section in morning. Advance party entrained at ABBEVILLE at 2-30 pm for CHOCQUES. Transport should entrain at 8/10/16, at ABBEVILLE Stn by march route at 4-30 am.	
"	7/10/16		Personnel at 5-30 am. Arriving at ABBEVILLE Stn by march route at 4-30 am.	

3353 Wt W3544/1454 700,000 5/15 D.D. & L. A.D.S.S./Forms/C. 2118.

WAR DIARY

INTELLIGENCE SUMMARY

65th Field Ambulance
October 1916
Page 2

Army Form C. 2118.
Vol. XIII

Place	Date	Hour	Summary of Events and Information	Remarks and references to Appendices
HAUT RIEUX	8/10/16	12 mn	Completed entraining at ABBEVILLE at 5.30 a.m; departed at 6 a.m + arrived CHOCQUES 12.20 p.m; left station by march route + arrived HAUT RIEUX 2 p.m + went into billets. Transport (less 2 G.S. 2 hooded waggons + 1 water cart left behind at ABBEVILLE) arrived 3.30 p.m. Remainder of Transport (small) arrived 12 midnight + 3 A.M. 9.10.16.	Ref. MAPS HAZEBROUCK 5A + LENS 11 (1/100000)
"	9/10/16	"	2 Mot. Cars from 24th Field Amb. reports 8.30 a.m + were employed in collecting Sick from units of 1st & 11th Brigades. Meeting of 2nd 2/Lieuts of LABOURSE + ADSM at the BREWERY VERMELLES + arranged for relief of A.D.S. "R.A.M.C. O.O. No. 29" received 8 p.m (envelope)	
"	10.10.16		4 Busses + the Sanitary lorry reported at 10.15 a.m. to the proceeding of B + C section with Captains Storms, McFARLANE, + Lieut EASTON to VERMELLES where the ADSM at the BREWERY + CHATEAU were taken over from 24th + 26th field ambulances respectively. The take over was completed by 5 p.m. Captain Steel + Lieut EMBLEM with 12 O.R. of "A" section left as an advanced party to take over 24th field amb. at LABOURSE.	

W. Kemp

WAR DIARY
INTELLIGENCE SUMMARY
(Erase heading not required.)

Army Form C. 2118.

65th Field Ambulance
October 1916.
Page 3. Vol. XIII

Instructions regarding War Diaries and Intelligence Summaries are contained in F.S. Regs., Part II. and the Staff Manual respectively. Title pages will be prepared in manuscript.

Place	Date	Hour	Summary of Events and Information	Remarks and references to Appendices
LABOURSE	11-10-16	12 mid night	Remainder of personnel ('A' Section) with transport left HAUT RIEUX at 10.15 am by march route & arrived at LABOURSE at 2.15pm at which hour man Dressing Station was taken over from 24th Field Ambulance 8th Div.	MAPS HAZEBROUCK 5A LENS 11 (1-100000)
"	12.10.16	"	Visited the ADStations at CHATEAU, BREWERY, VERMELLES with ADMS. Captain McFARLANE + 35. O.R. of 'C' section returned to H.Q. at 7.30 p.m. + went round Trench posts in QUARRY sector + went round Trench posts in HOHENZOLLERN sector	
"	13.10.16	"	Visited ADS at CHATEAU & went round instructions from the ADMS. Took over the CHATEAU LABOURSE from ADMS 8th Divn as an officers Mess for 65th Field Amb. Captain A.S. MOORE departed on 14 days leave to ENGLAND.	
"	14.10.16	"	MT/ASC with Cars & 2 motor cycles were transferred to 63rd Field Amb. & exchanges for the MT/ASC personnel trans. of that unit under instructions from the ADMS. Captain E.V. RUSSELL R.A.M.C. reported for duty, two taken on the strength.	
"	15.10.16	"	Captain G.B. Richardson was transferred to 40th Divn for duty & was struck off the strength of the Field Amb. accordingly. Capt. A.G. McFARLANE was posted for temporary duty as MO/MC from 6th LEICESTERS (in relief of Lieut JOHNS RAMC) on 14th inst.	

W. [signature]

WAR DIARY

Army Form C. 2118.

65th Field Ambulance
October 1916.
Page 4   Vol. XIII

Place	Date	Hour	Summary of Events and Information	Remarks and references to Appendices
LABOURSE	16/10/16	12. midnight	Lieut S. POOL has proceeded for Temporary duty to 9th KOYLI in relief of Lieut MALSEED R.A.M.C (proceeded on leave). ADMS visited. 52 sick + 3 wounded remaining.	
"	17/10/16	"	Lieut SHANKS proceeded to ENGLAND on expiration of contract + was struck off strength accordingly. DADMS visited, Inspected WARDS cook houses + mens W.C.s. ADMS visited ADSn + went round Trenches in QUARRY Sector. Visited ADSn in afternoon. Started a library for patients in main Dressing Stn. HQ. 54 sick + wounded remaining.	
"	18/10/.	"	Cases reviewing. 41 sick, 5 wounded.	
"	19/10.	"	DDMS + ADMS inspected Horse Trouing Stn + in afternoon the advanced Dressing Stations at BREWERY + CHATEAU. VERMELLES advanced Dressing Stations reviewing. 53 sick & 3 wounded.	
"	20/10.	"	Captain F. V. RUSSELL deputed to take up Temporary duty as DADMS 1st Corps. Personnel paid out. ADMS visited. Running sick 46 wounded 4. Visited ADSns + went round Posts in Quarry Sector.	
"	21/10	"	Posts (43) relieved both personnel from Commander's Trench main Dressing Stn. Myatt

Army Form C. 2118.

65th Field Ambulance
October 1916.

WAR DIARY
INTELLIGENCE SUMMARY.
(Erase heading not required.)

Page 5 Volume XIII

Place	Date	Hour	Summary of Events and Information	Remarks and references to Appendices
LABOURSE	22/10/16	12 mid night	DADMS visited & Thorny. Remaining 35 sick. 6 wounded.	
"	23/10/16	"	Visits A.D.S tw. Remaining 44 sick 5 wounded. Much rain.	
"	24/10/16	"	Remaining 36 sick. 1 wounded. Much rain.	
"	25/10/16	"	Visits ADS th. OC 64th Fd Amb, & DADMS visited him during Sm. Remaining 35 sick. 2 wounded.	
"	26/10/16	"	GOC 2/C Div & AA & QMG with DADMS visited ADS tw VERMELLES at 9.30 am & main Dressing Sn. LABOURSE at 11 am. 31 sick + 1 wounded Remaining.	
"	27/10/16	"	DADMS visited subsequently proceeding to British Red Cross depot at St OMER to obtain some necessary stores. Remaining 35 sick.	
"	28/10/16	"	Captain A G McFARLANE returned from Temporary duty with 8th Leicester Regt. accompanied by APM 21st Div visited ADS th in afternoon & fees Amb Posts in HOHENZOLLERN Sector. Remaining 43 sick. 2 wounded.	
"	29/10/16	-	Captain H S MOORE reported his arrival on return from leave. Remaining 47 sick. 2 wounded.	

WAR DIARY

INTELLIGENCE SUMMARY.
(Erase heading not required.)

Army Form C. 2118.

65th Field Ambulance
October 1916
Page 6 Volume XII

Place	Date	Hour	Summary of Events and Information	Remarks and references to Appendices
LABOURSE	30/10/16	12 mid^{night}	Captain T.S MOORE proceeded to A.D.S.A. To be attached there for 2 days prior to taking on a one day course at Divl Gas School. Lieut T.R Walker R.A.M.C (T.C) reported his arrival for duty, was posted to B section. Remaining 35 Sick 3 wounded	
"	31/10/16	"	Captain O.W.D. Steel detailed for duty with 46th Divn & was Struck off strength. Lieut Easton a relief of Lieut Walker returned to H.Q from A.D.S. A.D.M.S visited ment round hore lines. Visited A.D.S. in afternoon. Remaining 36 Sick 2 wounded.	

W. Thompson
Major
OC 65th Field Ambulance

140/943 Confidential
Vol 15

21st Div

Nov 1916

WAR DIARY.

OF THE

65th FIELD AMBULANCE.

FROM

NOVEMBER 1st 1916

TO

NOVEMBER 30th 1916.

VOLUME

COMMITTEE FOR THE
MEDICAL HISTORY OF THE WAR.
Date 13 MAR. 1917

65? Field Ambulance MEDICAL

Army Form C. 2118.

Vol. XIV Page 1

WAR DIARY

INTELLIGENCE SUMMARY.

November 1916

(Erase heading not required.)

Place	Date	Hour	Summary of Events and Information	Remarks and references to Appendices
LABOURSE	1/11/16	12 mid night	Captain E.V. Russell reported from Corps H.Q. where he had been acting as DADVS. Thomas visited a Divn (audit) on Canteen accounts. Personnel at 3 ASPs + Tramh Posts were relieved. Capt Shoven & Lieut Easton being relieved by Capt Morgan + Lieut Walker. Remaining Sick 52 Wounded 2.	
"	2/11/16	"	Visited ADS's Trench and Quarry + Hohenzollern sections. Captain R. Taylor RAMC (SR) reports for duty + no posted to command 1. @ section. Lieut W.C.C. Easton evacuated to West Riding CCS. Remaining Sick 68 Wounded 2. No 69501 Pte W. Jennings 2/1st DAC admitted in an unconscious condition died at 10.30 p.m. Personnel paid out. Lieut J.P. Carroll RAMC (T.C.) reported his arrival.	
"	3/11/16	"	Remaining 63 Sick, Wounded 4.	
"	4/11/16	"	Capt Russell attended P.M. on Pte Jennings at 33 CCS. would death due to Pontine Haemorrhage, (knee full of sugar). ADVms visited + inspected in afternoon. Remaining Sick 60 Wounded 6.	
"	5/11/16	"	Visited ADSm + Field Ambulance Posts. Remaining 52 Sick & 4 Wounded.	
"	6/16	"	Remaining 55 Sick + 3 Wounded.	
"	7/11/16	"	Lieut Pool relieved Lieut F. Walker at ADS. Pte Lacker reporting for duty with 64th Field Ambulance.	

WAR DIARY

65th FIELD AMBULANCE
NOVEMBER 1916
Page 2 Volume XIV

Army Form C. 2118.

Place	Date	Hour	Summary of Events and Information	Remarks and references to Appendices
LABOURSE	8/11/16	12 midnight	Visited ADSt. Remaining 58. sick. 2 wounded.	
"	9.11.16	"	Visited ADMS. Captain Taylor proceeded on leave to Scotland.	
"	10.11.16	"	ADMS visited huns Dressing Stn. Visited ADSt. & Estaminet Posts & Hulluch & Parts Alleys. Remaining 46. sick. Capt. K. Patano proceeded to Boulogne for Dental treatment.	
"	11.11.16	"	Personnel of Trench Posts relieved. OC 8th. Divl Supply Column inspected the Huts Ambulance of the Unit.	
"	12.11.16	"	ADMS visited. Visited ADSt in afternoon.	
"	13.11.16	"	6 men from Head Quarters were sent up to ADSt. for work on Trench Posts. ADMS visited. Remaining 55 sick. 4 wounded.	
"	14.11.16	"	Visited ADSt. ADMS visited Head Quarters.	
"	15.11.16	"	Personnel paid out. DDMS held a conference of ADMS's & OsC DMS. OC Sanitary Section on 1st Chateau LABOURSE. Capt Stevens was detailed for duty with 10th Yorks Regt in relief of Lieut Powell vacated. Sick.	
"	16.11.16	"	Corps Commander the ADMS & ADMS's inspected the Ambulance. Visited ADSt. both steps to move a Divn inside from the British house VERMELLES.	

Army Form C. 2118.

WAR DIARY
65th FIELD AMBULANCE
INTELLIGENCE SUMMARY. NOVEMBER 1916
Page 3. Volume XIV.

(Erase heading not required.)

Instructions regarding War Diaries and Intelligence Summaries are contained in F.S. Regs., Part II. and the Staff Manual respectively. Title pages will be prepared in manuscript.

Place	Date	Hour	Summary of Events and Information	Remarks and references to Appendices
LABOURSE	17/11/16	12 mid night	Captain McFarlane returned from BOULOGNE. DADMS visited in morning. Remaining 43. Sick + 6 wounded.	
"	18/11/16	"	Visited ADS's. Remaining 47 Sick + 7 wounded.	
"	19/11/16	"	Visited ADSms. Remaining 67 Sick + 6 wounded.	
"	20/11/16	"	All officers of the Field Ambulance attended a General Court Martial. Captain Brennan 63rd Field Ambulance reported for temporary duty for the day. Remaining 57 Sick + 2 wounded.	
"	21/11/16	"	Personnel in Trench Posts were relieved. DsMS 1st Army + DDMS 1st Corps visited ADSs. ADsMS visited ADSs in morning. Lieut J. P. Carroll proceeded to 64th Field Ambulance Headquarters to afternoon. Capt Russell proceeds to 33 C.C.S. + performed a P.M. there. Ambulance for duty.	
"	22/11/16	"	Visited ADS's + Trench Posts in Quarry Rector. Visited ADSms. Whompson Kanl.	Major Thompson 65th Field Ambulance
"	23/11/16	"	Major N Thompson proceeded on leave of absence for Ireland. Capt P. H. Russell assumed temporary command ADS. Limited no dressing station returned from leave. Remaining 50 sick and 1 wounded.	Capt P. H. Russell Capt RAMC P. H. Russell Capt RAMC

Army Form C. 2118.

WAR DIARY
or
INTELLIGENCE SUMMARY.

(Erase heading not required.)

65th Field Ambulance
NOVEMBER 1916.
Page 4. Volume XIV

Place	Date	Hour	Summary of Events and Information	Remarks and references to Appendices
LABOURSE	24/11/16	12 midnight	Visited Corps Rest Sta. at Labourse. Evac. improved later. Remaining S-69. W-4	
"	25/11/16		Visited Advanced Dressing Sta. O.O No 31 received	
"	26/11/16		Six return men sent up from main Dressing Sta. to St Hours Post for the purpose of effecting repairs to the roof (under supervision of R.E.) Capt Taylor proceeded to A.D.S. to relieve Lieut Pool who returned to H.Q. Fd. A. D.M.S. visited the main Dressing Sta.	
"	27/11/16		Lieut Pool proceeded to England on leave of absence. I visited the A.D.S. Remaining S.8 sick, wounded nil	
"	28/11/16		One Officer, Two R.C.O's. & four men reported to the Advanced Dressing Sta. Dressing from the 63rd Field Amb. for instruction in the Trench Posts, evacuation routes Etc of the Hohenzollern section.	
"	29/11/16		Personnel laid out. Remaining 32 sick.	
"	30/11/16		The A.D. Dressing & Trench Posts in the Hohenzollern section were taken over by the 63 F.A. Personnel from the Trench Posts returned to H.Q. A.D.M.S visited the main Dressing Sta. Remaining 49 sick 1 wounded	

E.U. Russell
Capt. R.A.M.C.
for O.C. 65th Field Amb.

140/1942

21st Div.

65th Field Ambulance

Dec. 1916

COMMITTEE FOR THE
MEDICAL HISTORY OF THE WAR
Date 13 MAR. 1917

MEDICAL

65th FIELD AMBULANCE Army Form C. 2118.
DECEMBER 1916
Page 1.

WAR DIARY

INTELLIGENCE SUMMARY

Place	Date	Hour	Summary of Events and Information	Remarks and references to Appendices
LABOURSE	1/12/16	12 pm midnight	G.O.C. 21st Div and D.A.Q.M.G. 21st Div inspected transport at 11.15 a.m. Visited A.D.S. & parts of personnel. A.D.S & nearby returned to H.Q. The Château Journel were relieved from Main Dressing Stn. Capt H.S. Hone returned to H.Q. Capt. & Q. MacFarlane proceeded to A.D.S Château for duty. The room formerly used as Q.M. stores was handed over to the municipality on the 1st to be used as a schoolroom.	
"	2/12/16		A.D.M.S. visited Main Dressing Stn. Remaining 43 sick	
"	3/1/16		Visited A.D.S and French Posts (Quarry Sentry). Remaining 43 sick 1 wounded. Major F.I. Thompson returned from leave 12.20 am 3/12/16	
"	4/12/16		Remaining 46 sick	
"	5/12/16		Visited A.D.S. Château & Posts	
"	6/12		Arthur marked from Brens' St & inspected Hone Louis Lorrain St. Receiving 57 sick + 2 wounded - Visited ADSt.	
"	7/12		Visited 64th F.A. (Capt Ryd St). 10 km + 1 re-stables Lieut Hy. H. Symons Subtd to 62 Brig AR. h a working party reported ha arrived tonight. 6 reinforcements arrived. R.A.M.C. (T.C.) refugees	
"	8/12		Visits ADS. Remaining 52 sick.	
"	9/12		Visit ADTS. & French Posts (St Henry's) PM held on Shpt. Donner 1st inrolure at 33 C.C.S. attached below at 63rd Ft. BETHUNE Lieut S.Pool returned from leave.	

WAR DIARY

65th FIELD AMBULANCE Army Form C. 2118.

DECEMBER 1916.

Page 2. Volume XV.

INTELLIGENCE SUMMARY

(Erase heading not required.)

Place	Date	Hour	Summary of Events and Information	Remarks and references to Appendices
LABOURSE	10/12/16	12. midnight	Personnel of main Dressing Stn. took over the Stn. Chambre from 1st Hs. Small Box Respirators were received. 2 Stretcher-bearers & a Nursing Orderly admitted M.D.S.	
"	11/12/16	"	Captn. R. Taylor was detailed to tempy. duty with 10th Yorks in relief of Capt. Stevens who has proceeded to England on transfer. 3 Other Ranks returned to Coy. from hospital & admitted to Ambulance. Capt. Russell visited M.D.S. & Bearer Posts.	
"	12/12/16	"	Sent Pack mules to the Ghisk to 8th Leicesters & were struck off strength of the unit. Lieut. Escott was struck off strength of the Ambulance from 15 inst. on transfer to 46th D.A.C. 1 O.R. was admitted to hospital. Horses shoes from 22 inches to Company Commanders at their request. So The Personnel in Trench Posts were relieved (since 1/12 inst.). Remaining S.B. sick	
"	13/12/16	"	Visited M.D.S. & Trench Posts — Personnel pencil out.	W. McMahon Maj.

WAR DIARY

65th FIELD AMBULANCE
DECEMBER 1916.
Page 3. Volume XV.

INTELLIGENCE SUMMARY.

(Erase heading not required.)

Place	Date	Hour	Summary of Events and Information	Remarks and references to Appendices
LABOURSE	14/12/16	12. mid night	ADMNS & DADMS visited. 62 Sick remaining.	
"	15/12/16	"	Visited ADS Duray Sr. Capt Russell taken on strength of Ambulance. Visited BETHUNE F.A Hosp.	
"	16/12/16	"	Capt Russell promised on leave to England. Remaining 55 Sick. Letter which was not given.	
"	17/12/16	"	Visited A.D.S. & Trench Posts. 70. Sick remaining.	
"	18/12/16	"	O.C. 2d Div Train inspected Horses Harness & Transport. The Corps Commander DDMS. 1st Corps & ADMS inspected ADS. CHATEAU VERMELLES & Arrangements the 74 min during St.	
"	19/12/16	"	Visited A.D.S. & Trek on BREWERY VERMELLES & the Trench MDS in the HOHENZOLLERN Sector. 1 Sergt & 20 Rks were transferred from M.D.S. to Trek on their posts. Remaining 47 sick & 3 wounded	
"	20/12/16	"	One Horse & Ml wagon accompanied 6th & 7th Leicesters to AUCHEL. Starting at 9 am	

Signature

WAR DIARY

INTELLIGENCE SUMMARY

65TH FIELD AMBULANCE
(3rd W. Lancs T.F.)
DECEMBER 1916

Army Form C. 2118.

Page 4 of Volume XV

Place	Date	Hour	Summary of Events and Information	Remarks and references to Appendices
LABOURSE	21/12	midnight	Visited ADS. Lieut Symons posted to ADS for duty	
"	22/12	"	ADS visited. Lieut Bevan Sgt Ramminey S/S sick. 1 3 wounded	
"	23/12	"	Visited ADS & French Poste. R.O. No 33 received. Captain Storrs returned from leave	home
"	24/12	"	ADS visited. Captain Storrs returned to 10th Yorks. & Captain Taylor for purposes medical Charge) 10th Yorks. to ADS. Lieut Symons returning to Main Dressing Stn Greeat of the OS in being	
"	25/12	"	Xmas day. Visited ADS. ADMS DADMS present	
"	26/12	"	Callan Turner QMS Piry & 12 O.R. proceeded as an advance party to ALLOUAGNE to take over from 18 Field Ambulance Personnel I think hand out	

W. Humphreys
Major

WAR DIARY or **INTELLIGENCE SUMMARY**

Army Form C. 2118.

65th FIELD AMBULANCE
DECEMBER 1916
Page 5 Volume XV

Place	Date	Hour	Summary of Events and Information	Remarks and references to Appendices
LA BOURSE	27/12	12 midnight	Captain Russell returned from leave. 1 Officer & 15 O.R. from 16 Field Amb. proceeded to A.D.S. to learn evacuation routes etc.	MAP. France 36. B (1-40000)
"	28/12		1 Officer & 40 O.R. m. 16 Fd.Amb. proceeded at 9 a.m. to A.D.S. VERMELLES to complete taking on the Arrangements. half of 1 Officer & 20 O.R. moved to take over main Dressing Stn. standing on 21st Divn. completed by mid day. A.D.M.S. visited A.D.S. & Sick & wounded m to 16th Fd. Amb.	
"	29/12		The Field Ambulance marched off at 8-15 a.m. arriving at ALLOUAGNE at 12. noon. Personnel billeted by sections. Capt. McFarlane proceeded on leave.	
"	30/12		Visited 63rd Fd.Amb. AUCHEL.	
"	31/12		A.D.M.S. visited & and Ritchie & Stokes A.P.M. visited. Lieut. D.M. Surgeon proceeded on leave. W.Thompson Major R.A.M.C. O/c 65th Fd. Amb.

140/1943

21st Div.

65th Field Ambulance.

Jan 1917

COMMITTEE FOR THE
MEDICAL HISTORY OF THE WAR
Date 13 MAR. 1917

MEDICAL

WAR DIARY
INTELLIGENCE SUMMARY

65th FIELD AMBULANCE
JANUARY 1917
Page 1 Volume XVI

Army Form C. 2118.

Place	Date	Hour	Summary of Events and Information	Remarks and references to Appendices
ALLOUAGNE	1/1/17	12 midnight	Lieut. Smith Turck to the provided to leave to England. Visits. 63rd Field Ambulance AUCHEL. 2 Reinforcements arrived.	Map reference Sheet 36 B (1/40000) D7a.3.6
"	2/1/17		Visited H.Q'rs of LA BEUVRIÈRE. A.D.M.S. & A.Q.M.G. visited to investigate position of the 62nd Brigade using part of Hosp. accommodation. To entertainments.	
"	3/1/17		6 Reinforcements arrived from Base. Concert got up by the hunt in Evening.	
"	4/1/17		O.A.D.M.S. visits. Rtn. in of 64th Field Amb. at FOUQUIÈRES.	
"	5/1/17		A.P.M. visits. 19. Sick remaining that lunch.	
"	6/1/17		G.O.C. Div. & G.S.O. I. also Staff Captain 62nd Brigade visited with reference to use of a Room for lectures. Personnel of the Ambulance was kind nt. The Ambulance to take team defeats 23 C.C.S. team on the ground by 5 goals to 1.	
"	7/1/17		A.D.M.S. & D.A.D.M.S. visited. The former inspected the reserve harness rooms & inspecting the Horse Standings.	

W. Thompson
Major

WAR DIARY / INTELLIGENCE SUMMARY

65th FIELD AMBULANCE
JANUARY 1917
Page 2 Volume XVI.

Army Form C. 2118.

Place	Date	Hour	Summary of Events and Information	Remarks and references to Appendices
ALLOUAGNE	8/1/17	12 midnight	Sick remaining 10. Wounded nil.	Map reference Sheet 36 B. 1/40000 D.7.a.3.6.
"	9/1/17	"	Inspected billets & horses. Visited Lilliers & called on 57 FA.	
"	"	"	Officers & Major Innerdale S.C.F. (C of E) visited.	
"	10/1/17	"	Field Ambulance football team defeated 62nd Infantry headquarters team by 15. 2nd Divl General Entry lost on the Victoria Room & are holding nightly concerts.	
"	11/1/17	"	Captains C.D. Hollworth, H. Hume (T.C.), Captain H. Goodman (T.C.) & Captain T.W.R. Stooke (T.C.) reported here arrived for duty & were posted to A, B & C Sections respectively.	
"	12/1/17	"	The Field Ambulance football team defeated an R.F. Corps team by 5 goals to nil.	
"	13/1/17	"	Rodney inspected personnel of Field Ambulance in marching order. 17 sick remaining.	
"	14/1/17	"	G.O.C. visited with a representative of the Philippine Medical Service, who saw methods & formation of a Field Medical Unit.	
"	15/1/17	"	Attended lecture on Horse management by Lt Col Habel & Lt Hammon AAVC 1st Corps. Captain E.W. Revill was transferred for duty on D.A.D.M.S. 24th Divn & was struck off strength of Ambulance from this date.	
"	16/1/17	"	Field Ambulance football team defeated 18 C.C.S. by 4 goals to 3.	

Kennedy
Lt Col. Commanding

WAR DIARY
of
INTELLIGENCE SUMMARY.
(Erase heading not required.)

65th Field Ambulance Army Form C. 2118.
JANUARY 1917
Page 3. Volume XVI.

Place	Date	Hour	Summary of Events and Information	Remarks and references to Appendices
ALLOUAGNE	17/1/17	12 midnight	Capt. Lieut Symons proceeded on leave to England. Lieut H.A.M. Buckler returned from leave.	Map reference Sheet 36.B 1/40,000 D.7.a.3.6
"	18/1/17	"	Capt Hedsworth reported to 95th May A.F.A. for temporary duty in lieu of Capt Burns (sick). Personnel 1 Ambulance men leave met.	
"	19/1/17	"	Sick running 16. wounded nil.	
"	20/1/17	"	Capt McFarlane returned from leave (12 days extension).	
"	21/1/17	"	The Corps Commander presented medals to 62nd Brigade &c. Parade formed of 1 Officer & 40 O.R. from 65th Field Ambulance. 2 men (Mann) transferred to 63rd Field Ambulance.	
"	22/1/17	"	Visited 72nd Field Ambulance at BRAQUEMONT preparatory to taking on from that Unit. Visited Annexes on return. S.A.S.C. reinforcements reported for duty.	
"	23/1/17	"	O.C. & Quartermaster 72nd Field Amb. visited & went over Hosp. buildings & billets.	

Wilfrid Thompson
Lt. Col. R.A.M.C.

WAR DIARY

INTELLIGENCE SUMMARY
(Erase heading not required.)

65th FIELD AMBULANCE   Army Form C. 2118.
JANUARY 1917.
Page 4 Volume XVI

Place	Date	Hour	Summary of Events and Information	Remarks and references to Appendices
ALLOUAGNE	24/1/17	12 mid night	Le K nuaining 9.	Ref Maps HAZEBROUCK St A. Sheet 28. (1-40.000)
"	25/1/17	"	" 16	
"	26/1/17	"	Captain Taylor, Stads & 1 Sect Bearers with 24 O.R. proceeded on an advanced party to HQ 72nd Field Amb at Ash Dump, Ch LE BRESIS. Remainder left at 6 am & arrived 12 noon.	
POPERINGHE	27/1/17	"	Advanced party less beaters, Cooks & truck less transport proceeded at 4.30 pm arriving here & woke at 8pm & billeted at Chequers in POPERINGHE — HOPOUTRE 9pm & Warning at 11pm hoard to F Camp in POPERINGHE WOESTEN road. One 13th NF's here to enquire if all available accommodation according will (a) be retained. In Transport in charge of the team. 1 Copt & Orderly proceeded by road via NEUF-VERQUIN arriving at 7pm. Mess cars at 8pm 28th.	
"	28/1/17		Transport & baggage party arrived at Transport lines on POPERINGHE — ELVERDINGHE Rd (A 28 D Central)	

W. Mawsha
Lt. Col Rammer

WAR DIARY or INTELLIGENCE SUMMARY

65th FIELD AMBULANCE
JANUARY 1917
Page 5 Volume XVI

Army Form C. 2118.

Place	Date	Hour	Summary of Events and Information	Remarks and references to Appendices
POPERINGHE	29/1/17	12 mid night	The unit marched from Flanck 15 the Gruinell at St Michel HAZEBROUCK arriving there at 7 p.m. to the town of POPERINGHE.	Ref Maps St Michel HAZEBROUCK 5A (1:100000)
"	30/1/17	—	Visited D.D.H.Q. — A.D.M.S. at WORMHOUDT. A.D.M.S. & D.A.D.M.S. made inspection of H.Q. & hospital (L. Public buildings) intended (5) to be at the Open Club.	(1. 12th W.F. & 1. 62nd M.G.C.)
"	31/1/17	—	2 Officers transferred to No. 12 C.C.S. 4 Cases remaining sick.	

W. Thompson
Lt Col RAMC
OC 65 Field Ambulance

140/1991

21st Div.

65th Field Ambulance.

Feb. 1917

COMMITTEE FOR THE
MEDICAL HISTORY OF THE WAR
Date 4 APR. 1917

MEDICAL

Army Form C. 2118.

WAR DIARY
or
INTELLIGENCE SUMMARY.
(Erase heading not required.)

65th FIELD AMBULANCE
FEBRUARY 1917.

Page 1. Volume Vol 18

Place	Date	Hour	Summary of Events and Information	Remarks and references to Appendices
POPERINGHE	1/2/17	midnight	Rode to HERZEELE to draw pay from Fld Cashier for unit. The personnel at Headquarters were paid out at 4 p.m. ADMS & ADSMS 8th Corps visited.	R/f MAPS HAZEBROUCK S.A.
"	2/2/17	"	Visited Transport lines & paid A.S.C. (H.T. + M.T.) & a mule personnel there. One horse with shrapnel follock - will others to. Mules fit & in good condition. A clean clothing store now open at H.Q. to 62nd Div. (Supt numon places t/c) 12000 sets received. Officers Mess started in Convent premises, & quarters for Officers found in same building.	
	3/2/17	"	3 cars running to Hospl.	
	4/2/17	"	Visited P. & X. Camps on POPERINGHE — WOESTEN Rd with a view to utilising them in acts: dressing Stns in collecting Stn in event of certain contractions.	

W. Thompson
Lt Col Manual

WAR DIARY / INTELLIGENCE SUMMARY

65th FIELD AMBULANCE Army Form C. 2118.

FEBRUARY 1917.
Page 2. Volume XVII.

Place	Date	Hour	Summary of Events and Information	Remarks and references to Appendices
POPERINGHE	5/2/17	12 midnight	Visited EDEWAARTHOEK SIDING (Ypres) returning via to 65th Howard R.A. Subsequently visited Transport Lines met 7th Wor. 9th Inf. R.F.A. Hurd & Mr. McKids with Shrapnel Helbert evacuated train. Wd. see F.30. A.6.S. (Sheet 27). ADMS & DADMS visited in the morning. 55th Div. Band arrived & were billeted in 2 rooms in the Convent.	R.A. MAP HAZEBROUCK 5A Belgium Sheet 27 (1:20000) (60 Stony)
"	6/2/17	"	Has word spread in Convent. Visited No. 2 C.C.S. BAILLEUL.	
"	7/2/17	"	A.D.M.S. visited. Captain Stroke started on month's leave to England. Lent Sgt. H. Capt. McKenzie proceeded on a months leave to England. Sgts. — detailed for the Sick of No. 2 Coy D.T. Train at F.19.a.7.3. Syouro detached	
"	8/2/17	"	Staff Sgt. Reynolds & Capt Holland proceeded to England to take up commissions. Capt Mg. AFC arrived & was temporarily attached to the Unit. 9 DYS on DADMS visited.	
"	9/2/17	"	A.D.M.S. below by General Visited a Canor R.A. on "Recent Operations on the Somme".	
"	10/2/17	"	DADMS visited. Visited Transport Lines. Mr. Maugham Brevenal Bombing Office Wh has been attached Since to hunt reported to D.H.Q.	

W. Morrison
Lt Col Kenned

WAR DIARY
INTELLIGENCE SUMMARY

Army Form C. 2118.

65th FIELD AMBULANCE
FEBRUARY 1917
Page 3. Volume XVII

Place	Date	Hour	Summary of Events and Information	Remarks and references to Appendices
POPERINGHE	11/2/17	12 mid night	ADMS marked also DA & QMG VIII Corps verbal transport orders & 62nd Report. MAP	HAZEBROUCK S.A.
on the March	12/2/17		The unit moved by march route to HAZEBROUCK starting at 11.25 a.m. joined transport at 12 noon & arrived at billets 3 kilometers S.E. of HAZEBROUCK at 4.30 p.m. 1 Motor Ambulance Car handed on to MO att 12NF temporarily.	
"	13/2/17		Left billets at 6.25 am & marched via MORBECQUE - ST VENANT - ROBECQ - OBLINGHEM to BETHUNE, where the unit occupied ARCHIVE LIBRARY Place St BARTHELMY arriving there 2.25 pm. Lieut Symons proceeded for temporary duty with 2y_st D.A.C.	
BETHUNE	14/2/17	"	ADMS visited. 2 Serjts & 2 Cpls (reinforcements) arrived from RAMC Territorial Base Depot.	
"	15/2/17	"	Personal found out. Captain Hedworth Jackman attached to duty on to 1st Div in the Somme. 1 hrs & LILLERS - Communication Arrangements	
"	16/2/17	"	9. OR proceeded for duty at Battn ANNEQUIN	
"	16/2/17	"	Visited 64th Field Amb. at LABOURSE. 1 hrs & 9 OR attached to laundry BETHUNE	
"	17/2/17	"	1 hrs & 7 OR proceeded duty to Battn VERMELLES & 1 hrs & 7 OR to Battn NOVELLES.	

WAR DIARY

Army Form C. 2118.

65th FIELD AMBULANCE
FEBRUARY 1917
Page 4 Volume XVII

Place	Date	Hour	Summary of Events and Information	Remarks and references to Appendices
BETHUNE	18/2/17	12 midnight	Visit by Lieut.Col. LABOURSE. Capt. LeTULANE, referring to find Car provided fortnightly to 21st Divst Training at Mt. AUCHY-au-BOIS. Took medical charge of 21st Divst School FERFAY.	MAP HAZEBROUCK S.A
"	19/2/17	"	1 N.C.O. & 1 Pte proceeded to 62nd Fd. Amb. VERMELLES. 5 N.C.Os horses lent daily to Town Major BETHUNE for Sanitary work. Rode round to all available huts in the morning. Kit inspection in [illegible] afternoon. 1 Reinforcement arrived.	
"	20/2/17	"	O.C. & Chaplain horse attended burial of LILLERS in advance school on reference to Capts on the Somme.	
"	21/2/17	"	No 2231 Pte Johnson H.E. proceeded to report to O.C. Reinforcements near ROUEN to transfer to England (claimed as a minor American citizen). 2 Pts proceeded to Rock Store at Butts ANNEQUIN, & 2 Pt to 110 Major from host store VERMELLES. 2 N.C.Os & 13th proceeded for duty to 21st Div. Laundry BETHUNE. Civilian Gardener being posted to 25th Divst now struck up the strength of the Unit. Lieut E. O'Reilly (J.C.) reported his arrival for duty came taken in the strength from this day stated to be ten. Visits: OFFS. SALLY LABOURSE.	W.Rawson Lt.Col. Commdr OC 65 Field Ambulance

WAR DIARY

65th FIELD AMBULANCE Army Form C. 2118.

INTELLIGENCE SUMMARY

FEBRUARY 1917.
Page 5. Volume XVII

Place	Date	Hour	Summary of Events and Information	Remarks and references to Appendices
BETHUNE	22/2/17	12 mid-night	Visited to 1 Sec G.H. Reserve Park & inspected sanitary arrangements, turns, billets, accompanied by Lt. O/c of the unit. Capt. Huish A.S.C.M.T. proceeded to Humstation Depot BOULOGNE.	MAP. HAZEBROUCK 5.A.
"	23/2/17	"	Visited Corps Rest Stn FOUQUIERES.	
"	24/2/17	"	Officers visited. 1 Ypr & 4 Pts proceeded to Transportation Depot BOULOGNE. Lieut Symons regained from temporary duty with 21st D.A.C.	
"	25/2/17	"		
"	26/2/17	"	Actions visited & inspected huts Hazebrouck.	
"	27/2/17	"	Visited Actions at SAILLY LABOURSE. Ramc o/o no 38 received	
"	28/2/17	"	Personnel bathed & fitted out.	

W. Thompson
Lt. Col. Comm.
of 65th Field Ambulance

140/1042

21st Div.

65th Field Ambulance.

MO/1917 /51

COMMITTEE FOR THE
MEDICAL HISTORY OF THE WAR
Date 11 MAY. 1917

Army Form C. 2118.

MEDICAL

Vol 19

WAR DIARY
65TH FIELD AMBULANCE
MARCH 1917
Page 1. — Volume XVIII.

INTELLIGENCE SUMMARY.
(Erase heading not required.)

Place	Date	Hour	Summary of Events and Information	Remarks and references to Appendices
BETHUNE	1/3/17	12 mid-night	1. Horse Ambulance reports to 1st Lincolns at MAZINGARBE that about 1/2 march to BUSNES & another to accompany 10th Yorks Regt. from NOEUX-LES-MINES to same place.	MAP HAZEBROUCK 5 A.
"	2/3/17	"	1. Horse Ambulance reports to 12 & 13th NF's accompanied them from NOEUX-LES-MINES to ECLEME & proceeding next day to HAM-EN-ARTOIS.	
HAM EN ARTOIS	3/3/17	"	Ambulance left BETHUNE by heat route at 9.40 am & arrived at HAM-EN-ARTOIS at 1.30 pm & went into billets there.	
"	4/3/17	"	Owing to a confused house to take short accommodation for 9. Cars & 20 Horses marched 1 NCO & 7 men returned from NOYELLES. 1 NCO & 2 men from ANNEQUIN. 1 NCO & 9 men proceeded to Baths LILLERS.	
"	5/3/17	"	Unit went to a route march in afternoon.	
"	6/3/17	"	Visited 2/1st Det Training Depot at AUCHY-au-BOIS. Route march in afternoon.	
"	7/3/17	"	Attended Dilletin family reports to Staff Captn 63rd Div at LIGNY-LEZ-AIRE at 11 am. & took over billets. Foot & kit inspection held by Capt Thomas RAMC	

WAR DIARY or INTELLIGENCE SUMMARY.

65th FIELD AMBULANCE   Army Form C. 2118.

MARCH 1917

Page 2   VIme XVIII

Place	Date	Hour	Summary of Events and Information	Remarks and references to Appendices
HAM EN ARTOIS	8/3/17	12. midnight	A.D.M.S. noted. Route march in afternoon. Adm.O.D. no. 128 ref. MAPS	MAPS HAZEBROUCK S.A. to LENS 11.
LIGNY LEZ AIRE	9/3/17	"	The unit left HAM EN ARTOIS at 12 noon by march route & arrived at LIGNY LEZ AIRE at 2 p.m. & went into billets there.	
VALHUON	10/3/17	"	Adm. O.D. no. 129 arrived at 2 a.m. The unit left LIGNY LEZ AIRE at 11·15 a.m. & arrived at VALHUON at 3 p.m. & were billeted there. Adm. O.D. no. 130. Adm.O.D. at 11·5 p.m.	
HONVAL	11/3/17	"	The unit left VALHUON by march route at 8·10 a.m. & arrived at HONVAL at 1·30 p.m. 1 Officer & 42 OR of 21st Div. Cyclists Corps joined the Ambulance & were attached for Rations & Quarters.	
HALLOY	12/3/17	"	Adm. O.D. no. 131. Reveille 3·55 a.m. 7 cases evacuated to 6 Stationary Hosp. FREVENT (13th N.F.) & 17th 12th N.F.S. The unit left at 9·15 a.m. & arrived HALLOY at 3·15 p.m. & went into huts in C camp there. Road very heavy & many horses & waggons got stuck	Marching W. Off Lanes Marching W. Off Lanes

WAR DIARY / INTELLIGENCE SUMMARY

65th FIELD AMBULANCE
MARCH 1917
Page 3. Volume XVIII

Army Form C. 2118.

Place	Date	Hour	Summary of Events and Information	Remarks and references to Appendices
HALLOY	13/3/17	12 md night	Hospital that opened up, capable of accommodating 16 patients. A.D.M.S & D.H.Q Officer visited. 6 cases transferred to Z.L.S. (including 1 case of 1 [German hands]) 13 [illegible]	MAP. LENS (1).
"	14/3/17	"	2 cases that opened. 11 Batt: Beds were fitted to accommodate personnel of hospital. (Iron beds for 4 Officers). Personnel of the unit paid out k.. 28 remaining.	
"	15/3/17	"	3. Horse Amb: Wagon proceeded to GROUCHES under instructions from A.D.M.S. on duty between that village & LUCHEUX. Heavy rain has fallen during last 2 days. Capt Stroud rejoined the unit from 13th N.F.s. A.D.M.S. visited.	
"	16/3/17	"	A.D.M.S visited. Was that opened for patients. 11 Reinforcements arrived from Base. Unit parade to Div. Respirator Drill. Rode much in afternoon. Visited VII & VI. 2 [illegible]	
"	17/3/17	"	A.D.M.S visited. Pte Roberts & Pte G. returned sick. Visited from FERFAY. Cpl. Headquarters. Remaining in Ambulance 51. hour [illegible] Capt M? [illegible] & [illegible] An returned	
"	18/3/17	"	An N.C.O. proceeded to Brit: Gas School for 2 days course.	
"	19/3/17	"	Nurses visited. [illegible] Tent opened in a nursing room for patients [illegible] Drill. Visited DOULLENS. 2 N.C.O's & 15 O.T.R returned from Brit: Laundry BETHUNE.	

War Diary

65th Field Ambulance
MARCH 1917
Page 4.

Army Form C. 2118.

INTELLIGENCE SUMMARY

Volume XVIII

Place	Date	Hour	Summary of Events and Information	Remarks and references to Appendices
HALLOY	20/3/17	12 mid-night	Lieut. O'Kirk marched detachment consisting of 1 NCO & 12 NFS during absence of Capt Griffin, 1 NCO & 7 OR proceeded ahead to Bretts LUCHEUX. Route march in afternoon.	Reference Map LENS (11)
"	21/3/17		Capt Steele furled further party of 13 NFS during absence of Sunday evening. Capt d'Kenzie visited ADMS LUCHEUX.	
"	22/3/17		Lieut. Spiers visited No. 5. Labora en Milly with reference to wounded. ADMS visited. Route march in afternoon.	
"	23/3/17		2 hots of personnel taken on 7 am field ambulance also Officers' Mess Personnel & went bathed, arrived with them immediately. Pte Bradford proceeded to Thomophratten Depot DOULLENS	
"	24/3/17		Capt. Steele rejoined from 13th NFS adv/FA Summer Time at 11 pm. 11 pm becoming 12 midnight.	
"	25/3/17		Unit paraded to marching order at 10.10 am (advanced party consisting of 1 Officer & 10 OR left at 9 am) & proceeded by march route via PAS - HENU - SAUSANT - HUMBERCAMP to LACAUCHIE & took in turn 2/3 Home Counties Field Ambulance at 2.30 pm. The relieved unit marching out at 4 pm.	

[signature]

WAR DIARY
INTELLIGENCE SUMMARY

65th FIELD AMBULANCE Army Form C. 2118.
MARCH 1917
Page 5   Volume XVIII

Place	Date	Hour	Summary of Events and Information	Remarks and references to Appendices
LACAUCHIE	26/2/17	12 midt	Capt McShield, Lieut Symons & 20. O.R. proceeded as an advanced party to A.D.S. at Super Secteur, BOIRY St. RICTRUDE X.24.a.9.1. (Sheet 51.C) A.D.M.S. visited also ADVms & D.ADms 38th Divn. 32 sick taken on from 2/3rd H.E. FIELD Amb. An advanced party of 1 m.o + 3 N.C.'s with 4 G.S. wagons arrived from 63rd Fd Amb	Ref MAP LENS (I) (1:100,000) 51-C 1-40,000
	27/3/17	"	Capt McFarlane & remainder of B Sec'n personnel & transport also 3 motor amb. cars proceeded & took over the A.D.S. at BOIRY. The advanced party 1, 2 Officers & 20 O.R. arrived from 63rd Fd Amb & took over. Lieut Em Blum & 20 O.R. with C. Sec'n Transport proceeded to HUMBERCAMP to take on from 2/3rd H.E. Fd Amb. 1 m.o & 3 Pts 15th M.U attached party at BERLES AU BOIS. Accompanied by O.C. 65th Fd Amb, visited A.D.S. at BOIRY. The horse cycle attached to A.D.M.S. office returned to the unit.	
"	28/3/17	"	Handed over to 63rd Fd Amb 31 hospitals + tooth on 51 from 1/3rd H.E. Fd Amb. A.D.M.S. 2 Div'n Army & R RAPS accompanied by ADMS & DADms visited the ADS. 2 Dean park & R RAPS returning to HUMBERCAMP at 9.30am.	E. Ringler Lt Col

WAR DIARY

65TH FIELD AMBULANCE
MARCH 1917.
Page 6. Volume XVIII

Army Form C. 2118.

INTELLIGENCE SUMMARY.
(Erase heading not required.)

Place	Date	Hour	Summary of Events and Information	Remarks and references to Appendices
HUMBERCAMP	28/3/17	12 midnight	The Transport of the unit marched off at 10·30 a.m., & the Personnel arrived at MDS: DOISY St RICTRUDE (Super Factory) at 12·40 & 1·40 pm respectively. A rear party of 9·1 Officer & 20 OR remained at HUMBERCAMP to hand over to relieving unit at S 11. c 3·10. Another Section of S 30. c 1·3. +1 to S 11 c 3·10 - workshop. An Officer Sent to Workshop. The had & 3 men arrived from BERLES au BOIS. 1 Another Section visited the Dump Post at HAMELINCOURT & received back all Med. equipt (25/3/17) & belong.	Ref MAP LENS (11) 1:100,000 & St. C. 1:40,000
DOISY St. RICTRUDE	30/3/17	"	Capt hour 1 Staff Sergt + 9 men proceed to 15 Reserve Park S.30.c.1.3. 2. M.T. Party Cars parked in village of BOISIEUX au MONT S.10 c 9.6 to evacuate sick from S.11. c. 3.10 110th Bdy Post at VERNELLES 10 men rejoined from HUMBERCAMP. O.C. 65 & 64th Field Amble also the rear party from HUMBERCAMP visited & went round front line.	
"	31/3/17	"	Lieut Symons + 24 Reserve proceed to Reserve Park S. 30 " C 3·10 - 30 Officers & Nothing a RC. 64th Field Ambulance Visited. 2. Reinf Substrainers reported from 65th Field M.C. visited Reserve Park.	

W. Murphy Lt

CONFIDENTIAL

Vol. 20

14/7036

21st Div.

WAR DIARY
OF THE
65TH FIELD AMBULANCE
(3RD W. LANCS. T.F.)

FROM APRIL 1ST 1917.
TO APRIL 30TH 1917.

VOLUME
(PAGES.)

COMMITTEE FOR THE
MEDICAL HISTORY OF THE WAR
Date −6 JUN. 1917

April 1917

5

B.E.F.

SUMMARY OF MEDICAL WAR DIARIES FOR 65th F.A. 21st Divn. 7th Corps, 3rd Army.

WESTERN FRONT. April- May. '17.

O.C. Lt. Col. W./Thompson.

SUMMARISED UNDER THE FOLLOWING HEADINGS.

Phase "B" Battle of Arras- April_ May. '17.

1st Period Attack on Vimy Ridge April.
2nd Period Capture of Siegfried Line May.

B.E.F.

65th F.A. 21st Divn. 7th Corps. WESTERN FRONT.
O.C. Lt. Col. W. Thompson. April. '17.
3rd Army.

Phase "B" Battle of Arras- April- May. '17.
1st Period Attack on Vimy Ridge April.

1917.   Headquarters. at Boiry St. Rictrude.

April. 1st.   Moves Detachment: Medical Arrangements:

                1 and 1Br S.D. to Coll. F. Hamelincourt.

                1 " 1 Br. S.D. to Coll. P. S.11.C/5.10.

                1 " 9 to 20th C.C.S.

                Remainder of Unit at A.D.S. Boiry St. Rictrude.

2nd.   Casualties: Evacuation: 4 and 72 wounded evacuated
                by Ambulance car to C.M.D.S.

3rd.   1 and 18 wounded evacuated.

4th.   Moves Detachment: Medical Arrangements:
                1 and 13 to St. Leger formed Coll. P. at T.28.a.3.3.
                with Br. P. at T.29.a.4.10. Returned to A.D.S. on 7th.

5th.   Casualties. 0 and 13 wounded evacuated.

7th.   Medical Arrangements: 1 and B & C Br. S.Ds. reported
                to O.C. 63rd Field Ambulance for collection of
                wounded in front line.

                Assistance. 50 men of Divn. reported at A.D.S. for
                loading and unloading ambulance. Returned to Units
                on 18th.

8th.   Transport. Ambulance cars of 63rd and 64th Field
                Ambulances attached to A.D.S.

9th.   Operations: 21st Divn attacked 4.15 p.m.
                Casualties. 0 and 25 wounded admitted.

10th.   Casualties. Evacuation: 16 and 152 wounded and 4 W.
                P.O.W. evacuated by Ambulance cars of 3rd M.A.C.
                1 and 4 and 1 P.O.W. died of wounds.

B.E.F.

65th F.A. 21st Divn. 7th Corps.   WESTERN FRONT
   O.C. Lt. Col. W. Thompson.   April. '17.
      3rd Army.

Phase "B" cont.
1st Period cont.

1917.

April.11th.   Casualties. 14 and 115 wounded admitted and evacuated.
              Moves: Medical Arrangements: A.D.S. moved to S.10.d.
              5.8. (Sheet 51B)

    12th.   Casualties. 2 and 22 wounded evacuated.

    13th.   Moves: Medical Arrangements: A.D.S. moved to S.12.d.7.4.
              (on Arras- Bapaume Road).

    14th.   Casualties. 1 and 37 wounded evacuated.
              0 and 3 died of wounds.

    15th.   Military Situation: 21st Divn. relieved by 33rd Divn.
              Medical Arrangements: A.D.S. handed over to 99th Field
              Ambulance.
              Moves: To Boiry St. Rictrude.

16th- 23rd.   Operations R.A.M.C. Routine, sick of 64th Bde. collected.

    25th.   Moves: Medical Arrangements: To Boyelles S.18.b.8.7.
              (Sheet 51B)
              2 and "A" and "C" T.S.Ds. took over A.D.S. St. Leger
              T.27.b.4.0. from 101st Field Ambulance.
              "B" Section T.S.D. proceeded to A.D.S. Henin N.32 D.10 under O.C. 63rd F.A.

    26th.   1 and "A" Section Br. S.D. took over L. Sector of
              Front line from 19th Field Ambulance.
              1 and "C" Section Br. S.D. took over R. Sector of Front
              line from 101st F.A.

    27th.   8 Brs. attached to each Battln. in the line.

2.

B.E.F.

65th F.A. 21st Divn. 7th Corps.   WESTERN FRONT.
O.C. Lt. Col. W. Thompson.   April. '17.
3rd Army.

Phase "B" Battle of Arras- April- May. '17.
1st Period Attack on Vimy Ridge April.

1917.	Headquarters. at Boiry St. Rictrude.
April. 1st.	Moves Detachment: Medical Arrangements:
	1 and 1Br S.D. to Coll. P. Hamelincourt.
	1 " 1 Br. S.D. to Coll. P. C. S.11/5.10.
	1 " 9 to 20th C.C.S.
	Remainder of Unit at A.D.S. Boiry St. Rictrude.
2nd.	Casualties: Evacuation: 4 and 72 wounded evacuated by Ambulance car to C.M.D.S.
3rd.	1 and 18 wounded evacuated.
4th.	Moves Detachment: Medical Arrangements:
	1 and 13 to St. Leger formed Coll. P. at T.28.a.3.3. with Br. P. at T.29.a.4.10. Returned to A.D.S. on 7th.
5th.	Casualties. 0 and 13 wounded evacuated.
7th.	Medical Arrangements: 1 and B & C Br. S.Ds. reported to O.C. 63rd Field Ambulance for collection of wounded in front line.
	Assistance. 50 men of Divn. reported at A.D.S. for loading and unloading ambulance. Returned to Units on 18th.
8th.	Transport. Ambulance cars of 63rd and 64th Field Ambulances attached to A.D.S.
9th.	Operations: 21st Divn attacked 4.15 p.m.
	Casualties. 0 and 25 wounded admitted.
10th.	Casualties. Evacuation: 16 and 152 wounded and 4 W. P.O.W. evacuated by Ambulance cars of 3rd M.A.C.
	1 and 4 and 1 P.O.W. died of wounds.

B.E.F.

65th F.A. 21st Divn. 7th Corps.   WESTERN FRONT
O.C. Lt. Col. W/Thompson.   April '17.
3rd Army.

Phase "B" cont.
1st Period cont.

1917.

April 11th. Casualties. 14 and 115 wounded admitted and evacuated.
Moves: Medical Arrangements: A.D.S. moved to S.10.d.
5.8. (Sheet 51B)

12th. Casualties. 2 and 22 wounded evacuated.

13th. Moves: Medical Arrangements: A.D.S. moved to S.12.d.7.4.
(on Arras- Bapaume Road).

14th. Casualties. 1 and 37 wounded evacuated.
0 and 3 died of wounds.

15th. Military Situation: 21st Divn. relieved by 33rd Divn.
Medical Arrangements: A.D.S. handed over to 99th Field
Ambulance.
Moves: To Boiry St. Rictrude.

16th- 23rd. Operations R.A.M.C. Routine, sick of 64th Bde. collected.

25th. Moves: Medical Arrangements: To Boyelles S.18.b.8.7.
(Sheet 51B)
2 and "A" and "C" T.S.Ds. took over A.D.S. St. Leger
T.27.b.4.0. from 101st Field Ambulance.
"B" Section T.S.D. proceeded to A.D.S. Henin N.32.D.10 under O.C. 63rd F.A.

26th. 1 and "A" Section Br. S.D. took over L. Sector of
Front line from 19th Field Ambulance.
1 and "C" Section Br. S.D. took over R. Sector of Front
line from 101st F.A.

27th. 8 Brs. attached to each Battln. in the line.

MEDICAL
XIX

65TH FIELD AMBULANCE   Army Form C. 2118.
APRIL 1917
Page 1. Volume

WAR DIARY
INTELLIGENCE SUMMARY.
(Erase heading not required.)

Place	Date	Hour	Summary of Events and Information	Remarks and references to Appendices
BOIRY St. RICTRUDE	1/4/17	12. midnight	1. New Quarter for 65th with Capt Brennan in command proceeded to Collecting Post HAMELINCOURT. The other with Capt Grey to Tournament S.11.C.5.10. Lieut Andrews proceeded to Collecting Post & entrainment. Capt McFarlane & 9.O.R. proceeded to Tournament dug out to 20.CCS. Visited with others the Collecting Post. 3 amb. waggons from 63rd & 64th Fd Amb into 3 Cars from each reported for duty & the formed were sent up to Collecting Post 3 to each to work between them & MDS.	Ref MAP 51.B;&51E (1-40000)
"	2/4/17	"	8. amb. cars arrived & reported to hut from no 3 M.A.C. also 2. Lorries. 2 Douglas & 3 Small transports were put to use for transporting wounded. Motors & others visited — Walked Collecting Posts. Capts Cummnets visited hut 5th in afternoon up to midnight 4. Officers & 72. OR. (wounded) were evacuated to Caps horse Dress Stn.	
"	3/4/17	"	Lieut S. O'Reilly reported from 12.RNF. Officers walked — work up to Collecting Posts. 1 hit & 5 OR. proceeded to S.11.C.5.10. to receive & attend to following in Craters at K.M. & S.12-c & S.12.G. 1 M wounded from 12 87st Hospl in Craters at K.M. & S.12-c & S.12.G. 1 Officer & 15 OR. (wounded) were evacuated.	

WAR DIARY

65th FIELD AMBULANCE
APRIL 1917.
Page 2. Volume XIX

Army Form C. 2118.

INTELLIGENCE SUMMARY

Place	Date	Hour	Summary of Events and Information	Remarks and references to Appendices
BOIRY St. RICTRUDE	4/4/17	12 midnight	Capt Hackworth & 13 OR. proceeded to St LEGER & formed a Collecting Post at T28A.33 with a Bearer post at T29A.4.10. Made a reconnaissance of St LEGER – BOYELLES – CROISILLES, BOYELLES & CROISILLES – BOIRY roads. 12 OR. returned from S.M.C.S.10. OC 63rd Fld Ambl. ADMS. 7th Div. visited.	Ref. 17AP 51. B. (1-A.D.S.03)
"	5/4/17	"	DDMS VII Corps. ADMS. 7th Div. visited; worked Collecting Posts. 13 OR. (wounded) evacuated.	
"	6/4/17	"	With ADMS visited 64th Fld Ambl dugout under 8th A S.E. Central. Visited OC 63rd Fld Ambl at Advanced Collecting Post BOYELLES. 10 Bearers & 3 wheeled stretchers worked jointly by OC 63rd Fld Ambl & Capt. Rec'd Capt from (C.F. reported in charge of MDS.)	
"	7/4/17	"	OC 63rd Fld Ambl took over the collection of casualties from the front near Capt Hackworth returned to the MDS. Lieut Symes reported sick with 15 C. Division, stretcher bearers to OC 63rd Rear Ambl. The B Horse Ambl Waggons reported at 11 am to OC 63rd Fld Ambl at BOYELLES. 2/L Rice & 50 men reported to MDS. Capt Stoner + 1 OR (clerk) reported for duty. Capt Henderson RAMC London Amb workshop RAMCOO hq arrived	

WAR DIARY

INTELLIGENCE SUMMARY

65th FIELD AMBULANCE Army Form C. 2118.
APRIL 1917.
Page 3 Volume XIX

Place	Date	Hour	Summary of Events and Information	Remarks and references to Appendices
BOIRY S.M. BIACHE	8/4/17	12 midnight	Instructions from 63rd Bde H.Q. ards to join 58th Div near Ficheux temporarily. 1 O.R. reports from Surplus Kit Store MONDICOURT.	MAP. 51.B. (1:40000) & LENS 11 (1:100 000)
"	9/4/17		ADMS visited. 3 O.R. reports from Bath. LUCHEUX. 1 N.C.O. + 3 G.S. wagons (the Artillery Coln) proceeded towards from S.F. at 1.15 p.m. B. H.Q. Divn sent on Store Lorries to O.C. 63rd Fd Amb. BOYELLES. 25 O.R. wounded arrived at M.D.S.	
"	10/4/17		8 Cars reported from H.Q. 3 M.A.C. to assist in Evacuation. ADMS visited VII Corps. visited. 16 Officers + 152 O.R. + 4 Germans wounded + evacuated. 1 Officer. 4. O.R. + 1 German died.	
"	11/4/17	6 p.m.	ADMS + DADMS visited. Received orders to S.10 d.S.E. Bec Section (Horsed transport + motor transport) marched up at 4.30 p.m. Horses + self inspected. Rode for M.D.S. subsequently with Brig. General. 14 Officers + 115 O.R. wounded admitted + evacuated. (from midnight 10th to 6 p.m 11th) 1 German died.	
"	12/4/17		2 Officers + 22 O.R. wounded evacuated during previous 24 hrs.	
"	13/4/17		The Field Ambulance moved to S.12.d.7.4. (on ARRAS-BAPAUME Rd) 21 Bell, 3 Operating Tents, + 1 Marquee pitched. Wounded began to arrive at 12 noon. 64th Fd Amb formed to Walking wounded Station alongside (immediately south of 65)	

WAR DIARY
INTELLIGENCE SUMMARY

65th FIELD AMBULANCE — Army Form C. 2118.
APRIL 1917
Page 4 Volume XIX

Place	Date	Hour	Summary of Events and Information	Remarks and references to Appendices
S12.d.7.4 BOYELLES	14/4/17	6 p.m.	ABtars visited Hermies, & Beaumont & Cemetery HENIN. 1 Officer & 3 OR wounded Hermies. 3 OR sick. Received news that the Div. was being relieved by 33rd Div. 12. 1 Off & 2 Mounting Troops struck in preparation for departure. RAMC OxD hos 45 received.	MAP 51.B. (1 - 40,000)
"	15/4/17	"	Handed over to 99th Field Amb. 33rd Div. had marched off at 12 noon & arrived at Sapin Farm Boiry St RICTRUDE at 1.25 p.m. 5 wounded handed over. The unit is dealing with the sick of 64th Brig II. 1 European picked up sleeping quick.	
BOIRY Sᵗ RICTRUDE.	16/4/17	"	8. Sick evacuated from 64th Brigade. 8ut Dunberry Officer & 21 OR. Infantry admitted to unit.	
"	17/4/17	"	DADMS visited ADG New CQE 3rd Army visited.	
"	18/4/17	"	ADMS visited. Capt Hume proceeded for Temporary duty evacuated their 10 Officer & 21 Rice & 43 OR 2 Yorks Regt whether been attached for dealing with per returning to their unit.	
"	19/4/17	"	No 3 M A C. Stretchers Horse Headquarters at Sapin Factory & Cafe hear Brewery St. found it Muckfields 5.12.a.1 at 6am 20th inst. Lieut HHSymons signed it back from 60th Field Amb.	
"	20/4/17	"	Corps MAS established at S.2.b.q.u.	

W. Wright Major
O.i/c

WAR DIARY / INTELLIGENCE SUMMARY

65th FIELD AMBULANCE
APRIL 1917.
Page 5. Volume XIX

Army Form C. 2118.

Place	Date	Hour	Summary of Events and Information	Remarks and references to Appendices
BOIRY ST. RICTRUDE	21/4/17	6 p.m.	Rec'd forward outfit for duty in front line. Held 3 O.A.D.M.S. (TC) 2/1st London Field Ambulance reported for duty.	MAP 51.B (1:40000)
"	22/4/17		Captain Irvine proceeded to h/o home during O/C for temporary duty. A/F W.3121 submitted.	526.9.11 AIX.ILL, LENS 11.
"	23/4/17		64th Brigade attaches to 50th Div. Mulquetis N.7.d.4.4. 110th Div moved from BASSEUX area to BLAIREVILLE - FICHEUX area.	
"	24/4/17		R.T.M.C. O.O. No 48 received —	
"	25/4/17		Captains Peter, O'Connor & Irvine returned from leave. Capt'n Peter posted temporarily with 21st D.A.C. & rejoined at BOYELLES at 2 pm. R'd instructions from Supeur Factory BOIRY ST. RICTRUDE at 12 noon & arrived at BOYELLES 5.15 & 8. at 1.15pm. Captain Taylor & Hollsworth with A & C First Section proceeded to ADSs ST LEGER T.27.b.4.d. & took over from 101st. Field Amb. 33rd Div at 3pm. B lee: Ted vehicles reported to Pte 65th Fd Amb. NADS HENIN N.32.d.1.0.	
"	26/4/17		Head: Recon Sector H.52 & Square Post on left sector 1 front line (N.34-T.5-T.12) from 14th H.L.A. b. relief completed at 9 am. Cres Reserve Section W.2 & L.5 D Lively took on R. Scotr Lvnt time U.7 - U.13.b - U.14.b from 101st Fd Amb.	

WAR DIARY

INTELLIGENCE SUMMARY

65th Field Ambulance Army Form C. 2118.
April 1917.
Page 6. Volume XIX

Place	Date	Hour	Summary of Events and Information	Remarks and references to Appendices
BOYELLES	28/4/17	6 pm	3 Motor Amb Cars & 17 Horsed Amb waggons attacked 65th ADS, St LEGER. 1 Motor Car 65th 2CCS & 1-1 pm 63rd Fd Amb attached to left sector. Loading Post of 54 C.C.S. 2. also Motor car to each place. Visited RAPs by _N_ Bearer Posts of both sectors. Bearer Subdiv. attached to Right sector & Reliefs to each RAP.	St Leger M+P St B (1 M.O & 50 ORs)
"	29/4/17		Reconnoitred 1 63rd & 64th Amb left Bearer + Dressing Relief of 1 A+C section 65th FA + 1 M+ left & right sectors at 8am+ relieved Bearer Posts + RAPs on both sectors. Motor Amb waggon + 4 hand car (hg) & 2 motor cyclist attached to it ADS St LEGER. Visited ADS St LEGER + Bearer posts + RAPs on left sector (HENIN)	
"	30/4/17		2. Reconnoitred 63rd & 65th Amb left & right sectors 25 prisoners (19 sector) 63rd HQ Amb attached to Right Bearer being completed by 9am. Visited MDSs St LEGER + RAPs 1st Lincolns & 10th Yorks also Bearer Posts. Capt. R.C. Horne reported for temp. duty to 1/30. C.C.S.	

CONFIDENTIAL.

WK 21

COMMITTEE FOR THE
MEDICAL HISTORY OF THE WAR
Date 10 JUL. 1917

WAR DIARY
OF THE
65TH FIELD AMBULANCE.
(3RD W. LANCS T.F.)

From 1/5/1917
To 31/5/1917

VOLUME
(PAGES).

B.E.F.

SUMMARY OF MEDICAL WAR DIARIES FOR 65th F.A. 21st Divn. 7th Corps, 3rd Army.

WESTERN FRONT. April- May. '17.

O.C. Lt. Col/ W. Thompson.

SUMMARISED UNDER THE FOLLOWING HEADINGS.

Phase "B" Battle of Arras- April- May. '17.

1st Period Attack on Vimy Ridge April.
2nd Period Capture of Siegfried Line May.

B.E.F. 1.

65th F.A. 21st Divn. 7th Corps.　　　WESTERN FRONT.
O.C. Lt. Col. W. Thompson.　　　May. '17
3rd Army.

Phase "B" Battle of Arras- April- May. '17.
2nd Period Capture of Siegfried Line. May.

1917.
May. 3rd.　　Operations. 21st Divn. attacked 3.45 a.m.
　　　　　　Casualties: Evacuation: wounded from front line cleared
　　　　　　and evacuated by 11 a.m.- about 200 wounded from L. Sector.
　　　　　　Ambulance cars cleared from Coll. P. N.35.d.5.0.
　　　　　　Two buses evacuated sitting cases from A.D.S. St. Leger
　　　　　　to C.W.W.S. at Mercatel- Ambulance cars evacuated lying
　　　　　　cases to C.M.D.S. at S.2.b.9.4.
　　　　　　Casualties. R.A.M.C. Capt. Little M.C. attached 6th
　　　　　　Leicesters wounded.
　　　　　　Capt. Wallace attached 7th Leicesters wounded.
7th.　　　　Operations. Artillery very active.
11th.　　　Medical Arrangements: A.D.S. St. Leger and R. Sector
　　　　　　Front line taken over by 101st Field Ambulance-L. Sector
　　　　　　Front line taken over by 99th Field Ambulance.
　　　　　　Moves: To Basseux.
12th-23rd.　Operations R.A.M.C:-
　　　　　　Routine.- Collection of sick of 64th Bde.
24th.　　　Decorations:-
　　　　　　Sgt. Jones　)
　　　　　　　　　　　　) awarded M.M.
　　　　　　Pte. Maguire)
25th.　　　Moves Detachment:-
　　　　　　O and 9 to 20th Casualty Clearing Station.
26th-30th.　Operations R.A.M.C. Routine.

31st.　　　Moves : Medical Arrangements:/

B.E.F.

65th F.A. 21st Divn. 7th Corps.
O.C. Lt. Col. W/Thompson.
3rd Army.

WESTERN FRONT.
May. '17.

Phase "B" cont.

2nd Period cont.

1917.
May. 31st   Moves: Medical Arrangements. To St. Leger and took over A.D.S. and Br. Ps. from 101st Field Ambulance.

B.E.F.　　　　　　　　　　　　　　　　　　　　　　1.

65th F.A. 21st Divn. 7th Corps.　　　　WESTERN FRONT.
　　　　　　W.
O.C. Lt. Col./ Thompson.　　　　　　　　May. '17

3rd Army.

Phase "B" Battle of Arras- April- May. '17.
2nd Period Capture of Siegfried Line. May.

1917.
May. 3rd.　　Operations. 21st Divn. attacked 3.45 a.m.

Casualties: Evacuation: wounded from front line cleared and evacuated by 11 a.m. about 200 wounded from L. Sector. Ambulance cars cleared from Coll. P. N.35.d.5.0.

Two buses evacuated sitting cases from A.D.S. St. Leger to C.W.W.S. at Mercatel- Ambulance cars evacuated lying cases to C.M.D.S. at S.2.b.9.4.

Casualties R.A.M.C. Capt. Little M.C. attached 6th Leicesters wounded.

Capt. Wallace attached 7th Leicesters wounded.

7th.　　Operations. Artillery very active.

11th.　　Medical Arrangements: A.D.S. St. Leger and R. Sector Front line taken over by 101st Field Ambulance L. Sector Front line taken over by 99th Field Ambulance.

Moves: To Basseux.

12th-23rd.　　Operations R.A.M.C:-

Routine.- Collection of sick of 64th Bde.

24th.　　Decorations:-

Sgt. Jones　　)
　　　　　　　) awarded M.M.
Pte. Maguire)

25th.　　Moves Detachment:-

O and 9 to 20th Casualty Clearing Station.

26th- 30th.　　Operations R.A.M.C.　　Routine.

31st.　　Moves : Medical Arrangements:/

B.E.F.

65th F.A. 21st Divn. 7th Corps.　　　　WESTERN FRONT.
W.
O.C. Lt. Col./Thompson.　　　　　　　　May. '17.

3rd Army.

Phase "B" cont.

2nd Period cont.

1917.
May. 31st　　Moves: Medical Arrangements. To St. Leger and took over A.D.S. and Br. Ps. from 101st Field Ambulance.

WAR DIARY

65th FIELD AMBULANCE Army Form C. 2118.

MAY 1917.

Page 1. Volume XX.

INTELLIGENCE SUMMARY

Place	Date	Hour	Summary of Events and Information	Remarks and references to Appendices
BOYELLES S.18.d.7.5.	1/5/17	6pm	Opened O.R.T.M.O. and D.R. Bearers on Right Subsection also A.D.S. ST LEGER.	MAP S.I.B. (1:40000)
"	2/5/17		Near Station on L.H.Cubitts relieved. (48 hr relief). Michel dressed right section. Capt H.P.S. Moore returned from temporary duty with 10 K.O.Y.L.I.	
"	3/5/17		Wounded from front line were cleared forward & everything two wounds & 11 am — Ambulance motor left Relief Collecting Post N.35.d.5.0 about 200 casualties from left reaches up to 7pm. Two Bearer wounded sitting cases from A.D.S. ST LEGER to Capt. talking hands D.R. at MERIATEL Lyn's team in front lines to Capt M.D.St at S.2.b.9.4. Colan have reported for temporary duty with 6th division Cpl Little M/c (wounded).	
"	4/5/17		O.T.M.O. worked. Marked H.R.P. Returns. Dr O'Reilly reported to Company, Duty 15 7 Leicesters. Lt Wallace (Canadian)	[signature]

WAR DIARY

65th FIELD AMBULANCE
MAY 1917
Page 2. Volume X.

Army Form C. 2118.

INTELLIGENCE SUMMARY

Place	Date	Hour	Summary of Events and Information	Remarks and references to Appendices
BOYELLES	5/5/17	6 p.m.	62nd Bde. behind 110th Bde in Left Sector. N E of Hindenburg Line. – 110th Bde took over position from 62nd Bde & Hindenburg Line in Right Sector. Recon. information re Sucl centre (Leer heavin attacks & Bathm) relieved at 6 p.m. Visited RAPs & Recon Post in Left sector, & ADS St LEGER.	Ref. MAP S.I.3 (1-40,000) S.I.C. (1-40,000)
"	6/5/17	"	Visited Recon. & Regt MOs in the Line. Everything very quiet.	
"	7/5/17	"	Visited ADSt St LEGER also Left Sector. Our artillery very active especially on BULLECOURT & CHERISY. All Recon in Eastric relieved at 6 p.m.	
"	8/5/17	"	Heavy enemy bombing night of 7.8" – morning of 8. Front very quiet. Visited Right Sector.	
"	9/5/17	"	Visited Recon & RAPs in Left Sector; & half-platoon Recon in Right Sector	
"	10/5/17	"	OC 101st Fd Amb. visited Lect & ADSt. St LEGER and doing their	
"	11/5/17	"	HQrs.2 in MDSt. St LEGER & Recon in Right Lect. Recon in Left (HENIN) sector handed over to OC 101st Fd St.AL. relief completed by 11 am. Recon in Right Lect taken over by 101st Brit. Ambulance. The unit marched from BOYELLES at 12 noon, arrived at BASSEUX at 5.50 p.m. & went its billets there. Everything sick from OC "B" Myst Rest area	
BASSEUX	12/5/17	"	Lieut. J.L. Johnston Kane (T.C) reports his arrival from England & was taken to Kirkington 9th trench.	

WAR DIARY

INTELLIGENCE SUMMARY

65TH FIELD AMBULANCE
MAY 1917
Page 3. Volume XX

Place	Date	Hour	Summary of Events and Information	Remarks and references to Appendices
BASSEUX	13/5/17	6 p.m.	Lt. J.L. Thruston posted for temporary duty to 1st East Yorks Regt. in relief of Captain Raine. Promoted to Hon. Lt 331499 Sergt. E. Dixon proceeded to England to take up a commission. Lieut. S. O'Reilly leaves here posted to technical charge of 7th Division from 4th Inst. (vice Capt Wallace wounded) — struck off the strength of the Ambulance from that date. Capt. A.D.N. Mackenzie was posted to the unit on 6th inst. & taken on strength. D.A.D.M.S. visited corps. ADMS was visited.	MAP 57. C (2 wounds)
"	14/5/17	"	DDMS & DADMS visited corps visited. Unit paid out.	
"	15/5/17	"	Captain Mackenzie reported for permanent duty with 65th August R.F.A. 7th Ash. Cylinders for unit on arrival at FC 28 Kite Balloon Section. ADMS visited.	
"	16/5/17	"	Visited VIII corps H.Q. at DUISANS. DADMS visited. Rained all day.	
"	17/5/17	"	3 huns walking wounded and 10 Officers Leeds St. BARLY. 1 Pte (Australia) reported proceeding to ARRAS.	
"	18/5/17	"	Captain H's home visited the unit from 6th Division.	
"	19/5/17	"	64th Inf Brigade Sports. The Ambulance won 3, 1sts & 1, 2nd Prize.	
"	20/5/17	"	Captain K. Taylor proceeded on leave to England. 21/5/17 to 31/5/17.	
"	21/5/17	"	ADMS held trial on P.B. son of 76th Brigade at Hulstmed who shot her.	

Wilson ? Major
? RAMC

WAR DIARY

INTELLIGENCE SUMMARY

65th FIELD AMB<u>ce</u>
MAY 1917
Page 4 Volume XX

Army Form C. 2118.

Place	Date	Hour	Summary of Events and Information	Remarks and references to Appendices
BASSEUX.	22/5/17	6pm	Staff Sergt Boxall proceeded on leave to England.	MAP 51 C (1-40,000) & 51 B (1-40000)
"	23/5/17	"	The Pte proceeded on leave to to England. Received 2 O.R's from D.D.C. 2 O.R's for duty from 4 Pte Magazine	
"	24/5/17	"	A.D.M.S. visited. Staff Sergt & 1st Inspector inspected the building occupied by Corps Commander. 2 him proceeded to 3rd Army Rest Camp Boulogne. 1 man detailed temporarily in medical orderly to 35 Kite Balloon Sec<u>tn</u>.	
"	25/5/17	"	1 N.C.O. & 6 O.R proceeded to No 20 C.C.S. for temporary duty, in relief of original party being duty there.	
"	26/5/17	"	A.D.M.S. inspected personnel & Trenches order. 1 hurt hand not on employment.	
"	27/5/17	"	A.D.M.S. inspected Transport. 1 Pte proceeded on leave to England.	
"	28/5/17	"	3 reinforcements arrived. 1 Pte returned to duty from Train on leave relieved from employment Co. O.C. Div Train inspected Transport.	
"	29/5/17	"	1 Pte transfered to 1/3rd F.A. Field Amb. BARONS visited. D + C section with hospital proceeded by motor ambulances to ST LEGER. Austerlitz & Pail A ac? left BASSEUX at 7am. arrived ST LEGER 11.30am & took over A.D.S.	
"	30/5/17		hand Pat? from 101st Fd Amb. 33rd Div visited Rilon Pt CROISILLES.	
"	31/5/17			

Confidential.

Vol 2.2

140/2230

WAR DIARY.
OF THE
65ᵀᴴ FIELD AMBULANCE.
(3ʳᵈ W. LANCS. T.F.)

From 1ˢᵗ June 1917
To 30ᵗʰ June 1917.

VOLUME XXI.
(5 Pages).

COMMITTEE FOR THE
MEDICAL HISTORY OF THE WAR
Date -7 AUG. 1917

6
June 1917

Army Form C. 2118.

MEDICAL

65th FIELD AMBULANCE
JUNE 1917.
Page 1. Volume XXI

WAR DIARY / INTELLIGENCE SUMMARY
(Erase heading not required.)

Place	Date	Hour	Summary of Events and Information	Remarks and references to Appendices
ST LEGER	1/6/17	6 p.m.	A.D.M.S. visited Kench round Relay Post, Croisilles + R.A.P.s of Staff[?], L. Front Line i.e. 12th N.F. on right & 13th N.F. on left. R.A.P.s at T.18.d.9.6 respectively. 1st lines in reserve with R.A.P. at T.23.a.3.6. A.D.S. at St LEGER T.27.b.5.1. Lieut P. Hall-Smith reported his arrival & was posted to A sec. Captn Shade rejoined from Corps brain Dressing Str. at 7 p.m. 3/5/17.	MAP. 51. B.
"	2/6/17	"	Lieut Johnston rejoined from Pensbury leaf with 15th E. Yorks.	
"	3/6/17	"	A.D.M.S. + D.A.D.M.S. visited .. Captn Taylor returned from leave, visited th Corps H.Q. D.V.I.S.A.M.S.	
"	4/6/17	"	Captn Shade proceeded for duty to report to D.D.M.S. 2nd Army. 4. Reinforcement arrival. Proceeded on leave to England. Lieut Hawston now Captain Taylor.	
	After Note:			Whittern[?] Lieut reserve[?]
"	4/6/17	"	At A.D.S. In St Leger. T.27.b.5.1 (Map 57 B. sw) five R.A.M.C. personnel were wounded, one of which died shortly afterwards	

Taylor Capt
for O.C. 65th F.A.

Army Form C. 2118.

WAR DIARY

INTELLIGENCE SUMMARY

(Erase heading not required.)

65th FIELD AMBULANCE
JUNE 1917.
Page 2. Volume XXI

Place	Date	Hour	Summary of Events and Information	Remarks and references to Appendices
St Leger	5/6/17	6 p.m.	D.A.D.M.S visited.	
"	6/6/17	-	A.D.S. St Leger was heavily shelled in the evening, one man being slightly wounded.	
"	7/6/17	-	D.A.D.M.S visited. 110th Brigade relieved 62nd Brigade.	
"	8/6/17	-	D.A.D.M.S visited also D.D.M.S and A.D.M.S VII Corps. A.D.S shelled again. One advanced dressing of A.D.S. One ambulance car was marked by a shell. No casualties. Advanced removal of A.D.S. One ambulance was removed to T 25 d 4.4 (Map 57b S.W) under Pro Headquarters of Field Ambulance. One tent subdivision remained at A.D.S and Captain Nightingale R.A.M.C. One man was posted to transportation troops depot Boulogne. Hollesworth in charge. One man was evacuated.	
"	9/6/17	-	New Advanced Dressing Station commenced at T 27 d 6.7 (Map 57b Sw) Work was continued at new A.D.S. by working parties from H.2 and 110th Brigade. Also a party from 63rd Field Ambulance.	
"	10/6/17	-	D.D and D.A.D.M.S VII Corps visited new A.D.S. R.A.M.C O.O 48 received. Also 110th Brigade O.O. 68. There were later performed in the evening new A.D.S at T 27 d 6.7. (Map 57b S.W) was opened to receive patients. Two men wounded on 4/6/17 reported from C.C.S	
"	11/6/17	"	D.A.D.M.S visits 112 and A.D.S and R.A.P.s of Batts with Capt Taylor.	
"	12/6/17	"	One man evacuated to Base with A.F.C.	
"	13/6/17	"	D.O.D.M.S visited.	
"	14/6/17	"	Capt. Hollsworth proceeded — have 15 days leave. Col. Thompson returned from leave & assumed command of the Unit.	

WAR DIARY

65th Field Ambulance
JUNE 1917
Page 3. Volume XXI

Army Form C. 2118.

INTELLIGENCE SUMMARY

Place	Date	Hour	Summary of Events and Information	Remarks and references to Appendices
St LEGER	16/6/17 6p.m	—	1st & 2nd N.F's attacked Tunnel Trench (Hindenburg Support Line) at 3.10 a.m. Casualties began to arrive at A.D.S. at 4.15 a.m. D.D.M.S.; A.D.M.S., D.A.D.M.S. visited M.D.S. & reinforcements arrived. Casualties from 16th to noon 15th = 11 Officers + 283 OR wounded.	M + P. S + B.
"	17/6/17 6p.m	—	Visited R.A.P's in Hindenburg front Line & field Ambulance Relay Posts in Quarry T.18.d.10.7 & CROISILLES. T.23.d.2.7. A.D.M.S. visited + Aus. Shell Shock arr. Casualties to noon 17th = 3 Officers + 128 OR wounded.	
"	18/6/17	.	Officers visited Advance Posts 1/ 101st Infantry arrived at H.Q. Casualties to noon 18th = 3 Officers + 20 wounded	
"	19/6/17	.	1 Officer & Bearer Relief 1 64th Field Amb. reported. Their went visited A.D.S. + Relay Posts CROISILLES. Queen Posts & Quarry. Relay Post CROISILLES + A.D.S. handed over to 101st Field Amb. Relief completed at 6p.m. Transport under Capt Taylor marched M. at 6.25p.m. + arrived BASSEUX at 10.5p.m. remainder 1 unit marched M. at 7.5p.m arrived BASSEUX 10.30p.m. Casualties to noon 19th = 10 Sick + 5 wounded	[signatures]

WAR DIARY
65th FIELD AMBULANCE
JUNE 1917
Page 4 Volume XXI

INTELLIGENCE SUMMARY
(Erase heading not required.)

Army Form C. 2118.

Place	Date	Hour	Summary of Events and Information	Remarks and references to Appendices
BASSEUX	20/6/17	1pm	Ambulance opened up. Various patients in. Had paid not...	MAP 51. C
"	21/6/17	-	NCOs visited who DDMS & DADMS on 11th inst. visits 64 2/2 L La Cauchie. A/B action reinoculated.	
"	22/6/17	-	Captain + A/Sgt H.T. + N.T. reinoculated. Lieut W.H. Embrey promoted Capt.	
"	23/6/17	-	A/B men trialled.	
"	24/6/17	-	Corps Commander visited. Capt F.W. Rigby. Home T.C. expected home arrival now probable L/S dist.	
LA CAUCHIE	25/6/17	-	The Field Ambulance moved K to Cauchie ASR on the D.R.S. Station from 64" AAA to relief completed by 12 noon. Pte Owen. Attack + Burgess were awarded the Military Medal for their fine work in Trenches 7 15 – 16" inst.	
"	26/6/17	-	DDMS DADMS on 11th corps visited. Captain D. Hedworth returned from leave. To 9 p.m. + 164 D.R. remaining a D.R.S...	
"	27/6/17	-	Troops visited	
"	28/6/17	-	Lieut & Johnstone proceeded to Ste Pol. duty to 9th KOYLI	
"	29/6/17	-	3 horse Amb. Wagons accompanied Rollers 1 64 Army from Rest Area to MOYENVILLE Capt F.W. Rigby + 10 O.R. proceeded to GAUDIEMPRÉ + took over Rgt S/x from 15th Field Amb. 1st Half-Company proceeded to Linepay dat with 3rd H. Section.	W.Spain Capt W.K.W. O

WAR DIARY

INTELLIGENCE SUMMARY

65 Field Ambulance
JUNE 1917
Page 5 Volume XXI

Army Form C. 2118.

Place	Date	Hour	Summary of Events and Information	Remarks and references to Appendices
DHQ La Cauchie	30/6/17	6p	Capt Tutt Stroke regained the march from J.D. to Louin. Capt Hodworth +40 OR Regt 8r Gaudiempré. 13 Officers & 233 OR remaining in Rest Bt	M > P S/16 (1.40 000) & LENS II (1.100 000)

Wingham Keane
Lt.Col.
65th Fld Ambulance

No. 65. 7. a.

COMMITTEE FOR THE
MEDICAL HISTORY OF THE WAR
Date   10 SEP. 1917

WAR DIARY

INTELLIGENCE SUMMARY
(Erase heading not required).

65th FIELD AMBULANCE   Army Form C. 2118.
JULY 1917
Page 1. Volume XXII

Vol 23

MEDICAL

Place	Date	Hour	Summary of Events and Information	Remarks and references to Appendices
LA COMTE	1/7/17	6 p.m.	Lt. Colonel Newman returned from leave.	MAP ST. C 1-40,000
"	2/7/17	"	Nothing. Orders 33rd O.R. visited. Lt. Lyman proceeded on leave. Lt. Johnston rejoined from Ecfan. duty with 9th K.O.Y.L.I. 1 O.R. rejoined from C.C.S. And	
"	3/7/17	"	Lunch hour notes. 1 O.R. transferred to tent from 63rd Fd Ambulance.	LENS 11 (1-100,000)
"	4/7/17	"	Capt 2nd Rgh & 1 D.R. rejoined from GOUDIEPRÉ Red Staln. Three to work place of 48th Div. Lt Burton rejoined from tent visiting workers party at COUIN.	
"	5/7/17	"	6 Officers & 204 O.R. remaining	
"	6/7/17	"	Capt. Woldsmith & 40 O.R. Manual rejoined from COUIN	
"	7/7/17	"	Orders visited. The cricket team defeated VII Corps Officers Rest Stn team by 48 runs to 33.	
"	8/7/17	"	Heavy Thunderstorm during night. 6 Officers & 252 O.R. remaining	
"	9/7/17	"	Genl. Skinner & 38 O.R. proceeded to Antanzas & 20. C.C.S. S.2 & 9.4 Strength 53-20. Court of Enquiry held.	
"	10/7/17	"	Cricket match v Officers Rest Stn. B.A.S.C. Hrs won	
"	11/7/17	"	" v VIIth Corps School. Won by 2 wickets. 6 Officers & 226 O.R. remaining.	
"	12/7/17	"	" v Divisional School. Won by 46 runs	

WAR DIARY

65th FIELD AMBULANCE
July 1917 — Page 2, Volume XXII

Army Form C. 2118

Place	Date	Hour	Summary of Events and Information	Remarks and references to Appendices
LA CAUCHIE	13/7/17	6 p.m.	ADMS visited School Holiday. Arrived & Inspected Training. 6 Officers & 227 O.R. remaining.	MAP 51.C (1:40,000) LENS 11 (1:100,000)
"	14/7/17		Lieut. Seymour returned from leave. Ambulance Cricket team defeated the R.O.D. team by 46 runs.	
"	15/7/17		The C of S Commander visited in the morning. DDMS & DADMS VII Corps visited in the afternoon.	
"	16/7/17		Cricket team defeated Lewis Gun School by 67 runs. S. Officers & 206 O.R. remaining.	
"	17/7/17		DDMS VII Corps visited.	
"	18/7/17		Lt Seymour proceeded to the horse duty with 14th N.F.'s – visited VII Corps HQ. Sergt Maj. Shaw proceeded to England to take up a commission in the R. Aust Inf Corps.	
"	19/7/17		5 Officers & 212 O.R. remaining.	
"	20/7/17		ADMS visited. Capt. F.W. Ruff proceeded on leave to England.	
"	21/7/17		4 Officers & 206 O.R. remaining. 1 NCO & 4 O.R. proceeded to Rest Station GOUDEMPRE.	
"	22/7/17		OC 64th Fd Amb. visited.	
"	23/7/17		2 Officers & 220 O.R. remaining. 10 O.R. transferred from 20 CCS & 49 CCS.	W. Wharton Lt Col

WAR DIARY

INTELLIGENCE SUMMARY.

(Erase heading not required.)

Army Form C. 2118.

65th Field Ambulance
July 1917
Page 3 Volume XXIV

Place	Date	Hour	Summary of Events and Information	Remarks and references to Appendices
LACAUCHIE	25/7/17	6 p.m.	226 O.R. remaining	MAP LENS II (1:100,000)
"	26/7/17	"	Captain A.W.B. Duncan taken on strength & to remain at Le Souich. RAMC	
"	27/7/17	"	3 O.R. transferred to No. 4 Stat'y Hospl. as dental mechanics. 1 Officer & 230 O.R.	
"	28/7/17	"	A.D.M.S. Marked G.S. Waggon competition (1st hut Turn Out). by " "	
"	29/7/17	"	2 Officers + 263 O.R. remaining. Lieut. Stanton walked 65 miles in 17 = 27.	
"	30/7/17	"	Tent Competition (1st hut Tent Garden). 2 Officers + 252 O.R. remaining.	
"	31/7/17	"	2 Officers + 221 O.R. remaining. Heavy rain started at 6 p.m.	

Murphy Lieut
Vincent the Ponds
O.C.

CONFIDENTIAL.

V.d. 24

140/204

WAR DIARY.

OF THE

65TH FIELD AMBULANCE.

(3RD W. LANCS T.F.)

From 1st August 1917
To 31st August 1917.

VOLUME XXIII.
(3. PAGES)

COMMITTEE FOR THE
MEDICAL HISTORY OF THE WAR
Date -1 OCT.1917

3
Aug '17

WAR DIARY

65th FIELD AMBULANCE
AUGUST 1917
Page 1. ~~XIII~~ MEDICAL

Army Form C. 2118.

INTELLIGENCE SUMMARY

(Erase heading not required.)

Place	Date	Hour	Summary of Events and Information	Remarks and references to Appendices
LA COMTHE	1/8/17	6pm	3 Officers & 233 OR Remaining.	MAP LENS 11 (1:100000)
"	2/8/17	"	5 " & 209 " "	
"	3/8/17	"	7 " & 221 " "	
"	4/8/17	"	5 " & 212 " " Captain Few Res'y returned from leave	
"	"	"	Proceeded to Tenspeakes duty to 7th Leicestershire Regt. Lieut Hall Smith reported from 1st Leicesters	
"	5/8/17	"	Captain H.W. B. Dumahu joined from VIIth Corp Reinforcement Depot Le Souich	
"	6/8/17	"	8 Officers & 202 OR remaining	
"	7/8/17	"	Captain H.W.B. Dumahu proceeded to report to A.D.M.S. 34th Div. two struck off the strength from this date. D.D.R 3rd Army visited	
"	8/8/17	"	A.D.M.S. 21st Div. visited & inspected horses. Lieut Symons proceeded	
"	"	"	for temp. duty with 14th N.F.A.	
"	9/8/17	-	Captain C.D. Aldsworth proceeded to temp. duty with 94th Brig R.F.A.	
"	"	"	4 Officers & 221 OR remaining	
"	10/8/17	-	DDMS & MDMS VIIth Corp visited. Cricket match v. R.C.E. Beaumetz	
"			Won by 2 runs	

WAR DIARY
INTELLIGENCE SUMMARY.
(Erase heading not required.)

65th FIELD AMBULANCE
AUGUST 1917
Page 2. Volume XXII.

Army Form C. 2118.

Instructions regarding War Diaries and Intelligence Summaries are contained in F.S. Regs. Part II. and the Staff Manual respectively. Title pages will be prepared in manuscript.

Place	Date	Hour	Summary of Events and Information	Remarks and references to Appendices
LA COMTIE	11/8/17	6pm	A Theatre Horse Show Humorating Competitions at D.H.Q. Visited 64th Field Amb. Unit was fallen out.	MAP. LENS. 11 (1/100,000)
"	12/8/17	"	6 Officers & 210 OR Leaving	
"	13/8/17	"	DDMS 2nd Army, DDMS 1st Corps & ADMS hospital. 1st Trench noted to the R.F.C. no.13 Squadron then by 2 cinemas	
"	14/8/17	"	Cricket held v. 183 OR Running	
"	15/8/17	"	7 Officers & " "	
"	16/8/17	"	7 " & 195 " "	
"	17/8/17	"	Lieut Hull-Smith proceeded to England duty. O.C. 12/13th N.F. ADMS visited	
"	18/8/17	"	1st Corps Horse Show. O.C. 64th Field Amb. & DADMS visited.	
"	19/8/17	"	Capt Rush rejoined from 2nd Leicesters	
"	20/8/17	"	Lieut Johnston proceeded home to England	
"	21/8/17	"	7 Officers & 167 OR training	
"	22/8/17	"	Capt Hucklesworth rejoined from 94th M.G. RFA. bath hut out.	
"	23/8/17	"	ADMS 21st & 16th Divisions visited. I.M.T. inspected mechanical transport	
"	24/8/17	"	Rations O.O. 54. received.	
"	25/8/17	"	Advanced Party from 113th Fd Amb arrived to take over	

W[signature]

WAR DIARY
INTELLIGENCE SUMMARY

65th Field Ambulance
August 1917
Page 3 Volume XIII

Place	Date	Hour	Summary of Events and Information	Remarks and references to Appendices
AVESNES LE COMTE ("E")	26/8/17	1 pm	40 O.R. transferred to 113th Fd Amb. 12 hrs marched from LA CAUCHIE – 2.30 pm. Capt. Geo Pugh proceeded to report to OC 4th Cav Div'l – 40 OSD	M.A.P. S.T.C.
"	27/8/17		Major Storms proceeded (North Section Railhead Div Details) at HAUTEVILLE. Capt. T. W.R. Stroud + 27 O.R. reported from 20 CCS.	
"	28/8/17		Held P.B. South. (No. 1 Labour Coy)	
"	29/8/17		Tug-of-war with 12/13th N.F.	
"			(No. 18-D) " a " Lieut. Hall Smith reported from Tring leave with England & here. + 4 O.R. reported from 119 Labour Coy	
	30/8/17		Route march to afternoon – 35 O.R. remaining.	
	31/8/17		Gas visit parade. 47 O.R. remaining.	

Wheeler Capt RAMC
Act OC 65 F.A.

CONFIDENTIAL.

WO/95/

140/24/66

WAR DIARY

OF THE

65th FIELD AMBULANCE.
(3rd W. LANCS. T.F.)

From 1/9/17
To 30/9/17.

VOLUME XXIV.
(3. PAGES)

COMMITTEE FOR THE
MEDICAL HISTORY OF THE WAR
Date - 5 NOV. 1917

WAR DIARY
or
INTELLIGENCE SUMMARY.

65th FIELD AMBULANCE Army Form C. 2118.
SEPTEMBER 1917
Page 1. Volume XIV

MEDICAL

Place	Date	Hour	Summary of Events and Information	Remarks and references to Appendices
AFESNES-LE-COMTE	1/9/17	6p.m.	P.B. Bowman Tell at 2.30 p.m. Marchu. Visit Thompson Capt. Hedworth.	MAP 51.C.(1:10000) & LENS 11 (1:100000)
"	2/9/17	"	Door Reports still. 1 Officer + 66 OR remaining.	
"	3/9/17	"	Route march. 72 OR remaining	
"	4/9/17	"	Rec Reports still. Infantry till 11a	
"	5/9/17	"	ADMS & DADMS visited MO i/c 64th Fd Amb. Lt Hill undtd V. 64 & 2d Amb. Wm & 4 pol. Unit hand over — ADMS DADMS visited also re 63rd Hosmt Brit Gas Hosmt inspected	
"	6/9/17	"	Bee Reports of visit.	
"	7/9/17	"	DDMS + DADMS XVII Corps visited 1 Officer + 116 OR remaining	
"	8/9/17	"	high march with Respirators on. Battle hostels v XVIII Corps Sports. hrs 2-4.	
"	9/9/17	"	1 Officer + 129 OR remaining	
"	10/9/17	"	Dist Sportsmen at WAGONLIEU.	
"	11/9/17	"	64th Field Ambulance Sports.	
"	12/9/17	"	ADMS visited	
"	13/9/17	"	ADMS visited. Lieut J.L. Johnstone returned from leave. 1 Officer + 96 OR remaining	

W. Magdjance
Lieut Col

WAR DIARY

Army Form C. 2118.

65ᵗʰ FIELD AMBULANCE
SEPTEMBER 1917.
Page 2. Volume XXIV

INTELLIGENCE SUMMARY.

(Erase heading not required.)

Instructions regarding War Diaries and Intelligence Summaries are contained in F.S. Regs., Part II. and the Staff Manual respectively. Title pages will be prepared in manuscript.

Place	Date	Hour	Summary of Events and Information	Remarks and references to Appendices
AVESNES LE COMTE	14/9/17	6 pm	1 Other ranks to 55 OTR returning.	MAP LENS (1:100,000) HAZEBROUCK S.A. (1:100,000)
"	15/9/17	"	ADMS visited. 1st Lieut H. Gauss U.S.M.C. reported to duty.	
"	16/9/17	"	Captain Squires departed to England to report to Commandant Rouen Training Centre. Blackpool then struck off strength of Ambulance accordingly. Handed over to a detachment from 17th Divn. at 6 pm. Remaining Nil.	
PRADELLES	17/9/17	"	Transport of unit moved off at 10 pm at 11-40 pm & dismounted personnel at 11.40 pm & proceeded by march route to AUBIGNY & thence arriving at CASSEL at 8 am & proceeded at 9.30 am by march route to PRADELLES arriving there ch. 12.30 pm where the unit went into billets.	
"	18/9/17	"	ADMS visited. Captain C.D. Holdsworth proceeded to temporary duty to X Corps Rest Stn.	
"	19/9/17	"	1st Lieut Gauss U.S.M.C. proceeded for duty with 20th Divn Horse Shoe. Nothing Gr of Unit from this date. March route out DADVS worked	
"	20/9/17	"	16 OTR returning.	
"	21/9/17	"	5 Rdn Horses handed in to 33 to V. Section	

Whittaker
Lt Col

WAR DIARY

INTELLIGENCE SUMMARY

65th FIELD AMBULANCE
SEPTEMBER 1917
Page 3. Volume XXIV

Place	Date	Hour	Summary of Events and Information	Remarks and references to Appendices
PRADELLES	22/9/17	6 p.m.	Staff Captain 41st Div. Rained in Billets. 10. O.R. returning sick. B.O.29.	MAP HAZEBROUCK S.A. (1:100,000) Sheet 27 (1:40,000) & Sheet 28 (1:40,000)
"	23/9/17	"	Unit marched Hd.qrs at 10.45 am arrived at R.32.d.4.5. at 12.30 pm. Proceeded to Billets. Remounts & Horses.	
"	24/9/17	"	A.D.M.S. D.A.D.M.S. visited. Rained. O.C. hosp. arrived. 1 Officer & 20 O.R. proceeded at 2 pm on an advanced party to take on Divl. Rest Sta. at BOESCHEPE.	
BOESCHEPE	25/9/17	"	Unit marched Hd.qrs at 10.15 am & arrived at BOESCHEPE 11.30 am. took on 41st D.R.St. from 138th Fd Amb. Captain Pot. Raine Kame reported for duty from 1st E. Yorks. Rept. on being relieved by Lieut. Johnston who was struck off strength & Ambulance from that date. Captain J.P. Davies Kame rejoined for duty & was taken on the strength from this date. Lieut. Hall Smith having been posted to duty in England was
"	26/9/17	"	A.D.M.S. visited. Unit strength from 19th inst. 73. O.R. remaining. (sick)	
"	27/9/17	"	1 N.C.O. & 6 O.R. proceeded on holding party to Corps Walking Wounded Stn. LA CLYTTE.	
"	28/9/17	"	2. O.Rubes (N) proceeded to Infantry duty to each of the 3 Brigades for Cops. R.A.M.C. O.O.S.B. Second	
"	29/9/17	"	Bearer Divs. (91.O.R.) reported for duty to Lt. Col. 64th Field Amb. at Woodcote House (I.20.c.5.2.) Sheet 28.	
"	30/9/17	"		When from Woodcote Home

CONFIDENTIAL.

MEDICAL Vol 26

40/2499

COMMITTEE FOR THE
MEDICAL HISTORY OF THE WAR

Date —8 DEC. 1917

WAR DIARY

OF THE

65th FIELD AMBULANCE.
(3rd W. LANCS. T.F.)

From 1/10/1917.
To 31/10/1917.

VOLUME XXV
(4 PAGES).

[Stamp: 65th FIELD AMBULANCE ORDERLY ROOM]

WAR DIARY

INTELLIGENCE SUMMARY

65th FIELD AMBULANCE Army Form C. 2118.
OCTOBER 1917
Page 1. Volume XXI

Place	Date	Hour	Summary of Events and Information	Remarks and references to Appendices
BOESCHEPE (R.1D.a.2.B) (sheet 27)	1/10/17	6 pm	Captain R.T. Rome Lieut O'Reilly went to Rest Hut at WOODLOTE HOUSE. Captain F. Montgomery returned to DDMS X Corps, also B.DTR (holding party) from LA CLYTTE.	Army Reference Sheets 27 & 28 (1 = 40,000)
"	2/10/17		Captain Denis Holdsworth & 1 Trnst Subaltern reported for duty. To OC 3) CCS GODWAERSVELDE. 2 clerks reported for duty to Central Queries. REMY SIDING. - 3 Big Guns & 1 Trnst reported for duty to OC 64th Fd Amb.	
"	3/10/17		127 OTR returning; A OTD 59 received. 1 Motor cyclist reported for duty to OC 3) CCS. Captain Stodo reported for duty to OC 64th Fd Amb.	
"	4/10/17		133 O.R. returning.	
"	5/10/17		136 OTR returning.	
"	6/10/17		Winter Time started at 1am clock put back to 12 midnight.	
"	7/10/17		Lieut O'Reilly was posted to 3/4 Queens from 3rd Unit in which 2 Capt A.E. Mackenzie (wounded). Captains Stodo & Keith Cohen returned from 64th Fd Amb. Manc. 00 to Rest.	
"	9/10/17		Transport + HQ 1 unit moved off at 9.55am to manned MOULIN FONTAINE (Sheet HAZEBROUCK 5A) at 3.40 pm. Captains Stodo + Keith Cohen + 17 OR left at BOESCHEPE in a holding party.	Westhoeve West name

WAR DIARY
INTELLIGENCE SUMMARY.

65th FIELD AMBULANCE.
OCTOBER 1917
Page 2 Volume XIV

Army Form C. 2118.

Place	Date	Hour	Summary of Events and Information	Remarks and references to Appendices
LA BELLE HOTESSE	10/10/17	6 p.m.	Captain R.T. Rowe + Rear party arrived from 64th Field Amb. at 4 p.m. but Rear Str. BOESCHEPE hurried on to 43rd Field Amb. at 10 a.m. Rear party arrived at Headquarters	MAP HAZEBROUCK SA (1:100 000)
"	11/10/17	"	ADMS visited. Captain T. McCririck whd'd for duty. Captain Keith Cohen departed (proceeding on leave). Horse standard	
"	12/10/17	"	2. O.R. reported from 62nd Machine Gun Coy: Captain Shade proceeded on 1 months leave. 1. MD Horse Evacuated to 33 MV Section	
"	13/10/17	"	1. O.R. " " 64th " .... ADMS visited	
"	14/10/17	"	2. " " 11D 7th "	
"	15/10/17	"	Captain J.P. Davies reports to DDMS Roven fortnightly from 37. CCS. ADMS visited. Roulemarch in afternoon.	
"	20/10/17	"	Captain McCririck joined temporary duty to Heavy Artillery Camp to WIZERNES. 6 Carts from GOC Division received. Routemarch in afternoon.	
"	18/10/17	"	10. OR Reinforcements arrived. 4 by cars (Wheelers) and 6. 21st Divl 2AT2 Column. Pte Roberts reported from 10th KOYLI (attached for 1 months probation)	
"	19/10/17	"	DADMS visited. Capt Taylor Vicedad 65th 105th DICKEBUSCH Orientals con + 2 Fords also 2 Motor Cycles sent to 25th Div. L.A.F.S GR, 2 Pvy cars ; 1 Ford, + 1 Cycle received to ATTE 01D 61 Lecens	

Army Form C. 2118.

WAR DIARY

65th FIELD AMBULANCE.

OCTOBER 1917.

Page 3. Volume XXV

INTELLIGENCE SUMMARY.

(Erase heading not required.)

Place	Date	Hour	Summary of Events and Information	Remarks and references to Appendices
DICKEBUSCH HUTS	20/10/17	6 pm	Transport moved up from the highway at X18.b.2.5 (sheet 2) to Moulin Fontaine at 10 a.m. to billets transport personnel under Capt Taylor. Returned at EBBLINGHEM at 10 p.m. & arrived DICKEBUSCH at 5 a.m. 21st. Advance party under Capt Raine proceeded by cars (2) & arrived at 12 noon 20th & took over from 89th Field Amb. 23rd Divn.	Sheet 27, 28, 29 — D.S. ORD
	12/10/17		Transport arrived 2.30 p.m. Capt Raine — 89 D.R. (Senior MO) proceeded to École Bienfaisance I.9.c.64 (Sheet 28), & was attached to 63rd Field Amb. Lieut G.M. Cameron reported his arrival for duty, & was taken on the strength accordingly. DADMS visited; O.C. 44th Field Amb. visited Lieut J.H. Cochran U.S.M. Corps reported for duty & was taken on the strength from this date. O.C. 20 M.A.C. visited. Capt Le Grice.	
	22/10/17		DADMS visited.	
	23/10/17			
	24/10/17 25/10/17		Captain Hickson TF & 146 O.R. evacuated from 37 CCS 54 evacuated to CCS, + 19 F. 21 DRS WESTOUTRE.	
	26/10/17		DDMS X' Corp visited. 62 cases to CCS + 18 to DRSt.	
	27/10/17		53 Cases evacuated to CCS + 24 to DRSt Lieut Cameron attached for temporary duty to 63rd Field Ambulance.	

ADMS 63rd Division [signature]

WAR DIARY

65TH FIELD AMBULANCE.
OCTOBER 1917
Page 4.

Army Form C. 2118.

INTELLIGENCE SUMMARY.

Place	Date	Hour	Summary of Events and Information	Remarks and references to Appendices
DICKEBUSCH H.34.a.0.8.	28/10/17	6 p.m.	A.D.M.S. visited. Mr Talbot Park van damaged by shell fire. Amy/br 1 Rawling 62nd Regiment was killed. 46 cases to C.C.S. + 20 to D.R.St.	Sheets 28. (1:40000) HAZEBROUCK 5.A (1:100 000)
	29/10/17	-	Capt. Holdsworth + 15 O.R. proceeded to Enfirmy huts to 37 C.C.S. Applied to D.A.D.M.S. rendered funeral Any for Rawling attended by R.C. at 3 p.m. 65 cases to C.C.S.; 2) to D.R.St.	
	30/10/17	-	Medical Board held by A.D.M.S. P.B. men attached to 63rd + 65th Field Ambulances. Lieut Tucker U.S.M.C. reported for duty two taken on the Strength. 36 cases to C.C.S., r.44. to D.R.St.	
	31/10/17	-	Unit head part: 66 cases evacuated C.C.S. + 59 to D.R.St.; 1 Riding Horse killed by bomb.	

Wraysford
Lieut Colonel

CONFIDENTIAL.

MEDICAL
Vol 27

40/2573

COMMITTEE FOR THE
MEDICAL HISTORY OF THE WAR
Date   17 JAN.1918

WAR DIARY

OF THE

65th Field Ambulance.

(3rd W.Lancs T.F.)

From 1/4/1917
To   30/11/1917

Volume XXVI
4 Pages

WAR DIARY
or
INTELLIGENCE SUMMARY.
(Erase heading not required.)

Army Form C. 2118.

65th FIELD AMBULANCE.
NOVEMBER 1917
Page 1. Volume XXVI. MEDICAL

Place	Date	Hour	Summary of Events and Information	Remarks and references to Appendices
DICKEBUSCH	1/11/17	6 p.m.	The DADMS & Capt. Taylor proceeded on leave to England. 66 cases evacuated to CCS & DRSt. Pte. Roberts proceeded to England 6 p.m. and others cadet course.	Sheet 28. 1:40,000 HAZEBROUCK (5A)
"	2/11/17	"	42 cases to CCS + 31 to DRSt.	
"	3/11/17	"	57 " " 24 "	
"	4/11/17	"	ADMS visited. OC Motors visited DRSt WESTOUTRE. 38 cases to CCS + 15 to DRSt.	
"	5/11/17	"	Lieut Cameron reported from temporary duty with 63rd Field ambulance. Visited Divl Rest Pt. WESTOUTRE. 28 cases to CCS. + 8 to DRSt.	
"	6/11/17	"	OC Motors & staff visited. ADS at ECOLE on MENIN Rd. ADMS visited.	
"	7/11/17	"	30 cases to CCS + 23 to DRSt	
"	8/11/17	"	32 " " 21 " "	
"	9/11/17	"	DADQMG 21st Divn visited. Lieut Cameron posted to temporary duty to 4th Leicester Regt (Capt. Elephant on leave).	
"	9/11/17	"	Have DO hot B2 received. 30 cases to CCS. 15 to DRSt. ADMS visited. Sick returnee from 3) CCS & 2 Australian Casualty hosp. Poperinghe.	

W. Taylor
Lt. Col.

WAR DIARY or INTELLIGENCE SUMMARY

65th FIELD AMBULANCE (2nd W. LANCS T.F.)
NOVEMBER 1917
Page 2. Volume XVI.

Army Form C. 2118.

Place	Date	Hour	Summary of Events and Information	Remarks and references to Appendices
DICKEBUSCH	14/11/17	6 pm	41. DR. 1 Driver has reported this Unit no duty.	Recd L8 (W.D.2070/179) re Hazebrouck 5A
"	14/11/17	"	Advance party from 6th N.Z.F.Amb. arrived. Staff of 65 D.R. went to no 39 Camp. Remainder of party went to L/Cpl. T.W.R. Sharks regiment from base.	
G 21 c 6.7	15/11/17	"	Transport left DICKEBUSCH at 9.15 am. Division Dismantled party at 9.30 am arrived at No. 39 Camp at 11.20 + 11.35 am respectively. Capt. Rowe rejoined. 1 Horse died. 1 Wagon horse passed 11/3 LNFS + 1 to L. bathing	
"	16/11/17	"	110th Brigade O.O. 2099 received.	
"	17/11/17	"	Lieut Cochrane U.S.M.C. reported to S.O. 9th Divsn. Lt to Temporary duties. Military Lieut Cameron Rowe (Sick) Capt. H. Taylor rejoined from leave. 110 th Brigade O.O. no 100 received.	
DOULIEU	18/11/17	"	The unit left Camp no 39 at 10.30 a.m. and marched to DOULIEU, arriving at 5.50 p.m. Command passed from Lt Col Taylor Thompson to Capt Taylor.	
"	"	"	Lt. Col. Thompson and Captain Rowe proceeded on leave to England.	
LA COURONNE	19/11/17	"	Unit left DOULIEU at 9.30 am and marched to LA COURONNE arriving at 10.45 am. 110 Brigade O.O. no 101 received.	

A.D.S.S./Form C. 2118.

WAR DIARY

65th FIELD AMBULANCE

Army Form C. 2118.

INTELLIGENCE SUMMARY

NOVEMBER 1917

Page 3 Volume XXVI

(Erase heading not required.)

Place	Date	Hour	Summary of Events and Information	Remarks and references to Appendices
ANNEZIN	21/11/17	6 pm	The unit left LA COURONNE at 9 am, and marched to ANNEZIN arriving at 3 pm. 110th Brigade orders 102 received.	Hazebrouck S.A.
BARLIN	22/11/17		The unit left ANNEZIN at 8.15 am and marched to BARLIN arriving at noon. The G.O.C. 21st Division inspected the unit "en route", and A.D.M.S. marches that day also. One Army draught horse evacuated on receipt from base. Capt. McGuirk and Tent Sub division of "C" Section proceeded to XIII Corps Rest Station for duty (temporary). Twenty four other ranks of 9th Leicesters were evacuated. Jaw or other plates died on the third Ambulance as the result of their lillets being shelled. The unit had inspection of Kit.	L Ero 11.
"	23/11/17	"	110th Brigade O.O. 103 received.	
"	24/11/17	"	The unit left BARLIN at 8.45 am and marched to MINGOVAL arriving at 1.5 pm. A.D.M.S. and S.N.D.M.S. visited. Orders received to complete all equipment (Field Ambulance and personal) by 30th inst.	
MINGOVAL	25/11/17	"	O.C. Conference held by A.D.M.S. at 63rd Field Ambulance attended.	
"	26/11/17	"	N.C.Os and men on leave ordered to return on 30th inst. One riding Horse (W) received from 10th KOYLI. All Officers have been ordered to report in 3D1	

[signature]

WAR DIARY

INTELLIGENCE SUMMARY.

65th FIELD AMBULANCE Army Form C. 2118.
NOVEMBER 1917
Page 4 Volume 8x11

Place	Date	Hour	Summary of Events and Information	Remarks and references to Appendices
MINGOVAL	27.11.17	8pm	ADMS visited me. Called for me at 11pm to motor to Dijon. (Major 23 Div Amm Sub Park was photographed visited. Photographed.)	LENS 11 (1:100,000)
	28.11.17	-	ADMS visited	
	29.11.17	-	Lt Cotham reported for temporary duty with 9th Inn Field Ambulance. Attached not.	
	30.11.17		Capt McCormick + Lt Cotham reported from XIII Corps Rest Stn. Capt McCormick proceeded to 3rd Div. tomorrow. Lt Cotham reported from 3rd Div. Lt Col Thompson reported (medical officer). Ambulance proceeded of the unit marched off at 7.30pm to Buchan ct Sary actually entrained at 9.30 + arrived at Tincourt at 6am 1st Dec. Transport marched off at 7.30am 30th Proceeded to ARRAS where the billetted for the night arriving Tincourt on 1st Dec.	

W. Thompson Major
Lt Col RAMC

CONFIDENTIAL.

28
MEDICAL

COMMITTEE FOR THE
MEDICAL HISTORY OF THE WAR
Date −1 FEB. 1918

WAR DIARY

OF THE

65th Field Ambulance.

(3rd W. LANCS T.F.).

FROM 1/12/1917
TO 31/12/1917.

VOLUME
(PAGES).

Army Form C. 2118.

WAR DIARY
or
INTELLIGENCE SUMMARY
(Erase heading not required.)

65th Field Ambulance
DECEMBER 1917.
Page 1. Volume XXIII

MEDICAL

Instructions regarding War Diaries and Intelligence Summaries are contained in F. S. Regs., Part II. and the Staff Manual respectively. Title pages will be prepared in manuscript.

Place	Date	Hour	Summary of Events and Information	Remarks and references to Appendices
HAMEL	1/12/17	6pm	Went into billets alongside 1/3 WR hvrs RED ANC.	MAPS 57 E & F.1.C 1:40000
	2/12	—	ADMS visited Revd Hamel. D.O. to B5th transport moved 5pm. Capt Shook V McCarland & 12 OR proceeded on advanced party to DDS. ENEMY AC raided after dark with bombs & m.g. fire. RAPs of W. Yorks.	
TINCOURT	3/12	—	R.A.M.C. entraining with L. Tucker. He proceeded at 12 noon to take over post from detachment of 1/3 WR hvrs Transport 2 lorries & 2 buses to rebuild latest to half the VC visited & mules and RAPs. I left estm. M.R. & A section engrs to Rolled in TINCOURT I Major Capt & 2nd Lts for half 15 MDS. VILLERS FAUCHON. Capt Raine & the Staff hqrs reported from leave.	
	4/12/17	"	ADMS visited north OC visits no 5CCS. Capt Raine proceeded to ADS. Temp. V. Cameron Somervelle to CCS (NYD injuries) 3 wheeled stretchers sent up to MDS & 4 with the bearer pty.	
	5/12/17	"	OC & ADMS visited ADS. Walk vans new RAPs of left sector.	W Murphy Carpt & Sim Maur proceeded on leave England. Capt Taylor visited MDS. I AD Sim received. RAMC

WAR DIARY

Army Form C. 2118.

65th Field Ambulance
DECEMBER 1917.
Page 2. Volume XXVII

INTELLIGENCE SUMMARY

Place	Date	Hour	Summary of Events and Information	Remarks and references to Appendices
TINCOURT	2/12/17	6 p.m.	Visited A.D.S. & R.A.P.s of Division. Affairs worked along. Visited O.C. D.A.D.M.S. Visited by the A.A. Col. R.T. Rivers arranged the visits from + Pte. H.B. Taylor the bombardier. Severe head. Capt. Taylor visited the A.D.S. Three shorts used up.	Sheet 62. c & 57. c (1–40000)
"	5/12/17		O.C. D.A.D.M.S. visited A.D.S. wound room R.A.P. & left Regt. 2 & S transport but to S.C.C.S. to convey supplies to the 65th M.G. returned by A Maj in left Auto. Three continuing visited motors. Capt Taylor today football used up to HAPTS.	
"	10/12/17		Visited A.D.S. wound room R.A.P.s	
"	11/12/17		Officers worked Visited 64th Regiment Capt McCormick proceed on leave	
"	12/13/17		Visited A.O.S. R.A.P. of Regt. Lakholm & Centre R.A.P. of left Brigade.	
"	14/12/17		Acting Medical Ambulance. Capt Taylor visited A.D.S. & Heart. C.C Tucker applied lieutenant to 10th YORKSHIRE REGt. during absence on leave of Capt. Shorter. Capt. Jour + 16 Mums proceed to A.D.S. & relieved a similar number who returned to T.H.R.	

W. Morgan V.C. OC M.O.65 [signature]

WAR DIARY
INTELLIGENCE SUMMARY
(Erase heading not required.)

65th Field Ambulance
DECEMBER 1917
Page 3, Volume XXVIII

Army Form C. 2118.

Place	Date	Hour	Summary of Events and Information	Remarks and references to Appendices
TINCOURT	15/12/17	4pm	Inst. hand out. visited A.D.S. Pn. to R.A.P.s in R district. Revd. Ambulance Messrs Marshall & Rafter.	A.D.S. 37, O & 3rd C (1 - 40 - 30)
"	16/12/17		Rafters visited. A.D.S. horse in 2 65 waggons attached to 65 F.A. to move under O.C.Capt Rickmouth reported from 93rd Fd. Amb. - own token in charge.	
"	17/12/17		Walked up to A.D.S. with Capt Heldsworth. Horse hype a road on path down to see ?seriously wounded. Relay Post off. into Ralph left Royce VC Lieut to be & refull. 1 killed (Pt Sellars) & 4 wounded. 4th Ambulance received Pres 24/717. Lt Cochran V.S.M.C. relieved LT in Heartand as A.D.S. to take responsibility. 2 GS wagons sent to S.C.C.S. to draw stores for that month.	
"	18/12/17		Visited A.D.S. & Right Ante. No RAPs. There were sent from TINCOURT to LONGAVESNES.	
"	19/12/17		A.D.S. visited. Capt Taylor visited ADS. came front returning	
"	20/12/17		Visited ADS. & Regt. Antic. & left Ranieu posts & left Centre. Went to seek butler returned from leave worked Dud AR & accompanied by ADDSp proceeded to LIERAMONT & Chore visits to Audg. Heart Junction. visited 65 Fd Amby.	
"	21/12/17		Visited ADS & RAPs of Rt Brigade. village & EPEHY & recently 2 ADS had been heavily shelled. having night light 23 px with 5.9. The shells having fallen btwn 3.30 & 4pm 24 th Letter returning to ADS	

W Manfrot
Lt Col

WAR DIARY
of
INTELLIGENCE SUMMARY

65th Field Ambulance
DECEMBER 1917.
Page 4. Volume XXVII

Army Form C. 2118.

Place	Date	Hour	Summary of Events and Information	Remarks and references to Appendices
TINCOURT	25/12/17	6 p.m.	Visited A.D.S.'s a 4.2 shell blew in a portion of truss frame W.30.C.5.2. wounding 2 nurses. Visited R. Regt. R.A.P. 1 left Brigade.	MAPS 57c + 62c (1.40000).
"	26/12/17	"	Visited A.D.S. & R.A.P.'s of right & left sectors. Capt. Raine, two 3rd Queens Regt. relieving Lt. O'Reilly who reports sick at A.D.S. pending transfer to England on expiration of entire Capt. Short's leave. Transferred sick to C.C. Station (64 Cas. Ambl.) Telephonic communication available between A.D.S.'s & D.H.Q.	
"	27/12/17	"	Met R.E. Officer at 9.30 am at LIERAMONT. Discussed + arranged sites for Field Amb. Huts. 1 hut & 3 tour holes on a farm at this site. Will take two people.	
"	28/12/17	"	Visited A.D.S. with Lt. Col. Ar. E. Hau, accompanied by Capt. Taylor visited R.A.P.'s & Field Amb. Nurse huts of left sector. Lt. O'Reilly transferred on leave to England (from A.D.S.) on expiration of enlisted Capt. Hollsworth posted to right sector of Lincelles Regt. Junior section. Capt. Kirk & Coln. 2 drivers Cars arrived from base.	
"	29/12/17	"	Collected Capt. Warth's horses, repacking & disability.—Visited Lebaust, Silo at LIERAMONT.	
"	30/12/17	"	Visited Road at D.H.Q. & accompanied by him visited A.D.S. & R.A.P's + Nurse huts of Rt. sector.	
"	31/12/17	"	Rode to LIERAMONT + visited proposed field Amb. site. Erection of huts has been to be Standstill. Water only 1 hut being completed.	

W. Thompson
Lt Col R.A.M.C.
O.C. 65th Fd Amb

Confidential.

MEDICAL

Vol 29

WAR DIARY
OF THE
65th Field Ambulance.
(3rd W. Lancs T.F.)

From 1/1/18.
To 31/1/18.

VOLUME XXVIII.
(4 Pages).

January 1918

WAR DIARY

65th Field Ambulance Army Form C. 2118.
JANUARY 1918
Page 1 Volume XXVIII.

INTELLIGENCE SUMMARY.

Place	Date	Hour	Summary of Events and Information	Remarks and references to Appendices
TINCOURT	1/1/18	6 pm	Visited D.H.Q. & Ambulance site at LIERMONT. Enquired at 64th F.S.A. & M. Moislains. L.t. h. Cavelands situation from troops difft. to 63rd F.S.A.	Map 57.C & 62.C. (included)
"	2/1/18	"	Visited A.D.S. + R.A.P's + Rear posts. Lewis Rack + left Autos called at F.A.R. return. Entraine 1 cwch. 1 Enquiry relative to 64 F.S.A.	
"	3/1/18	"	Visited D.H.Q. interviewed D.A.D.M.S. re Billets accommodation reached Huts at LIERAMONT wind instructions to move 1st to 7. Billets TINCOURT etc. D.A.C. visited. Found post entirely unsuited removal of transport very difficult. Stand fustw moved to h.q. 7 & 14 Billets HAMEL. Visited A.D.S. & R.A.P's on left Sector.	
HAMEL	4/1/18	"	Visited A.D.S. at LIERAMONT. The F.A. are always employed. Huts are extremely heated. May be a trench booster Baths. Bombing party from the west advancing infancy 2.5 to F.A.R. Thinks Cookham provided from A.D.S. to 7 Leicesters in Frefis huts.	
"	6/1/18	—	Visited A.D.S. accompanied by A.D.M.S. Earlham. Went round R.A.P's & R.A.s etc. taken on by 64th Amb. from 110th Amb. arrived 1 4-5.	

W. Humphrys
V.R. Maurice

WAR DIARY

INTELLIGENCE SUMMARY.

Army Form C. 2118.

65th Field Ambulance.
JANUARY 1918.
Page 2. Volume XXVIII.

Place	Date	Hour	Summary of Events and Information	Remarks and references to Appendices
HANEL	2/1/18	6 pm	Lt W. Cleveland reported from 63rd Heavy Arty. Capt. W. Duncan RAMC has taken mushingh & remains att. to VIIth Corps Convalescent Depot.	Maps 57 c & 62 (& corps)
	5/1/18		Lt W. Cleveland + 6 OR (Rein) proceed to att. to ADS. Capt. W. Searle MOISLAINS re conf. of Surgery. 2 hours motor proceeded for staff to VIIth Corps Rivm. Forward Camps. at SOREL LE GRAND. 1 OR proceeded on am. of lorry. Lt. Amn School & Cookery	
	9/1/18		Visited MDS accompanied by Capt Taylor met & invest RAP's & sewer hotels of both sections. Snowing fairly heavily.	
	10/1/18		O.C. proceed on a course of instruction to VIIth Corps Gas School.	
	11/1/18		Accompanied by MDMS, visited ADS's & Bielow, selected a new site for RAP of 9th LRB RMF, 1 R.S. Batter.	
	12/1/18		Visited ADS's + D. 2. LORB RAP's & sewer hotels of LRB Batts. #3 ? In Cavalry formed for hols with 5th H.D. Regt. & now returned to the Shingle to the balance. J.W. Beckman reported from Camp duty with Drs. Lancashire.	
	13/1/18		Capt Hedsworth reported from Divis. Arty with 8th Divinities 1/1st Lochrum was reported to 3rd division. Capt Twose Shute posted to 6th Heavy Arty. Proceed to HQ post out.	W. Henderson

Army Form C. 2118.

WAR DIARY
of
INTELLIGENCE SUMMARY.
(Erase heading not required.)

65th Field Ambulance
JANUARY 1918
Page 3. Volume XXVIII

Place	Date	Hour	Summary of Events and Information	Remarks and references to Appendices
HAMEL	14/1/18	pm	Visited ADSt & R.Rector. Revd P/G. 1 n.c.o. proceeded to 2/0.7. Vol 3	heavy. SJ 4, 62c (1:40000)
"	15/1/18	"	Kept fit exercise & instruction. Visited ADSt. Left Rector.	
"	16/1/18	"	LIERAMONT (D.18.6.6.6) on a holiday party. 1 n.c.o. & 6 men proceeded to camp at	
"	17/1/18	"	Marked ADSt. & LIERAMONT where work was commenced in camp. Capt Cameron rejoined the unit from hospl. Men taken on the strength.	
"	18/1/18	"	Capt Cameron proceeded to ADSt. for duty. Visited ADSt. & R.Rector. 1/4 Tuckin USMC rejoined from leave 3 ½ days with 10th Yorkshire Regt.	
"	19/1/18	"	Visited ADSt. & Left Rector. Capt Cameron posted temporarily for duty to 1.E.Yorks. vice Capt Winster (sick).	
"	20/1/18	"	Visited LIERAMONT + ADSt. Capt Aselsworth proceeded on leave to England.	
"	21/1/18	"	Visited ADSt. & Revd P/G. or RAP. on Left Rector. 1/4 Tuckin proceeded for duty to ADSt. + Capt hr Cornick rejoined HQ. from there. DDMS VIIth Corps visited	
	22/1/18	"	Visited LIERAMONT + ADSt. + Right Rector + D.H.Q. in afternoon.	
	23/1/18	"		
	24/1/18	"	Visited LIERAMONT	
	25/1/18	"	Visited ADSt. Left Rector + MDS in afternoon.	
LIERAMONT	26/1/18	"	Headquarters of the Ambulance & Transport moved from HAME L. Visited ADSt. + ADS in Kitchener	Wilson from VIII Corps

WAR DIARY
INTELLIGENCE SUMMARY

65th Field Ambulance.
JANUARY 1918.
Page 4. Volume XXVIII.
Army Form C.2118.

Place	Date	Hour	Summary of Events and Information	Remarks and references to Appendices
LIERAMONT D18.b.8.6.	22/1/18	6pm	Visited ADSt & R. Posts. Capt. McCurdie returned to ADSt on duty relieving Capt Taylor who rejoined Headquarters. Captain J.L. Johnston reported for duty from Canton this strength for this date. Personnel at ADSt band out.	MAPS. 57.c x 52.c (1 week)
"	23/1/18	"	1 OR attached to 6 Division for instruction (prior to joining an Officer Cable Coy). Visited ADSts & Relief Posts. ADSt motors visited 133rd Regiment M.O.	
"	24/1/18	"	Visited 134 Fd Amb at HEUDICOURT & accompanied by OC visited their Posts & RAPs on top sector. Personnel at these Posts on the rota were relieved by 134th the Amb personnel. Relief completed by 4 p.m.	
"	25/1/18	"	4 ORs rejoined from "D" 8th Immobilly Coy. Visited ADSt & known posts on R. sector. ADSts visited. MO visited Train & S.S.O 21st Divn visited.	

W Thompson
Lt Col RAMC
OC 65th Fd Amb.

CONFIDENTIAL

WA 30

COMMITTEE FOR THE
MEDICAL HISTORY OF THE WAR
Date — 8 APR 1918

WAR DIARY

OF THE

65th Field Ambulance.

(3rd W. Lancs T.F.)

From 1/2/1918
To 28/2/1918.

Volume XXIV.
(3 Pages).

Army Form C. 2118.

65th Field Ambulance
FEBRUARY 1918.
Page 1. Volume XXIX

WAR DIARY
INTELLIGENCE SUMMARY.
(Erase heading not required.)

MEDICAL

Place	Date	Hour	Summary of Events and Information	Remarks and references to Appendices
LIERAMONT (D.16.b.8.6. sheet 62.c)	1/2/18	6pm	G.O.C. D.W. accompanied by A.A. & Q.M.G. + D.D.M.S. visited the Hornes Transport Lines & Ambulance visited A.D.S.	Sheets 62.C, 62.b, & 57.S.(1-40000)
"	2/2/18		Visited D.D.S. & R.A.P. Scheme for 62nd Division: R.A.P's attached for duty with 62nd, 64th, 110th & 237th Infantry Bgds:- 1 horse ambulance, 1 horse cycle, 1 horse attached, 1 N.C.O. + 3 men to duty. Sent Pte Hornes noted from consciousness to D.D.S. ETERN HAUT ALLAINES. Capt Taylor M.C. went forward to relieve Capt Whitesides reported H.Q. Advance H.Q. G, 1, 2, Moeuvre. 1/2 O.R. 63rd Fld Amb arrived at A.D.S.	
"	3/2/18		D.D.S.s been for & our R'bals handed over to 63rd Field Ambulance. The whole being completed by 10:30am. Capt de Chirnies + 2 M.Os also attached for duty to 63rd Fld Ambulance. 63rd O.R. proceeded to Etricourt for duty to 64th Reserve at MOISLAINS. The party were found at their bivouacs & 1 N.C.O. + 12 ptes attached for duty to 110th N.F.s (P) were to work on R.A.P. 6" x 25' central (approx) kitchen attached for duty by 11th N.F.s (P) respectively by 95th Fld R.F.A. (waggon lines by yff Twickey). 1 O.R. arrived on reinforcement from 1st Field Jokes Depot. Took on Conf. at but H.Q. proceeding back to the here made others took part of, when took some that HE.	

W Thompson
Lt Col RAMC
O/c 65 FA

Army Form C. 2118.

WAR DIARY
INTELLIGENCE SUMMARY.
(Erase heading not required.)

65th Field Ambulance
FEBRUARY 1918
Page 2. Volume XXIX

Place	Date	Hour	Summary of Events and Information	Remarks and references to Appendices
LIERAMONT COVERCOAT CAMP.	5/2/18	6pm	Unit fried out. Hrs. Inspection. K.O.R. took half Coy Mountain	MAPS 5th Army 57.c + 62.c (1-40,000)
"	6/2/18	"	Captain Hollworth rejoined from leave.	
"	7/2/18 to 11/2/18	"	64th Left. Army relieved 110th Inf. Brig in the line. Captain Jehnek provided scheme to English Capt. Hollworth detached to the Sick & Subway Sanitation 6, 12/13th N.F's Camp. D 28.b. Sheet 62c. Sgt. Summerwick the M.T. reports 6/o 21. Brit. S. Column on Transpo Scheme Staff. 1. hos N.6 F.R relieved a Landing party within hrs 142 N.F. (7) 14.E.P.2.4y.	
"	9/2/18	"	Captain R. Stenn reported for duty from 10th Yorkshire Regt.	
"	12/2/18	"	1/Lieut J.H. Cochran USMC reported for training duty with 1st Leicesters. DADMS visited. Area Commander visited. Stood for attached party of 64th Res. Amb. 1.O.R (Pte Williams) transferred to hd 3. M.A.C. - 1.F.R attached for tuberm. hit 15 237. W.E.Cog. MOISLAINS.	
"	13/2/18	"	1. O.R reinforcement reported for duty from hd 3. M.A.C. Captain R. Taylor was provided for Emb & hd. duty with 9th KOYLI. Capt & Holdsworth attached to 13/13th N.F's at Camp in D 28.b. Capt E McCormick rejoined from 13th F.Amb. War 2 bylaw.	

W. Hunt Ejean Lt.lot Rainel?

WAR DIARY
or
INTELLIGENCE SUMMARY.
(Erase heading not required.)

Army Form C. 2118.

65th Field Ambulance
FEBRUARY 1918
Page 3. Volume XXIX

Place	Date	Hour	Summary of Events and Information	Remarks and references to Appendices
LIERAMONT COVERCOAT CAMP	15/2/18	6 pm	1/Lieut G.H. Cochran proceeded on 14 days leave to Paris. Captain G. McKerron reported from 1/E Yorks.	MAPS 57c & 62c (1:40000)
	16/2/18	"	Veterinary Officer visited. Transport for heard sent into Captain Feniuck & 3 O.R. proceeded to 5th Army School of Instruction. + 2 O.R. to 5th Army School of Sanitation 1 Evacuation wired 64 Field Amb. Wit. Find out Port continuing.	
	18/2/18	"	attested labour on "Inculine" + 9 fractures at 5th AMD horse lined at 4 p.m.	
	20/2/18	"	A.D.M.S. visited. Captain Stores proceeded to 2/DR C for Lient's duty. 1 days leave + 1 off. Truck attached to 1/E Yorks. (O.B.U.) Shell 62 C. Shaw R.F.A.	
	21/2/18	"	Captain Fenwick returned from 2/DR C. OC 64 Field Amb + DADMS visited, lined.	
	22/2/18	"	A.D.M.S + O.C 21 DR C Coleman visited re Brigade Bn Ambulance Cars + A.D.V.S. visited.	
	23/2/18	"	1/Lieut C.C Treka proceeded on 14 days leave to Paris.	
	24/2/18	"		
	25/2/18	"	2/Lieut 3 O.R. NCO proceeded on leave. 60 OR 67 received.	
	26/2/18	"	Capt. T. Fenwick reported from 5th Army School of Sanitation, + returned to OC 65 FA ant. to duty.	
	27/2/18	"		
	28/2/18	"		

W. Thompson
Lt Col RAMC
65 FA

CONFIDENTIAL.

Vol 31

140/2849

WAR DIARY
OF THE
65th Field Ambulance
(3rd W. Lancs. T.F.)

From 1/3/1918
To 31/3/1918

VOLUME XXX
(6 Pages)

COMMITTEE FOR THE
MEDICAL HISTORY OF THE WAR
Date 12 MAY 1918

WAR DIARY

INTELLIGENCE SUMMARY
(Erase heading not required.)

Army Form C.
65th Field Ambulance
MARCH 1918
Page 1 Volume XXX MEDICAL

Place	Date	Hour	Summary of Events and Information	Remarks and references to Appendices
LIERAMONT	1/3/18	9pm	Actual march	MAPS Paris Plans 57c & 62c (1-4:2000)
"	2/3/18	–	4.5 O.R. rejoined from 6th Field Ambulance, also 1 O.R. from 8th Lincolns	
"	3/3/18	–	hides. 6 O.R. rejoined, 13th Field Ambulance at HEUDICOURT	
"	4/3/18	–	3 O.R. proceeded to 3rd Army 11 Ame School of Instruction at 4.4.1/4	
"	5/3/18	–	Visited A.D.M.S.HQ. & shepherd O.C. 83rd Field Ambulance.	
"	6/3/18	–	Visited A.D.S. at EPÉHY. Captain Taylor reported from 7th K.O.Y.L.I.	
			Bearer Posts on left sector at X.13.c.3.6 & W.18.d.2.3. taken over from 63rd Field Amb. Car collecting Post established & comforted at Sucrerie (W.16.d.6.1) Car relief post 24 bns road & A.D.V.S. rested. Rear headquarters site selected at N.13.a.5.1. (Ref. sheet 57c).	
	7/3/18	–	Accompanied by Capt. Taylor visited left Batt. HQ. & Menen Posts	
			D.A.D.M.S. visited	
	8/3/18	–	21 O.R. joined S.D. to 1st DS at VILLERS FAUCON to work in an RAP	
			at E.11 Central. Heut. Cochrane evacuated the 7/3/5 for sickness	
	9/3/18	–	Proceeded on leave to England. Much handed over to Capt. R. Taylor but	
				Williamson VAD Nurse

WAR DIARY
INTELLIGENCE SUMMARY.
(Erase heading not required.)

"65th" Field Ambulance
MARCH 1918.
Page 2. Volume XXX

Army Form C.

Instructions regarding War Diaries and Intelligence Summaries are contained in F.S. Regs., Part II and the Staff Manual respectively. Title pages will be prepared in manuscript.

Place	Date	Hour	Summary of Events and Information	Remarks and references to Appendices
Suzanne	10/3/18	6 pm	A.D.M.S. and Capt R Taylor R.A.M.C. wrote letter on return to left sector; I.O.R. proceeds to I.V. Army A.M.C. School of Instruction. On arrival H.Q. attached for duty at our collecting Post at N.18.d.3.1.	maps 57c & 12c
~	11/3/18	~	1st Lieut. C.E. Yunker U.S.M.C. M.C.R.C. from Paris Base. Capt Cameron & C. Sutton wrote the leave forms.	
~	12/3/18	~	1st Lieut. C. Ochrane U.S.M.C. was attached to 96th Bde R.F.A. for temporary duty. Court of Inquiry convened to investigate the absence of no. 1184 Pte Platts M.T. R.A.M.C. (yst Hants A.S.C. (M.T.) proceeds to England for admission to R.F.C. Cadet Unit. Capt. Cameron and 1st Lieut Yunker represented the area behind Bienvinal A.D.M.S. wrote.	
~	13/3/18	~	A.D.M.S. wrote. Motor Cyclist attached to A.D.M.S. H.Q. D.M.S. visits. Recent raid felt from Peronne.	
~	14/3/18	~	Capt Hollsworth and 20 O.R. reinforces left sector for night raid by 17/13 N.F. Capt Hollsworth being relieved from that unit by Capt Griffin R.A.M.C. Bearers of the left sector was relieved, 10 men of working party attached to M.D.S Villeret Lower Informal.	
~	15/3/18	~	Capt Stevens and Co English reconnoitre ground and tent reserve A.D.S.	
~	16/3/18	~	Reconnoitre of working party from M.D.S. Villeret Lower regions. A working party of 2 N.C.O's and 20 O.R. proceeds to E.12 central under Capt. Stevens. Capt Cameron and 1st Lieut Yunker proceeds to the same place for instruction in digging under A.D.M.S.	
~	17/3/18		Capt Cameron and 20 O.R. reinforces left sector for night raid by 2nd British which was subsequently postponed. 2 O.R. proceeds to I.V. Army R.A.M.C. School of Instruction.	

Major
for O.C. 65th F. Amb

WAR DIARY
INTELLIGENCE SUMMARY

65th Field Ambulance

MARCH 1918

Page 3   Volume XXX

Place	Date	Hour	Summary of Events and Information	Remarks and references to Appendices
Nurlu	18/3/18	6 pm	Capt Whayman went back with Capt Cameron to Cuperles Wall to 98th Sy R.B. for Company duty. 1st Lieut Tucker and 20 O.R. reinforced Capt Peter's Bn and Sgt 2nd Section which were carried out operations proposed.	Sheet 57c & 62c (1-40000)
	19/3/18	—	Capt Haddock - Sgt Major Parry Lowe under Headquart group with a view to establishing Power and car park there.	
	20/3/18	—	Nil	
	21/3/18	—	Working parties reported from E 12 (central). 1st Tucker + 20 O.R. 7th Leicesters to Saulcourt to evacuate wounded, 7th Leicesters from E 11 (central) to Saulcourt + thence by cars to ROS th LONGAVESNES - Capts Stevens & Holdsworth with our Fund Ambulance worked at MDS - q's m.o. at V18.c.2.9 for duty. Evac. in motors and in ambulances wounded 9 21st Divn. 2 O.R. + 2 limbless longexame transfer to 63rd Fand with wounded of Cuvignies 2 by Car at LONGAVESNES to Anvignes 9 wounded (sitting cases) 2 by Car forked at SUCRERIE were hit & damaged by Shell fire. 19 Kans won whereupon I asked but the other had to be abandoned at HEUDICOURT. Capt Cameron with the 2 other bus (one port motor 1st Tucker) proceeded to Rearer Relay Post on western edge of HEUDICOURT on HEUDICOURT-SORRLR) Evacuated some of that carriage + horse drawn wheeled stretchers to V18.c.2.9. In the evening Capt Cameron has returned by Capt Graham D.D.C 64 1/2 Amb. on big car proceed from V18.c.29 up the HEUDICOURT-VAUCELETTE FARM Rd + fell into the hands of Enemy. Whereupon Lieut Henry	

65th Field Ambulance
MARCH 1918

Page 4. Volume XXX

WAR DIARY
INTELLIGENCE SUMMARY.
(Erase heading not required.)

Army Form C. 2118

Place	Date	Hour	Summary of Events and Information	Remarks and references to Appendices
LIERAMONT	22/3/18	4pm	At 2am the transport & 1 Up-Par Section left Coucy & proceeded to BUSSU. Evacuation of cases from HEUDICOURT is V.18.c.2.9. was discontinued, & cases were conveyed from HEUDICOURT via LIERAMONT to ADS. LONGAVESNES. A Car Collecting Post was established mid-way between HEUDICOURT & LIERAMONT. The remainder of the personnel left at LIERAMONT, marched off at 11 am & rejoined the transport at BUSSU. The remaining Ambulance Cars were attached for duty to 63rd F.Amb, 1/1st Yorks & two Beaver reported.	Sheets 57c & 62c (1:40000)
BUSSU	23/3/18		The unit marched off from BUSSU at 11am on 23/3/18 arriving at QUINCONCE (W.9 PERONNE) at 2.30 am. Moving off again at 7am to MARICOURT arriving there at 4pm 23/3/18. Capts Shinnor & Hollingworth with the First Lieutenant rejoined at this place. An ADS² was formed on site of original Capts Rest Stn. The 3 Ambulances working in conjunction. This village has heavily bombed by enemy aeroplanes on night 23/24th.	

W Munro Lt. Col.

WAR DIARY / INTELLIGENCE SUMMARY

65th Field Ambulance
MARCH 1918.
Page 5. Volume XXX.

Army Form C. 2118

Place	Date	Hour	Summary of Events and Information	Remarks and references to Appendices
MARICOURT	24/3/18	6/7am	Unit moved off at 7.30 am & proceeded to BRAY arriving there at 10.30 am. The cars which had been attached to 63rd F.Amb. were transferred to 64th F.Amb. at MARICOURT	Sheets AMIENS (17) & LENS (11)
BRAY	25/3/18	"	Unit left BRAY at 4-45 am & proceeded along the BRAY-CORBIE Rd to X rds both of SAILLY-LE-SEC, arriving at 7-15 am. Captain Cameron proceeded for temporary duty to R/13" N.F's. The cars attached to 64th F.Amb. rejoined, & one was employed to patrol the rd from BRAY to H.Q of the Field Amb. for the purpose of picking up stragglers ill or wounded. Put in putts to reception & treatment of sick cases, which were subsequently transferred to 61. Stationary Hosp.	
SAILLY LE SEC	26/3/18	"	Unit marched off at 8 am & arrived at BAIZIEUX at 9.30 am. 1/W. Tucker proceeded for duty to 21 Div Reinforcement Depts. at RIBEMONT — Unit marched again at 4.35 pm & arrived at CONTAY at 6.15 pm & billeted there.	
CONTAY	27/3/18		Casualties in the unit to date have 9 missing, 5 wounded R.A.M.C. + 1 Missing A.S.C. M.T. Whatever.	

65th Field Ambulance
MARCH 1918.
Page 6. Volume XXX

Army Form C. 2118.

WAR DIARY
INTELLIGENCE SUMMARY.
(Erase heading not required.)

Place	Date	Hour	Summary of Events and Information	Remarks and references to Appendices
CONTAY	28/3/18	6pm	Lt Colonel Thompson reported from leave, also 1/Lt Tucker from 21st Divn' Reinforcement Depôt. A loading party of 2 hrs. 12.1 hrs proceeded in a lorry to LANEUVILLE (Near CORBIE) to salve kits + stores abandoned by a CCS.	Sheets AMIENS & LENS.
MOLLIENS-AU-BOIS	29/3/18		Unit left CONTAY at 7-45am. arrived at MOLLIENS-AU-BOIS at 9-40am. & transferred to a field immediately east of the Chateau. Which Cochran reported from 93rd Brig RFA. Killed D.G. Davies USMC. ½ Sept(?) Transport van taken in strength from this side.	
"	30/3/18		1/Lieut Cochran hope Invaided sick. 2 hrs tors arrived from Le Havre. 2 Cars were attached for that to B4 H.F. Amb.	
HANGEST SUR-SOMME	31/3/18		1. Car reported from 64 F.Amb. Transferred left MOLLIENS-AU-BOIS at 6.30 am. & marched via COISY – BERTANGLES – S' SAUVEUR – LA CHAUSSÉE – BOURDON – HANGEST, & billetted in Farm midway between the little place & SOUES arriving there at 3.30 p.m. distance 21 miles. The Horsemen transferred personnel marched Mollens (am) & proceeded to PICQUIGNY. Embussing there at 2 p.m arriving at Billet (arr) at 6pm.	

Wm Thompson Lt Col

CONFIDENTIAL

MEDICAL

WAR DIARY
OF THE
65th Field Ambulance
(3rd W Lancs T.F.)

From 1/4/1918
To 30/4/1918

VOLUME XXXI
(5. Pages)

COMMITTEE FOR THE
MEDICAL HISTORY OF THE WAR
Date 6 JUN. 1918

WAR DIARY / INTELLIGENCE SUMMARY

65th Field Ambulance
APRIL 1918
Volume XXXI Page 1.

Army Form C.2118
MEDICAL

Place	Date	Hour	Summary of Events and Information	Remarks and references to Appendices
HANGEST S/ SOMME	1/4/18	6h-	Unit remained at Billet -	Sheet 6 AMIENS 17
"	2/4/18		Grandhurst marched Off at 7am — Billeted at HANGEST St at 11am. Divisionals huwaned left at 9am. Returns by same Train. The [unit?] detrained at PESCHOEK St at 12·30 am 3/4/18 & proceeded to Tutu Louis to MONT DES CATS arriving them at 8am. Transport arrived at 7am 3/4/18	Sheet 27 (1×40,000)
MONT DES CATS	3/4/18	"	A.D.M.S. M.A & Q.M.G. visited: O.C 13. C.C.S visited. Sheet C.C. Trucks moved tonight with 6" Executive. 1 Dy.Ca reported from Mont Noir. O.O No 70 received.	
"	4/4/18	"	D.R.S.P. No taken over from 2nd Aust. F. Ambulance at 12 noon. 13 batels taken over. Captains Dunlop, Denton & Ferguson handed to Officers for duty. Horses taken in the Strength from them date.	
"	5/4/18	"	Unit formed part. 1) O.T.R reinforcements arrived from base	
"	6/4/18	"	Visited 13. C.C.S home O.O. No 71. received	
"	7/4/18	"	27. Cases transferred to 2.C.S. & 35 to Duty.	Without.... Lieut Colonel

WAR DIARY
INTELLIGENCE SUMMARY

Army Form C. 2118.

65th Field Ambulance
April 1918
Volume XXXI Page 2.

Place	Date	Hour	Summary of Events and Information	Remarks and references to Appendices
MONT DES CATS	2/4/18	6 pm	Capt. F. L. Johnston reports that from Caen (2 months)	Sheets 37 & 28
"	3/4/18		Whole O.O. No 72 received. 3 days leave allotted to B.R.C.S and Canadian Divs (1-4 Apr) & HAZEBROUCK. Ind'g 1 Officer & 25 O.R. Issued to DR8th WIPPENHOEK, & 1 Officer & 7 O.R. (L.23.C.3.0) O.C. notes 49th Div. DRSt stops leaving for (Corps Centre St. (L.23.C.3.0) O.C. notes 49th Div. DRSt stops leaving for hosts bicycles reported from F.8 Amb. A working party of 3 O.R. received from 27th Bn.	
WIPPENHOEK	10/4/18		Capt. C.D. Mitchell & 6 O.R. proceed at 5am to Officers Rest House EPERLECQUES. Capt. Taylor & 52 O.R. stands to 6am, reserve 2/3 MR. detail proceeded to Corps Sects St. Transport moved of at 6.15 am via GODEWAERSVELDE, WIPPENHOEK. Remainder of personnel moved off at 6.30 am arriving at 49th Div DRSt at 7-40 am. Relief was completed by 8am. The 3 WR. Hut Ant moved of at 10.30 am. 3 Officers & 291 OR taken on from 49 DRSt. & 253 which from XXII Corps Rest St. Clerk attached to Record host Bureau. 1 OR attached to hosp. Inspector Royer BOESCHEPE.	
"	11/4/18		3 Officers & 52 OR transfers to FCCS & 36 OR totally from DRSt. 73 admissions. 163 Rashin Cases to hosts from DRSt. 1 Evacuated FCCS & 1 disabled. 2 boys Son. attache to 64" Fd Amb. HQ Gate HQ V15 G.O. Pt. rd DDMS XXII G.O.Pt rd	

WAR DIARY or INTELLIGENCE SUMMARY

65th Field Ambulance Army Form C. 2118.
APRIL 1918. Volume XXI. Page 3

(Erase heading not required.)

Instructions regarding War Diaries and Intelligence Summaries are contained in F.S. Regs., Part II. and the Staff Manual respectively. Title pages will be prepared in manuscript.

Place	Date	Hour	Summary of Events and Information	Remarks and references to Appendices
WIPPENHOEK	12/4/18	6 p.m.	1 Officer & 40 O.R. (Reserve) reported for duty at 8 p.m. to O.C. 64th F.A. and returned. 41 cases evacuated to CCS. + 32 to duty.	Sheet (1-40,000)
"	13/4/18	"	WOODCOTE HOUSE. Officers rested. DDMS visited. 109 cases admitted to CCS. + 36 to duty. 3 Officers + 141 O.R. remaining.	
"	14/4/18	"	55 cases from Capt Sadie's S.F. evacuated to CCS, + 20 to duty. (re Total cases remaining). All personnel withdrawn to SRSF. - ½ hr stand fast on site of Capt Sadie's SF. - 77 cases transferred to CCS (from SRSF) + 3 Officers + 55 O.R. returned to duty. - 1 Officer + 91 O.R. remaining.	
"	15/4/18	"	35 cases returned to duty. 17 Officers + 48 O.R. to CCS. 2 Officers + 62 O.R. remaining.	40 cases Wippenhoek 15/4 [?] F mts 18/4
"				Issued 2 W bn/Js received
"	16/4/18	"	18 " 1 " 84 " 3 Officers + 29 O.R. remaining	
"	17/4/18	"	17 " 1 " 27 " 2 " 30 "	Unit paid out
"	18/4/18	"	12 " 2 " 63 " — 24 O.R. remaining	
			Captain J.L. Johnston proceeded at 7 p.m. to relieve Capt. C.D. Hollenworth at Officers Rest House EPERLECQUES. Capt Hollenworth departed for duty to 20 fd. hosp. turn struck of strength of unit from this date.	Wippenhoek Wipp Mess

WAR DIARY

65th Field Ambulance Army Form C.2118.
APRIL 1918
Volume XXXI Page 4.

INTELLIGENCE SUMMARY.
(Erase heading not required.)

Place	Date	Hour	Summary of Events and Information	Remarks and references to Appendices
WIPPENHOEK	19/4/18	6 p.m.	Captain J. Ferguson proceeded for ten days duty with 94th Bdy. R.F.A. Returning	Sheets for 27 & 28 (-4520)
"	20/4/18	"	C.R.A. 21st Divn. visited TERDEGHEM at 10 a.m. 10 Cases returned to duty & 42 transferred to CCS. 2 Officers & 115 O.R. remaining.	
"	21/4/18	"	28 Cases returned to duty — 8 Officers & 68 O.R. evacuated to CCS — 2 & 142 O.R. remaining. Capt. J.L. Johnston relieved his wound from Officer's Rest Home. EPERLEQUES. ADMS 49th Divn. marked also DADMS 21st Divn. 2 Cases totals 6 3 Officers & 3 Officers & life received KCCS — 2 Officers & 126 O.R. remaining. DDMS XXII left received 104 cases.	
"	22/4/18	"	35 Cases to duty. 3 Officers & 77 O.R. to CCS — 2 Officers & 116 O.R. remaining. DADMS 5 DADVS, DOC 64 Lts. Ambulance visited. About marked.	
"	23/4/18	"	34 Cases to duty. 72 to CCS. 5 Officers & 166 O.R. remaining. About marked.	
"	24/4/18	"	17 " " " 3 & 108 " " " 5 " " 166 " "	
"	25/4/18	"	19 " " " " " " 166 " "	
"	26/4/18	"	2 Officers & 69 O.R. to duty. 7 Officers & 150 O.R. to CCS. 51 O.R. remaining. ADMS & DADMS marked. 1 Instr Suffer 4. 9 Captain Brown attached temporary to 63rd Field Ambulance. 5 Officers & 50 O.R. transferred to KCCS; 16 O.R. transferred to 1st S.A. Field Ambulance. 6 to duty. 4/221 OR. ADM 21st Div Down marked. 28th Field Amb. arrived to spare marks. killed in spare marks.	

WAR DIARY

INTELLIGENCE SUMMARY.

65th Field Ambulance
APRIL 1918.
Volume XXVI. Page 5.

Army Form C. 2118.

Place	Date	Hour	Summary of Events and Information	Remarks and references to Appendices
WIPPENHOEK	22/4/18	6pm	1 Officer & 16 O.R. discharged to duty; 3 Officers & 102 O.R. to CCS. 1 Corpl. for duty. 1 Cpl. Sutton returned from 63rd F.Amb. 8 O.R. remaining. D.D.M.S. visited.	Sheets 27 & 28 (1:40000)
"	28/4/18	"	7 O.R. to duty, 2 Officers + 93 O.R. evacuated to CCS. 2 Officers & 27 R.S.	
"	24/4/18	"	10 " " 5 " " 141 " " - D.R.S. at WIPPENHOEK	
27/K19.C.4.4.			Closed. The unit less 2 Officers & the Bearer Div (who were attached to 63rd F.Amb.) moved to K.12.C.4.4. Sheet 27, & pitched camp in a field, arriving there at 3.30 pm. Subsequently the 2 Officers & Bearer Division returned to D.R.S. side WIPPENHOEK handed in a holding party.	
"	30/4/18		Transport moved April 8.15am & arrived at LEDERZEELE G.21.4.0.2. at 11.15am. O/c brought forward transport of 7 F.A. 8.45am[?] at about same time. Also wheel chl. Transport in readiness to take the sick of 62nd to 64th the [?]	
			Namur 0.0.76 Received. A.D.M.S. + M.O.V.S. visited. M. Unnatural[?] 1st Cpl. Jenkins O.C.45	

140/2493

No. 657a.

COMMITTEE FOR THE
MEDICAL HISTORY OF THE WAR
Date 9 JUL 1918

CONFIDENTIAL.
MEDICAL.
Vol 33

WAR DIARY
OF THE
65th Field Ambulance
(3rd W Lancs T.F.)

From 1/5/18.
To. 31/5/18

VOLUME XXXII
(6. Pages)

WAR DIARY

INTELLIGENCE SUMMARY

Army Form C. 2118.

MEDICAL

65th Field Ambulance
MAY 1918.
Page 1 Volume XXXII

Place	Date	Hour	Summary of Events and Information	Remarks and references to Appendices
LEDERZEELE	1/5/18	6 pm	Transport moved off at 8.15 am. & arrived at LEDERZEELE (Sheet 7.3) at 3.15 pm. Dismounted personnel travelled by T.L. at 6.45 am arriving at reserve Camp. All tentage pitched in readiness to take in sick. 9.52nd & 64th Brigades	Sheet 27 (1:40000) HAZEBROUCK S.9. SOISSONS (1:100000)
"	2/5/18	"	Name O.D. 77 received. Unit (less Bearer) standing out	
"	3/5/18	"	Captain W.P. Ondliffe RAMC (T.C.) posted to duty 15/12/13 NF¹ in relief of Captain G.M. Cameron who rejoined the Ambulance. Captain D de H. Dawson proceeded for duty with 9th K.O.Y.L.I. in relief of Captain Starling (passed) DADMS & DADVS visited	
"	4/5/18	—	Transport moved off at 1 pm & commenced entraining at 8 OVER at 3.10 pm Dismounted personnel marched off at 3.15 pm & entrained at 5.30 pm	
"	5/5/18	—	In the train —	
JONQUERY	6/5/18	"	Unit detrained at BOULEUSE at 4 am. Transport & dismounted personnel marched off at 6.50 am arriving at JONQUERY at 9.15 am & went into huts. ADMS & DADMS visited.	
"	7/5/18	"	A Hospital Hut opened & sick collected from 64th Brigade. Heavy rain during first 48 hrs.	
"	8/5/18	"	10 patients remaining. Rain continuing	

K Mounsen
Lieut Col
Comdg

WAR DIARY

INTELLIGENCE SUMMARY

65th Field Ambulance
MAY 1918.
Page 2. Vol. XXXII

Army Form C. 2118.

Place	Date	Hour	Summary of Events and Information	Remarks and references to Appendices
JONQUERY	9/5/18	6 p.m.	14 OR missing.	Sheet SOISSONS (1-100,000)
"	10/5/18	"	Visited Hôpital d'Evacuation at CHATILLON. RAMC OD 75 received. 22 patients transferred to 64th Field Amb.	
"	11/5/18	"		
"	12/5/18	"	7 cases where tent's An advance party of 2 Officers & 20 OR proceeded to ADS Stations at CAUROY & CORMICY starting at 12 noon. Main transport reached 9½ at 10.30 am via VILLE-EN-TARDENOIS – SAVIGNY	
PÉVY.			– JONCHERY – PÉVY. Where they billeted for the night arriving there at 4.15 p.m.	
VAUX – VARENNES (Château)	13/5/18	"	Unit marched off at 9.30 am arriving VAUX & VARENNES Château at 10.10 am. OC, Major Shaver + 1st sergt major visited the 2 ADS&m 2 NCOs + 10 OR (Reinfm) proceeded with 4 wheeled stretchers to ADS CORMICY. 9 OR proceeded with 1 wheeled stretcher to ADS: CAUROY. Unit fixed out.	
"	14/5/18	"	OC + D ram Ambler visited ADS&m. + Inspected some of the RAPs on left + right sectors – Major Taylor had moved in 9fm to ADSt CORMICY + ADSt. CAUROY 9 OR proceeded to CORMICY + 11 OR to CAUROY	

WAR DIARY / INTELLIGENCE SUMMARY

Army Form C. 2118.

65th Field Ambulance
MAY 1918
Page 3   Volume XXXII

Place	Date	Hour	Summary of Events and Information	Remarks and references to Appendices
VAUX VARENNES (Chateau)	15/5/18	6 pm	Accompanied by ADMS & DADMS, visited HERMONVILLE & established a Car Post there. (1 Big. Car parks permanently) & collect sick Offr from HERMONVILLE & MARZILLY areas. Visited ADS's at CAUROY & CORMICY. 1 Ford Car attached from 63rd F.Amb.	Sheet SOISSONS (1:100,000)
	16/5/18		Visited ADSs CORMICY & left Batt. R.A.P. & Rein. posts, 2 Big. Cars attached from 10th & B Wheeled Stretchers; also 2. Big Cars from Bde F.Amb. 2nd Blackmore rejoined from 21" W.G. Batt. Pte Rice from same Bath, proceeded on 1 months leave to England.	
	17/5/18		Visited ADSs CAUROY & accompanied men to the Rein. Posts of 6th Leicesters, 15th D.L.I. & 9th K.O.Y.L.I. Also visited DDMS Intelr RAP's	
	18/5/18		Arrived to Bn HQ, met D.D.M.S. 1X Corps + accompanied him to the 2. ADS's thence returning via HERMONVILLE to Amb AP which was inspected by DDMS. Colonel Blackham accompanied DDMS on Inspection.	
	19/5/18		Visit C.C. Tucker rejoined from furlough. Left with 6th Leicesters with 6 Leicesters + 7th Leicesters mens RAP's. Neuve Post 9/Lein + 7th Leicester. West Cochran proceeded for 8 days duty with 2nd Lewis	

K Mouston
Lt Col

Army Form C. 2118.

65th Field Ambulance

MAY 1918.

Page 4. Volume XXXII

WAR DIARY
INTELLIGENCE SUMMARY.
(Erase heading not required.)

Place	Date	Hour	Summary of Events and Information	Remarks and references to Appendices
VAUX VARENNES Chateau	20/5/18	6 p.m.	Visited ADSt CAUROY + RAPs. Thence to H.Q. Rt Sector. DDMS + DADMS visited.	Sheet SOISSONS (1-100000)
"	21/5/18	"	Visited ST H.Q. + accompanied by DADMS visited RAP + drew post of Left Batt of Left sector. Reconnoitred evacuation route (by day) from the RAP (12) via GERNICOURT to rd junction ¾ mile W of CHAPELLE - ADSt.	
"	22/5/18	"	Visited ADSt CAUROY + drew posts of Rt + Support Batts (Rt Sector).	
"	23/5/18	-	Visited both ADSs. Heavy thunder showers during the day have laid the dust. Lieut Cochran reported from 2. knos + proceeded to ADSt CORMICY for duty.	
"	24/5/18	"	Captain Cameron + 1/Lieut Tucker proceeded on 3 days leave to Paris. Accompanied by Lieut to A Pullen visited both ADSs + some of the heavy posts. MOHS + DADMS visited	
"	25/5/18	"	Visited both ADSs + RAPs of 1 E Yorks + 12/13th N.F's. Reconnoitred a route for evacuation of walking wounded by day from Left Batt of Left sector. 2 hy Cars proceed at 11 p.m. for emergency duty to ADSt CORMICY.	
"	26/5/18	"	Visited ADSt CAUROY. DDMS. visited ADSs at DHQ	

W Thompson
Lt Col comm.

65th Field Ambulance

MAY. 1918

Page 5. Volume XXXII

WAR DIARY

INTELLIGENCE SUMMARY
(Erase heading not required.)

Army Form C. 2118.

Place	Date	Hour	Summary of Events and Information	Remarks and references to Appendices
VAUX VARENNES Château	27/5/18	6 p.m.	Enemy offensive from SOISSONS to RHEIMS started at 3 a.m. shelling at 1 a.m. 16 Reserve + 2 Aylers shells to MDS & CORMICY + 16 shells (1:100,000) to 1. This Coy to MDS CORMICY at 12 midnight 26/27th. — Opening shelling was largely gas. Both ADSs were heavily shelled. Evacuated CORMICY at 6.45 a.m. + CAUROY at 11 a.m. Evacuation from forward MDSs difficult owing to most of roads + ambulance to MDSs being broken up, the two roads cleared but were kept going. Though evacuation from CAUROY looked smooth throughout, but HERMONVILLE had to be evacuated owing to roads through it being broken up, men were airflanking CORMICY in last month about 1 pm + at 2 pm ADSs there were evacuated. All personnel then falling away saw westwards thus leaving DMS at CHÂLONS LE VERGEUR. Rear personnel with left diff + centre diff. & 11/13 NF + 2 times wiring MO with forward diff reported to be a prisoner. To 9 at 7 p.m. an adequate nursing DHQ was handled about 2 p.m. to PROUILLY. CAUROY ADSs handed about 3 p.m. to about 4 S of 64 Div H.Q. about 1 mile west of HERMONVILLE. A continuous stream of visible 300 yd N of CHÂLONS — CHÂLONS — CORMICY R. then had to be withdrawn an hour or so, or about ½ way. The road but on R? water to MDS to la theing W. Petit Pery at 10 a.m. A.E.M.R. moved to Sparnshe	Sheet SOISSONS (1:100,000)

WAR DIARY / INTELLIGENCE SUMMARY

Army Form C. 2118.

65th Field Ambulance
MAY 1918.
Page 6. Volume XXXII

Place	Date	Hour	Summary of Events and Information	Remarks and references to Appendices
PÉVY & VILLE EN TARDENOIS	6/m	28/5/18	The unit moved from PÉVY at 3.15 am to French H.Q.E.N. PÉVY JONCHERY R.D. There at 6 am to French Amb. 1 mile South of SAVIGNY where it remained for 2 hrs overhauling convoy of FIRST VILLE EN TARDENOIS SOISSONS. at 4pm sent my ambulance with troops & transport horses L retiring (I–100000) to a loading theatre bus up to PÉVY & JONCHERY at 2 pm. 1 Pty Car which had proceeded at 4 pm 27" trees failed to return. Bus reported in FISMES at about the time & had held Pord to him in killed (GSW) rupture 1 27" between CHALONS LES VERGEUR & CORMICY. Lieut. C.C. Tucker reported from Paris leave.	[marginal notes]
MAREUIL LE PORTE	"	29/5/18	The unit marched off at 7.30 am proceeding via JONQUERY & CHATILLON arrived at MAREUIL LE PORTE. Col. Cameron rejoined from Paris leave. 1 Officer & 43 others provided by French route to CHAUMUZY to escort OC 64th Amb.	
VAUCIENNES.	"	30/5/18	Unit marched at 8 am & arrived at VAUCIENNES at 10 am. & bivouacked for the day. Heavy party rejoined from 64. F. Amb. The Division was relieved. Came out of the line.	
CHALTRAIT	"	31/5/18	Unit marched at 10 am & arrived at Ordination 1 kilometre & divouacked. Capt. Cameron reported to D.M.S. 62nd Corps hotfoot. Capt. Stanley reported to M.A.P. & Lieut. Tucker to 110 Fd Amb. Lieuts AODM & – DADMS briefed	

CONFIDENTIAL

MEDICAL 51 34
11/08/06

COMMITTEE FOR THE
MEDICAL HISTORY
Date 7 AUG. 1918

WAR DIARY
OF THE
65th Field Ambulance.
(3rd W. Lancs T.F.)

From 1/6/18.
To 30/6/18.

VOLUME XXXVII.
(4 Pages)

65th FIELD AMBULANCE

9
June 28.

WAR DIARY
or
INTELLIGENCE SUMMARY.

Army Form C. 2118.

65th Field Ambulance
JUNE 1918.
Page 1. Volume XXXIII.

MEDICAL

Place	Date	Hour	Summary of Events and Information	Remarks and references to Appendices
CHALTRAIT	1/6/18	6 p.m.	11 O.R. proceeded for duty with H.O.E. of EPERNAY. Lieut. HOEY proceeded to England to join an Infantry Cadet Unit. Transport of 63rd F.Amb. arrived & parked with this Unit.	MAPS CHALONS.
"	2/6/18		A.D.M.S. & D.A.D.M.S. visited. 1. O.R. proceeded to IX Corps H.Q. as clerk to D.D.M.S. 11 O.R. reporting from EPERNAY.	
CONGY	3/6/18		Unit marched off at 9.45 arrived at CENSE ROUGE farm (W.of CONGY) at 1-45 p.m. D.A.D.M.S. & D.A.D.V.S. visited.	
"	4/6/18		D.A.D.M.S., D.A.D.V.S. & O.C. 64 Field Ambulance visited.	
"	5/6/18		Visited 64th Field Ambulance.	
"	6/6/18		A.D.M.S. visited.	
"	7/6/18		Unit paid out. D.A.D.V.S. visited	
"	8/6/18		D.A.D.M.S. visited. 2 Cars returned for duty from 64th F.Amb.	
LES ESSARTS	9/6/18		Unit moved off at 12 noon in rear of 64th F.Amby, arrived at Les Essarts (1 mile S of LES ESSARTS) at 6 p.m. 1st D.A.C. near VAUCIENNES.	
"	10/6/18		D.A.D.M.S. visited. One Ford Car attached to 21st D.A.C. near VAUCIENNES.	
"	11/6/18		Major R. Strains have proceeded to England for duty in India. No promises by A.S.C. Base Depots.	
"	12/6/18		A.D.M.S. visited. 21st Div. Administrative Nurse is never received.	
"	13/6/18		Transport moved at 2 p.m. to CARROY S. of CONNANTRE	
"	14/6/18		Ambulance Cars proceed at 1 p.m. & parked for the night 2 miles East of CLERMONT.	

WAR DIARY

65th Field Ambulance
JUNE 1918
Page 2. Volume XXIII

INTELLIGENCE SUMMARY.

Army Form C. 2118.

Place	Date	Hour	Summary of Events and Information	Remarks and references to Appendices
	15/6/18	6 p.m.	Dismounted personnel left LES BORDES (Rd LES ESSARTS) & Embussed at LES ESSARTS Church (b¹¹⁰⁰) debussing at FERE-EN-CHAMPENOISE Stn at 4.30 p.m. Ambulance Car Convoy proceeds at 6.15 a.m. via POIX - OISEMONT-VISMES-AU-VAL	MAPS ABBEVILLE + (1:4)
PONT REMY	16/6/18		— HUPPY — PONT REMY arriving at Inft hand place at 2 pm. Parked at St DIEPPE. 64th Brigade detachment finished at 10 a.m. Dismounted personnel & the Ambulance + Transport arrived. The Transport (with 65" F. Amb. transport attached) (1:100000) marched off to PONT REMY & arrived at LAMBERCOURT at 3 pm. (at midday)	(16)
LAMBERCOURT	17/6/18		Dismounted personnel marched off at 12.30 pm arriving 4.15 pm. Unit went into billets in the village.	
	18/6/18		DADMS visited. Transport (with 65" F. Amb. attached) moved off at 6.20 a.m. via MOYENVILLE — HUPPY - OISEMONT - SENARPONT arrived at 1.45 pm. Dismounted personnel Embussed at 9.30 a.m. arriving at 1 pm. The Unit went into billets in NEUVILLE.	
NEUVILLE (at) FERGUEUSE	19/6/18		Sick from 62" & 84" Brigades + 14 KNF² collected by Amb. Cars. Raining steadily.	
	20/6/18		Captn Stanley was evacuated from 64" Brigade Det. Left Lancers he now goes to Division HQ. 2 2nd Lincoln Regt & 1 Hants Trackn to 1st Lincs Regt.	W Thompson Lt Col ?

2353 W. W2544/1454 700,000 5/15 D.D.&L. A.D.S.S./Forms/C. 2118.

WAR DIARY
INTELLIGENCE SUMMARY

65th Field Ambulance
JUNE 1918. Page 3. Volume XXXIII

Place	Date	Hour	Summary of Events and Information	Remarks and references to Appendices
NEUVILLE-COPPEGUEULE	21/6/18	4pm	Captain J. L. Photo. went with two motor lorries with 2 P/S NF Sgt Buchester, Corp. Brooks & Pte L. H. Smith were arranged the following kind to Abbeville on 23rd and on Pte Jamieson H/C MT 63rd F.Amb. (billeted 65") this F. had not.	MAPS ABBEVILLE DIEPPE 1:100,000
FLOCQUES	22/6/18		Transport moved off at 8.45am & Dismounted party at 8.55am. An advance party of 3 officers & 21 OR preceded by Car & Tenk on Hotchkiss ammunition at LA PIPE & FLOCQUES from B" Ford (30 cwt) Transport arrived at FLOCQUES at 7pm (Distance 7 months = 25 miles) Dismounted personnel marched 18 miles & were then picked up & carried on in the Amb. Cars, the last troop getting in at 6pm. HQ & A. Section & Transport billeted at FLOCQUES. B+C Sections at LA PIPE. DADMS visited.	
"	23/6/18		Visited personnel & Inspection Cases at LA PIPE.	
"	24/6/18		52 OR. remaining. Visited EU & LETRÉPORT.	
"	25/6/18		" Visited Convalescent Camp LA PIPE.	

[signatures]

WAR DIARY
INTELLIGENCE SUMMARY

65th Field Ambulance
JUNE 1918
Page 4 Volume XXXIII

Army Form C. 2118.

Place	Date	Hour	Summary of Events and Information	Remarks and references to Appendices
FLECQUES	26/6/18	6 pm	138. O.R. remaining. 74 of which were suffering.	MAPS. ABBEVILLE DIEPPE (1: 100,000)
	27/6/18		Visited Convalescent Camp LA PIPE. 35 Cars from there returned 4 sick + 5 to CCS. Found note.	
	28/6/18		147 O.R. remaining. 10 Officers + 11 O.R. to CCS, + 77 D.R. to duty. 16 Reinforcements reported today.	
	29/6/18		Visited LA PIPE. 115 O.R. remaining. 1 Officer + 9 O.R. to CCS. 49 O.R.T. duty.	
	30/6/18		86 Cars on hand. 15 to CCS. ordered per 29.6.18. 68. cars returned to duty. Transport has left. Unit has moved off at 10 am under Major R. Taylor + proceeds for the night to the OISEMONT area.	

V. Woolf Vincent
Lt Col. R.A.M.C.

CONFIDENTIAL.

MEDICAL.
Vol 35
140/3131.

WAR DIARY.
OF THE
65th Field Ambulance.
(3rd W. Lancs. T.F.)

From 1/7/18
To 31/7/18.

VOLUME XXXIV.
(4 Pages).

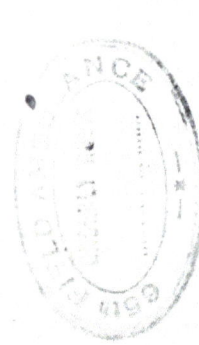

WAR DIARY
INTELLIGENCE SUMMARY.
(Erase heading not required.)

65th Field Ambulance
JULY. 1918
Page 1   Volume XXXIV

Army Form C. 2118.

MEDICAL

Place	Date	Hour	Summary of Events and Information	Remarks and references to Appendices
TALMAS	1/7/18	6 p.m	Personnel & Cooks Lorries moved off (from FLOCQUES) by M/T at a.m. being joined by rest at LA PIPE at 4.20 & arrived at EU Station at 5.20 a.m. Entraining at 8.30 a.m. & detraining at CANDAS (LENS sheet) at 4.30 p.m. Thence they proceeded by march route to TALMAS & took on Div. Rest. Stn. side (S.3 & 2.8) from a holding point, 9 53rd Field Amb. (17th Div.). Ambl. Cars Open Car attached to 95th Army RFA & on reopening of EU Station at 11.30 a.m., proceeded by road via OISEMONT — AIRAINES — LONGPRÉ — FLIXÉCOURT — FLESSELLES — TALMAS, arriving at 6 p.m. (all entrainment of 110th Army was completed)	Sheet ABBEVILLE DIEPPE LENS (II) 1:100,000
"	2/7/18	"	A.O.s & D.A.D.M.S. worked 1 Day. Car attached for temp. duty to 64th Fd Amb.	
"	3/7/18	"	Transport arrived at 6 a.m. All Trucks pitched as Hosp accommodation & having nearly started to duty & 21st M.T. Coy at BERNEUIL.	
"	4/7/18	"	81 ORs unwell. Influenza was prevalent but died out. DDMS of ...	
"	5/7/18	"	Visit W.S. Burgess MORC reported for duty. Cars taken on strength. Capt Parker Stk. taken on from 53rd Field Ambulance. Orders elsewhere to hosp.	
"	6/7/18	"	Colonel J McCammon M.C. rejoined from 2nd Army.	

W. Turnbull Lieut

65th Field Ambulance
JULY 1918
Page 2. Volume XXXIV

Army Form C. 2118.

WAR DIARY
INTELLIGENCE SUMMARY
(Erase heading not required.)

Place	Date	Hour	Summary of Events and Information	Remarks and references to Appendices
TALMAS	7/7/18	6p	Accompanied by Major Stanley, visited 63rd Div ADS at MAILLEY MAILLET & MDSt at ACHEUX. 1/Lieut 1 H Cochrane reported for temporary duty to 1/Works Regt in relief of Captain Chamberlain (sick)	LENS (?) 1,000,000
	8/7/18		144 QR remaining in 2nd Reft Stn.	
	9/7/18		152 " " " "	
	10/7/18		Capt S Parker, St. Johns & 60 tents advanced to Etrine procured for camp. Duty with 94th Heavy RFA in relief of Capt L Ferguson, RAMC. 64 tents, PUCHEVILLERS, also O.18.c.4.6.	
			& O.18.c.2.3. and N.5.a.8.7.	
			DADMS V Corp visited & inspected HQ and 1 - 63rd that Rd & Refreshmts tents at two bus school PUCHEVILLERS	
	11/7/18		1/Lieut L.S. Amps to RC reported for duty & duty at 52.36 CCS	
	12/7/18		DDMS V Corp inspected Coffee Feeder Stn & Bus Rest Stn	
	13/7/18		118 OR remain in DRSt ; + 71 OR in Rectn Stn.	
	14/7/18			
	15/7/18		5 OR reports in + reinforcements for duty. 16 Months leave	

Army Form C. 2118.

65th Field Ambulance
JULY 1918.
Page 3. Volume XXXIV

WAR DIARY
INTELLIGENCE SUMMARY.
(Erase heading not required.)

Place	Date	Hour	Summary of Events and Information	Remarks and references to Appendices
TALMAS	16/7/18	6 p.m.	1/Lieut. D.G. Dawrie W.O.R.C. reported from 94th M.G. R.F.A. PADMS visited	LENS (1) (1-100,000)
"	17/7/18	"	Captain Prather Snr R.S.A.M.C reported for a fortnight course of instruction	
"	18/7/18	"	173 O.R. remaining in D.R.St. - 1 Officer & 29 O.R. in Corps higher Stn	
"	19/7/18	"	142 " " " 2 " 86 "	
"	20/7/18	"	PDMS visited & inspected DRSt & CSSt - Kint hand out -	
"	21/7/18	"	134 O.R. remaining in DRSt - 2 Officers & 75 O.R. remaining in CSSt	
"	22/7/18	"	140 " " " " 68 "	
"	23/7/18	"	123 " " " " " - PADMS visited.	
"	"	"	2 Motor Lorries (1 MEO + 2 men in each) proceeded to Du Bois St at LE MESNIL & VACHEREUX. Then Mud - Ist lecture at BEAUQUESNES.	
"	24/7/18	"	Capt Cameron + 34 O.R. (Rear) with 3 Ambulances proceeded at 8.30 am to MDS ACHEUX & thence to ADS ENGLEBELMER	
"	"	"	Ry Capt with Ambulance C.P. proceeded MDS in hire car to ETAPLES	
"	25/7/18	"	2 Lg Cars attached to 63rd F.Amb. (MDS ACHEUX)	
"	26/7/18	"	ADMS visited. Capt Prather Snr reported to Rly from taken on the strength	
"	27/7/18	"	Lieut D.G. Dawrie posted to Ques Army R.F.A. Captain Ferguson relief has posted to this unit - Visited A.D.S. ENGLEBELMER	

W. Thyne [signature]

65th Field Ambulance
July 1918

WAR DIARY
INTELLIGENCE SUMMARY.
(Erase heading not required.)

Page 4. Volume XXXIV

Army Form C. 2118.

Place	Date	Hour	Summary of Events and Information	Remarks and references to Appendices
TALMAS	26/7/18	6 pm	10 O.R. returning to DR St.	LENS (1)
"	29/7/18	"	Capt Chamberlain + 11 O.R. proceed to duty to 63rd O.R. Rest St. + 66 O.R. transferred to Capt Parker St. 1 N.S. Cos attached. LE MENAGE + took on from 148th Field Amb. to duty DMS 3rd Army reenforcements to reinforce the DRSt + Scabies St + also Queen's medal ribbons. (to Capt Mayor + 8 O.R. Major R. Taylor R.C. proceeded on leave to England.	(1·100 O.Rs)
"	30/7/18	"	Pte C + DADMS visited, also OC 53 + Amb + ADMS 17th Divs. Lt Col S Sinclair visited DRS LE MENAGE officer Rest St. DONART.	
"	31/7/18	"	Colln. P. in Th. Satisfactory to OC 64th Fd Amb. on completion of fortnights instruction in the mining J. 2 O.R. St + Cap Parker St. 83 O.R. returning to DRSt. + 62 O.R. to Capt Parker St.	

W. Keen Barrett
Lt Col
RAMC
OC 65

CONFIDENTIAL

9/51 36
140/3200

WAR DIARY
OF THE
65th Field Ambulance
(3rd W Lancs T.F.)

From 1/8/18
To 31/8/18.

VOLUME XXXV.
(3 Pages)

COMMITTEE FOR THE
MEDICAL HISTORY OF THE WAR
Date 5 OCT 1910

Army Form C. 2118.

MEDICAL

WAR DIARY
INTELLIGENCE SUMMARY

65° Field Ambulance
AUGUST 1918.
Page 1. Volume XXXV.

(Erase heading not required.)

Place	Date	Hour	Summary of Events and Information	Remarks and references to Appendices
TALMAS	1/8/18	6pm	92. OR remaining in DRS. 1 Officer + 60 OR remaining in Corps bath at Beauval	
"	2/8/18	"	DDMS, ADMS + APM visited. The Rev. Capt A. Cory C.F. attached for duty. LENS(II)	
"	3/8/18	"	Capt Chamberlain + 14 OR rejoined from LE MENAGE.	1-100000
"	4/8/18	"	5 OR. Reinforcements rejoined for duty. Heavy rain for past 3 days.	
"	5/8/18	"	Lunch paid out — 117 OR. remaining in Brit. Rest. Stn — 1 Officer + 68. OR. in Corps baths Stn.	
"	6/8/18	"	2 NCO's + 32 Men promoted to APTS ENGLEBELMER + Wounded + Sick numbers returns.	
"	7/8/18	"	ADMS visited. Capt Chamberlain departs to 63rd F.Amb for duty + Capt Rhodes	
			from 63rd F.Amb rejoined this unit.	
"	8/8/18	"	Capt Ferguson leaves + 70 OR proceeded on a holiday trek. 63rd Dist	
			Rest Stn at LE MENAGE. 1 Sec W.S. Burgess M.O.R.C. reported from Tents?	
			duty at 36. CCS.	
"	9/8/18	"	Capt G.M. Cameron leaves proceeded on leave to England. Capt G.L.	
			Johnston proceeded on 7 days leave to ETAPLES. 1 Lieut. Becker	
			M.O.R.C. attached for duty from 64th F.Amb. 1 Officer wounded	
			daily to visit units of Corps Troops in the Area (present in an M.A.C. car at 9am)	
"	10/8/18	"	170. OR. remaining in DRSt. — 1 Officer + 90 OR. in Corps baths Stn	

WAR DIARY
INTELLIGENCE SUMMARY

65" Field Ambulance
AUGUST 1918.   Page 2. Volume XXXV

Army Form C. 2118.

Place	Date	Hour	Summary of Events and Information	Remarks and references to Appendices
TALMAS	14/8/18	6 p.m.	149 OR remaining in DRS. 77 OR remaining in Pope helm SA	Sheet
"	15/8/18	"	169 " " " 24 " " "	LEN S(1)
"	"	"		F DRSS.
"	13/8/18	"	ADMS + DADMS. visited	
"	14/8/18	--	Major Taylor reported from leave. Revd Capt Corry C.F. rejoined 63' Bay	
"	15/8/18	"	DDMS visited. Capt Johnston reported from leave to France	
"	16/8/18	"	ADMS visited. Wheat kitchen defects & rejoined b/w/ 2 Aust.	
"	17/8/18	"	DADMS visited. 145 OR remaining in DRSS 54 OR remaining in Drakes SA	
"	18/8/18	--	DDMS III Corps visited.	
"	19/8/18	"	kink head unit.	
"	20/8/18	"	drawn up in line relieved by a equivalent number to Drops. & 32.	
"	21/8/18	"	began starting we a 41 OR. (Scarers) proceeded in lorries of 9 pm 20th 15.	
"	"	"	ADSh Major MALLET. Capt Dufresne. +6 OR rejoined from LE MENAGE (6" DW-DRS?)	
"	"	"	1 hostler Cyclist attached to ADMS trains. -1 Lorhes out attached to 63' 2 Aust	
"	22/8/18	"	2 OR rejoined from Officers Rest St DOMART. All Stations Cars cleaned	
"	"	"	F.Amb, (A 52). - 150 OR rejoining in DRSh at 12 noon - S.R. 16 Duty. 16 CCS	
"	"	"	+ 62 on III dration.	

b. Heanfort Major

Army Form C. 2118.

65th Field Ambulance
AUGUST 1916
Page 3. Volume XXXV

WAR DIARY
or
INTELLIGENCE SUMMARY.
(Erase heading not required.)

Place	Date	Hour	Summary of Events and Information	Remarks and references to Appendices
TALMAS	23/8/18	6p	DDMS visited. 24 Bearers proceeded up the Line at 7.30	LENS(II) 1/40000
			Phd. Bearers att⁰ 63rd Amb. = 2 Officers + 101 OR. = 89 remaining from	
			DRS: - 18 womended BTCs; 24 totals; - 197 OR remaining	
"	24/8/18	"	" " " " 54 " ; 194 "	
"	25/8/18	"	72 Admissions, 21 " " " ; 54 " ; 194 "	
"			The unit proceeded to ACHEUX at 7am arriving at 11.2 am, and again marched	
MAILLY-MAILLET			off to MAILLY-MAILLET at 2/pm arriving at 3.15pm. Here the M.D.S. was	
"			Taken over from 63rd Field Ambulance. Two Officers and W.O.R. remained at	
"			TALMAS to dispose of 145 patients remaining in DRS, and to see sick of	
"			3 Corps Troops in the attack area and of 21 Div W'ing Capt. A H T	
"			Davies RAMC joined the unit from temporary duty with 63rd Field	
"			Ambulance at MAILLY-MAILLET and taken on the strength of the unit from	
"	31/7/18			
"			The Ambulance left MAILLY-MAILLET at 2.30pm to take over evacuations	
In the Line (M15607) SUISSE	26/8/18		from the Line and relieved 63rd "Field" Ambulance at the Quarry M15 b.0.9 (Sh57c)	
"			While the transport lines remained at MIRAUMONT with Major R. Taylor.	
"			Capt. B.M. Cameron MC joined the unit from leave	

WAR DIARY / INTELLIGENCE SUMMARY

Army Form C. 2118.

65th Field Ambulance
AUGUST 1918
Page 4 Volume XXXV

Place	Date	Hour	Summary of Events and Information	Remarks and references to Appendices
2nd Line (M.1,5,b,0,9.) Sheet 57.d.	27/8/18	9 pm	One Officer and 12 O.R. rejoined transport line from TAHITI S, all cases being disposed of from D.R.S. Capt. Johnstone and 4 O.R. remained to see sick from Corps Lorry.	Sheet 57 c
"	2/8/18	4	Corps Tanks and guard took over Corps Stores. Band provided the buses in the evening. Major Stirling M.C. joined the transport lines. A.D.M.S. visits Transport lines.	1/100.000 Sheet 57 c
"	"	"	In the evening OC 65th Field Ambulance with horses established HQ. Faulkner.	
M.23.a.9.3 sheet 57.c.	2/8/18	9	Forward at M.23. a.9.3. the Establishment consisted of horses from the three Field Ambulances & Officers of 64th Field Ambulance. Major Grey, OC 65th Y Amb. and Major Sodom of 64th Field Ambulance. Two water-carts and 10 cars under attached. The buses of everything which was now MIRAUMONT and MALCOURT.	
"	"	"	MAILLET was closed to POZIERES via BAPAUME - ALBERT Road.	
"	2/8/18	"	INC's and 2 O.R. proceeded to 4th Army H.Q. to await for instruction.	
"	3/8/18	"	Major Stirling M.O. rejoined the OC at M.23.a.9.3. and Capt A.R.T. Davis returned to transport Stables to ODone at M.15.b.0.9 m relief. Major Paton was sent to transport Lines. Lieut Chandler on P.A. U.S.	
"	"	"	Personnel during the Plague include 7 O.R. evacuation wounded. 20 R. wounded at duty	

MEDICAL CONFIDENTIAL. 2/1st 8*n*

WO 37
144/3259

WAR DIARY

OF THE
65th Field Ambulance.
(3rd W. LANCS. T.F)

FROM 1/9/18.
TO 30/9/18.

VOLUME XXXVI.
(4. Pages).

Part 1918.
9

Army Form C. 2118.

65th Field Ambulance
SEPTEMBER 1918
Page 1. Volume XXXVI

WAR DIARY
INTELLIGENCE SUMMARY
(Erase heading not required.)

Place	Date	Hour	Summary of Events and Information	Remarks and references to Appendices
1½ km Field	1/9/18	4pm	110th Inf. Bgd. attacks BEAULENCOURT & high ground North of. Attack starts at 2am. 1st Wounded (stretcher) Case N. 10. C.11. b. 70.5. POZIÈRES. A.D.S. been pushed	N.10. C.57 c 1.20 pm
	2/9/18		Began leaving wounded, also LUBRA COPSE. 1) Our cavalry & transport & advance to outskirts of ROCQUIGNY. 42 Div. took VILLERS AU FLOS.	
	3/9/18		Med. Supplies found. Wounded now transport times somewhat left P.U.O. any.	6" being shelled 10 other by shell
	4/9/18		Transport moved from MIRAUMONT to N.25.R.E.A. Being moved to U.9.b.5.0 refused owing to Detaches near & heavy shell fire V.16.d.2.R.	
	5/9/18		Hosts. moved to V.16.d.2.6. NURLU Rd.	
	6/9/18		Hosts. moved to V.16.d.2.6 (shrapnel LDS0) 3 killed + 2 wounded	
	7/9/18		Transport moved to U.8.a.5.R. at V.18.d.2.8. (shell hit one of the huts) Hostels moved to V.22.b.2.8. 65 F.Amb. Major Taylor be relieved Capt Ferguson who returned to transport lines	
	8/9/18		were wires to V.15. d.7.0. Capt Johnston & 3 OR. rejoined for duty with the	

WAR DIARY

Army Form C. 2118.

65th Field Ambulance
SEPTEMBER 1918.
Page 2. Volume XXXVI

INTELLIGENCE SUMMARY.

Place	Date	Hour	Summary of Events and Information	Remarks and references to Appendices
In the Field W.14.b.3.3.	9/9/18	6 p.m.	H. Quarters of F. Amb. moved to W.14.b.3.3. (On line HEUDICOURT R.) 64th Light Bury relieved 62nd Lf. Bry in the line. Brown Kelly took rations to Rosery (W.16.c.6.1) + W.16.a.5.5. Cars washed.	Sheet 57c S.E. 1:20000
	10/9/18			
	11/9/18		110th Bury relieved 64th Bury. & attacked on high ground E.2 HEUDICOURT by 4th Brigade. attacked on line CHAPEL HILL – PEIZIERE (50.100 Casualties) worked	
	12/9/18		Spent the day at Transport lines (15.A.7.0) Bury	
	13/9/18		Visited Reg.t. Posts & the line. Found various posts — had Xstlin. Capt. Ferguson broken leg (not but 2nd R.E.)	
	14/9/18		110 Bury A.P. Proceed to Transport Lines. Found and 6. Reinforcements reported.	
	15/9/18		119th Brigade relieved 110th Lf. Bry in the line. Night of 15/16 – 19 F.Amb. relieved 65th personel. Brown in the line. Relief completed by 7 p.m.	
	16/9/18		Leaving A.D.S. personel Returned to Transport lines V.15.A.2.0 (9 to 15 ?) The body moved back. 64 & 72nd Brown in the line kept Tramny lines to Brigade V.2.d.7.9.	
	17/9/18		A.D.S. personel returned to W.14.b.3.3. & took over from Stationary F.Amb. 1/Hert. F.Amb. & 1/2 E.R. reported for duty. 1/1 Cumberland A.D.S. V.11.a.2.2. 9.19th F.Amb. A.D.S. received of leave W.M.6.33. 1st W.22.b.8.7. 1.10 a.m.	
W.22.b.8.7.	18/9/18	—	2nd Div. attacked. S. 20 a.m. 4. Guard by these posts to relays N. W.24. b.88. 100th Stafford Division attacked. P.o.O. and returned to Corps Cam Tons in the line. Cars in arrivals from W.22.b.8.1. to V.11.a.2.2. Great Cap Curing over 1000 prisoners (Souta humi rex)	
	19/9/18	—	A.P.S. sent both Ni. Nalhecke at W.24.b.8.6 of 91 F.Amb. Voulelco ADS Cutinusies to take over.	

WAR DIARY / INTELLIGENCE SUMMARY

Army Form C. 2118.

65th Field Ambulance
SEPTEMBER 1918
Page 3 Volume XXXVI

Place	Date	Hour	Summary of Events and Information	Remarks and references to Appendices
W22 b 8.7	20/9/18	6 pm	ADS & Bearer posts were relieved by personnel from 99th 2nd Amb (33rd Div) at 8 pm. Sheet 57 C (1-40,000) In relief personnel & bearers returned to Tranes Port Camp (V.15.d.7.0)	Sheet 57 C SW (1-40,000)
T.32.central	21/9/18		Personnel & transport moved off at 9.30 & 9.15 am respectively & arrived at T.3.b (central) at 12.30 & 12.45 pm respectively. Took over ambulance like vacated by 19th F.Amb. Major Taylor acted as Prescriber at Court Martial to trial of Pte Jones. 5 O.R. attended ambulance.	
T.3.d central	22/9/18		Proceeded on 14 days leave England. Handed over the trust to Major R. Taylor R.E. 1st Lieut H.S.Burges M.O.R.C. was attached to 1st Field Battalion for temporary duty. Williamson Major	
	23/9/18		8 O.M.S. I Corps inspected the ambulance at Cont Martial two exchange. Wingfield Major	
	24/9/18		Capt & M. Dearing RAC & Jones were promulgated at 2 pm. Pte Jones being found guilty of ...... AD.S. Maryeffe leaves and returned to 2 years I.H.L. Ytr. cent marches off at 10 am and arrived at V.2.d.3.8 at 12.45 am a leading party of INCO & 2 O.R. (bearers) at 7.30 cent Capt & Johnston RAMC was attached to 6th Brigade Battalion.	
V.2.d.3.8	24/9/18		Capt & M Cameron MC and 10 Esperts proceeded to 65th Yield Amb & as front party for 110th Brigade. 2 Sports 1 musical were attached to each Battn 9/110th Brigade and 1 runner to Brigade Headquarters. Major Staley RAMC reports to ADS for duty & then 3 Capt & G Orr RAMC reports to 18 O.R. relieves	Wingfield RAMC
"	25/9/18		personnel 3 Capt to O Ord RAMC with 3 Yield ambulance at V.2.C	Wingfield RAMC

65th Field Ambulance
SEPTEMBER 1918.
Page 4. Volume XXXVI

WAR DIARY
INTELLIGENCE SUMMARY.
(Erase heading not required)

Place	Date	Hour	Summary of Events and Information	Remarks and references to Appendices
V 2 d 3 8 Contd	25/9/18	6/pm	2 D.R. reported from Buinval Post Station to Troops 1 and 2 also & party of T 3 a Central.	Sheet 57 C S.E. (1-10000)
"	26/9/18	-	1 Ford car was attacked & 63rd Field Amb. ADMS visited.	
"	27/9/18	-	During the night of 27/28th a bomb dropped on horse lines from enemy aircraft which resulted in the following casualties:- Killed Hot 1 H.D. 5 Riders - mules -	Died 2 Wounded M.V.S. 5 1 1
"	28/9/18	-	ADMS visited and Veterinary officer 13 H.D. horses were Mess from 21 Surveyed. 1 H.D. Lost returned from 33rd Mobile Veterinary Section for duty, after having been hit by shell fire on 16/9/18.	Tried to replace casualties fit for duty. Horse strengths
"	29/9/18	"	two heavy draught wounded and remaining at duty evacuated to 63rd Mobile V. Section one mule wounded and remaining at duty. 1 died at 3 am H.D 17 Riders 5 Mules 22	
"	30/9/18	-	There horsed ambulances attached to 63rd Fld Amb duty from 3 am to this Bn. were nightly being attacked by enemy Refugee Camp, and occupants made by Major Taylor to see their work daily. Three Horsed Ambulance which had formed during the night 29/30, were again sent to 63rd 4 and 1 A.DS. at W 2 c 6.4.	W.Mufiesh [signature]

Confidential.
MEDICAL
Vol 38
1493321

COMMITTEE FOR THE WAR
MEDICAL HISTORY OF THE WAR
4 DEC. 1918
Date

WAR DIARY
OF THE
66th FIELD AMBULANCE.
(3rd W. Lancs. T.F.)

From 1/10/18.
To 31/10/18.

VOLUME XXXVII.
(4 Pages)

9
Oct. 1918

WAR DIARY / INTELLIGENCE SUMMARY

65th Field Ambulance
OCTOBER 1918
Page 1. Volume XXXVII
Army Form C. 2118.

Place	Date	Hour	Summary of Events and Information	Remarks and references to Appendices
V.2.d.3.9	1/10/18	6 p.m.	Continued tour camp at Forêt. A.D.M.S. and Veterinary officers visits the unit.	57 @ appx
	2/10/18		Capt. A.H.T. Dann relieved Capt. Stowe in charge N.S. Bungalow. Lieut. R.C. White reported to unit, detailed to report.	57 B appx
	3/10/18			
	4/10/18			
N.4.b.6.8	5/10/18		The unit marched off at 06.15 hours to N.4.b.6.8 arriving at 08.00 hours. There heavy draught horses and two mule pairs received for the Base. Three Horsed Ambulances provided to 63rd F. Amb. A.D.S. and relieved the same day. Whilst there, cases sent in at midnight 5/6/18. With Capt. A.H.T. Dann in attendance. A/Corp. M.D.S. for S.O.S. The A.D.M.S. visited.	
	6/10/18		The unit moved at 13.30 hours to R.36.a.5..9. arriving at 16.30 hours.	
R.36.a.5.9	7/10/18		The unit handed on a mutton chest of Committee for military magazine. Pte Jones E. two infantry between 63rd & 65th Field Amb. seven, two transports sent to the unit.	
M.28.C.3.0	8/10/18		On 15.30 hours we moved to M.28.c.3.0 (short 57 B) again leaving leaves for the along; Capt A.H.Dann Dann and arrived at 5 Corps M.D.S. returned to unit, A/D.M.S. visits; new arrivals to N.23.c there also subsequently.	
	10/10/18	6 p.m.	Capt. Cameron to the Current Received. The unit opened LCC thereafter moved at 64 F Amb at N.24.d.0.4. (WALINCOURT) at 7.30 p.m.	
O.15.a.5.6	11/10/18		Left (at) CAULLERY (O.15.a.5.6) opening at 12.00 & W/L kpts. Kitbag... Waggonlin & Bearer opened (from Batt.). Unit sm field rest...	

WAR DIARY

65th Field Ambulance
OCTOBER 1918
Page 2. Volume XXXVI

Army Form C. 2118.

INTELLIGENCE SUMMARY.

Place	Date	Hour	Summary of Events and Information	Remarks and references to Appendices
CAULLERY	12/10/18	6pm	2 Lg Cars arrived from 65th F. Amb. Advd. party marked Beaumetz. Sheet Sh'y 8. TROISVILLES – INCHY – MONTIGNY villages from MDS. She. 1-4000.	
	13/10/18		ADMS & DDMS visited – Visited 17 sick & inj. at MONTIGNY hope station, all proceeded on leave to England. Cpt. Phelan reported from Transpt. duty with 6th Lancers Two	
	14/10/18		ADMS DDMS visited. 5 O.R. reinforcements whilst from Base Depot	
	15/10/18		The Ambulance Football team played 1st Welch & lost 3-0.	
	16/10/18		DDMS VIth Corps visited. Visited ADCS AUDENCOURT (5th Div.) 10 NCOs & men reinforcements arrived from Base Depot.	
	17/10/18		Heavy rain fell.	
	18/10/18		6th Bn (Welsh?) Conference & D.A. & L. Commandant at MDS Shee with view to starting sick to MDS; allowed cofference at 15.30. Heavy rain to last 2 days.	
	19/10/18		Viosyka INCHY amn note	
	20/10/18		ADMS visited	
	21/10/18		Lieut Brown our Lieut Cameron MC joined. 110th Inf. Brigade & marched to INCHY but marched off at 14.30 pm & bivouacked at J. 21.6.2.5.	Appendix
	22/10/18		Transport moved off at 15.30 & arrived at 16 km N. East from	

65th Field Ambulance
OCTOBER 1916
Army Form C. 2118.

WAR DIARY

INTELLIGENCE SUMMARY.

Page 3. Volume XXXVII

(Erase heading not required.)

Place	Date	Hour	Summary of Events and Information	Remarks and references to Appendices
INCHY	23/10/16	18 hrs	An advance party of 6 O.R. with 1 M. of L. & 1 water cart took over an ADSt site at K.7.d.6.8. at 6.30 pm. The remainder of Tent Sub personnel with 4 dy cars & 1 Ford proceeded at 3 am & took in at 3.30 am. Bgn 17 Std personnel evac. 200 lying & 550 sitting cases. Evac. treated evacuated by 15.30 hrs.	Wnd 57, B 1.40 rrs.
NEUVILLY VENDEGIES	24/10/16	"	Transport moved up from INCHY arriving at 7.30 am. ADS established at 5 pm at VENDEGIES (F.7.d.7.3.) From 15.30 hrs 23/10 to 18 hrs 24/10 approx 80 lying & 160 sitting cases evacuated.	
"	25/10/18	"	ADMS visited. To 53rd Fd Amb. abt OADMS. 17"Divn. No of lying cases evacuated to 18 hrs 24/10/ approx 20 lying & 66 sitting. We were relieved by 53rd F. Amb at 12 noon & marched to OVILLERS & bivouacked in a field (E.23.b.6.4.) arriving there at 13.00 hrs.	Wnd. OR. 100 R.C.
OVILLERS	27/10/16	"	Capt Stevens reported to 63rd Fd Amb for duty for 24 hrs, Captain Cameron & Alexei have reported, also 24 other bearers who proceed to join their own units.	
"	28/10/16	"	ADMS visited. Capt Hatfield RAMC marked	W. Morgan Lt Col RAMC

Army Form C. 2118.

WAR DIARY
INTELLIGENCE SUMMARY
(Erase heading not required.)

65th Field Ambulance
OCTOBER 1918
Page 4 Volume XXXVIII

Place	Date	Hour	Summary of Events and Information	Remarks and references to Appendices
VENDEGIES F74.73.	29/10/18	18 hrs	Unit moved from OVILLERS at 12:00 hrs & took over ADS & car Post in POIX du NORD from 53rd F.Amb. Relief was completed by 13:00 hrs.	Sh 57B 1-4 50000
	30/10/18		Visited RAP's 2. 2" Leins & 2 "Leinsters" at X.21.d.8.5. x.21.b.37. refreshing. class 110 & 62 half Bttn D.R.S. Stress makes 1.Tns Car hit & had to be towed to workshop.	
	31/10/18		Visited 62nd Lfs Brigade, RAP (12/D N.F.)Car park. D.D.M.S. visited.	

M Murphy
Lt Col. RAMC
O.C. 65 F.Amb.

Confidential.

MEDICAL

Vol 39
(1 of 340)

COMMITTEE FOR THE
MEDICAL HISTORY OF THE WAR
Date 20 JAN 1919

WAR DIARY
OF THE
65th Field Ambulance
(3rd W. Lancs T.F)

FROM 1/11/18
TO 30/11/18.

VOLUME XXXVIII.
(7. Pages).

65th FIELD AMBULANCE
ORDERLY ROOM

Nov 1918

WAR DIARY / INTELLIGENCE SUMMARY

Army Form C. 2118.

65th Field Ambulance
NOVEMBER 1918
Page 1. Volume XXXVIII.

MEDICAL

Place	Date	Hour	Summary of Events and Information	Remarks and references to Appendices
VENDEGIES	1/11/18	18.00	Visited 110th, 162nd Brig. H.Q. & Regtl Aid Posts. 2 Batt. of 3 Brigades. Majors Timlin and Ritchie returned from leave (Brig't 131st) 2 Horses on A.D.B's & Car Park	Maps 57.B. 1-40000
"	2/11/18	"	Handed over to 52nd Field Amb. Relief completed.	
"	3/11/18	"	R. ame OO 103. Received 2 clerks attached temp'y to MDS W.Sh. Capt. Davies reports for temp'y duty to Capt. M.D.8th. Capt. Cameron on leave. 65th Field Amb. wishes to O.C. 64 Field Amb during Evacuation, also Major Stanley, M.D. Heavy Office & 1 Brigade. Majors Taylor Irvine & Capt. Johnston also reported for duty attached to T.C. 64 & 1 Fd. Amb. 3 Brig. Group & 1 Fd Amb.	
"	4/11/18	"	F Amb & Field (This Div) returned Estrées (Expt.7.3) at 15.00 hrs. ADS. BAOMS. Transport Remaining at F.13.d.4.3. Fwd. Dressed Museum Officer killed.	
"	5/11/18	"	(A has worked)	
"	6/11/18	"	63 App. I HQ. Transport arrived at VENDEGIES. Lieut Bennett, U.S.M.C. reported his arrival. Sick remaining. (Out & road for a week)	
"	7/11/18	"	All sick evacuated to C.W.S. St FOREST to F.A Anderson. Sick & transport moved MOB 15 schs.	
"	8/11/18	"	C.W.S. St. Forest. 15.45 hrs. bivouacked in a Field.	

W. Thorney Sturt Lieut
A.D.S.S., Forms C. 2118.

WAR DIARY

INTELLIGENCE SUMMARY

65th Field Ambulance
NOVEMBER 1918
Page 2. Volume XXVIII

Place	Date	Hour	Summary of Events and Information	Remarks and references to Appendices
T.24.d.1.4.	9/11/18	18 hrs	A/Lieut. Colonel Brassett. V.S.M.C. departed for general duties being 1/5th N.F. Visited ADS's AULNOYE (64th F.Amb.) U.22.c.1.2 also ADS's 17th Div. U.29.a.3.7.	Sketch 51. S.W. 1:20000
	10/11/18		Ambulance parties ¼ 1 Bro. & 5 OR proceeded at 17:30 hrs 9th inf. took on billets in GRAND CARRIERE T.18.a.7.3.; knit moved at 09:45 hrs arrived there at 10:30 hrs Capt A.J. 17th Irish Reared TF replied for duty & was taken on the strength 2 other ranks from this date. DADMS visited. Irish knit sent.	
V.23.b.3.7.	11/11/18		Unit moved at 08:45 hrs to LIMONT FONTAINE V.23.b.3.7. arriving there at 13:00 hrs. Cessation of hostilities at 11:00 hrs Captain J.L. Johnston proceeded on leave to England. Capt Cameron sick & reaches required the unit at V.23.b.3.7. Major R. Taylor & & reported from troops duty with 64th F.Amb. Collection & sick from 64th & 110th brigades Commenced. 1 Rig Car & 1 Ford reported from 64 F.Amb.	
	12/11/18		4 Capts. Hew from troops sick to & for the Ambulance from this date in consequence 3 & 1 were not be required from their units.	
	13/11/18		Troops visited.	

W. Thompson Lt Col
RAMC

Army Form C. 2118.

65th Field Ambulance
NOVEMBER 1918
Page 3. Volume XXVIII

WAR DIARY
INTELLIGENCE SUMMARY.
(Erase heading not required.)

Place	Date	Hour	Summary of Events and Information	Remarks and references to Appendices
V23.b.3.9.	14/11/18	15hr	Capt J.W. Irvin posted for duty to 94th Bde. R.F.A. two thirds of strength	Sheet 51.
	15/11/18		Capt. P.H. Bevin was struck off the strength of the Amb. from 12th inst on	1.40000
			being attached to ["]command 125th F. Amb. Capt. J. Ferguson having reported	
			his arrival (on return from leave). Visited MAUBEUGE & Eversfield's Div.	
			viewed RAMC Plays "Reserf".	
	15/11/18	"	Capt Ferguson reported to ADMS for duty.	
			Capt Cameron proceeded on leave to Paris (10 days) OC 69th F.Amb visited.	
	16/11/18	"	Inspected hut in Jumohey adm—	
	16/11/18	"	Rook Stock Inspection. Rs into huwleung & inspected stock of Horne Club	
	19/11/18	"	Apparel inspected hut & Transport & stays to lunch.	
	20/11/18	"	Veterinary officer's monthly (Captain Hartfield)	
	21/11/18	"	Route March — kit clothing Inspection	
	1/11/18	"	Lecture on Demobilization - Football	
	2/11/18	"	ADMS. visited.	
	23/11/18	"	Route march	
	24/11/18	"		
	25/11/18	"	DADVS visited	

65th Field Ambulance
NOVEMBER 1918
Page 4. Volume XXXVIII

Army Form C. 2118.

WAR DIARY
INTELLIGENCE SUMMARY
(Erase heading not required.)

Place	Date	Hour	Summary of Events and Information	Remarks and references to Appendices
V23.b.3.7.	26/11/18	18 hr	Football match v. 63rd F. Amb. w.l. won 3-0. Horns 10 A.D.S. reached	Sheet 51. 1:40000
LIMONT-FONTAINE	27/11/18	"	Unit paid out.	
"	28/11/18	"	Horns L. walked - Route march in afternoon. 2 O.R. drawn bill.S.M.S proceeded to Sivresse	
"	29/11/18	"	2 O.R. (Minim) proceed to CAMBRAI for interview by Training Expert.	
"	30/11/18	"	Major Taylor & Statting visited 63" Field Ambulance - St Andrews Day -	

Lloyd Evans
Lt. Col. RAMC
65 F. Amb
O.C. F. Amb

CONFIDENTIAL.
MEDICAL
No U 40
140/3461

WAR DIARY
OF THE
65th FIELD AMBULANCE.
(3rd W. Lancs T.F.)

From 1/12/18
To 31/12/18.

VOLUME XXXIX
(2. Pages).

Dec 1918

65th Field Ambulance
DECEMBER 1918
Page 1 Volume XXIX

Army Form C.-2118.

WAR DIARY
INTELLIGENCE SUMMARY.
(Erase heading not required.)

Place	Date	Hour	Summary of Events and Information	Remarks and references to Appendices
LIPPONT FONTAINE	1/12/18	18 hrs	Officers visit	Photo 51
"	2/12/18	"	Parade, Football	Photos
"	3/12/18	"	Lecture on Demobilization & Finance of the War	
"	4/12/18	"	A.D.M.S. visited. Route march in afternoon.	
"	5/12/18	"	One Big Car attached to 14. N.F⁵.(?) for journey to her area.	
"	6/12/18	"	G.O.C. visited. 15 horses previous to CAMBRAI.	
"	7/12/18	"	Captain J.L. Johns R.E. travel was struck off strength from 29/11/18 on being posted to Horse Dpt.	
"	8/12/18	"	R.A.M.C. O.O. no 105 received. Route march in afternoon.	
"	9/12/18	"		
"	10/12/18	"	2 horses proceeded to CAMBRAI on Investigation.	
"	11/12/18	"	Unit marched off at 09.30 hrs & arrived BERLAIMONT 11.30 hrs	
"	12/12/18	"	" " 08.30 hrs " DYLLERS 13.15 hrs	
"	13/12/18	"	" " 09.30 hrs " INCHY 11.30 hrs	
"	14/12/18	"	Divisional Personnel Embarked at 06.00 hrs Amb Cars proceed at 07.30 hrs then fortier arrived at SAVEUSE at 14.00 hrs afford Transfort went off at 09.30 hrs & arrived AUBENCHEUL AU BOIS 14.30 hrs	

65th Field Ambulance
DECEMBER 1918
Page 2   Volume XXXIX

WAR DIARY
INTELLIGENCE SUMMARY
(Erase heading not required.)

Army Form C. 2118.

Place	Date	Hour	Summary of Events and Information	Remarks and references to Appendices
Bi Wood	18/12	18.00	Transport left AUBENCHEUL AU BOIS at 06.00 hrs arrived BUIRE	VALENCIENNES to ATHIES
"	19/12/18	"	W of TINCOURT at 15.00 hrs. Dismounted personnel finished at SAVEUSE	
			Transport left at 06.00 hrs arrived PROYART (ATHIENS halt) at 16.00 hrs	
"	20/12	"	Transport moved off at 07.00 hrs & arrived SAVEUSE (24 miles) at 16.00 hrs	
"	21/12	"	Transport personnel finished work. - Visited 64" F. Amb. at PISSY	
"	22/12	"	ADMS Office at MOLLIENS VIDAME DDMS & DADMS visited	
"	23/12	"	DADMS visited.	
"	24/12	"	Visited 110th Inf. Bgd. HQ., & 7th MMG & conference	
"	25/12	"	DDMS DADMS. T. half no work & comf. xmas dinner	
"	26/12	"	housed. Xmas festivities 72 Bde 2.1.6 Inspected.	
"	27/12/18	"	Visited Div HQ. G.O.C. 110th Brigade visited the Ambulance	
			Visited DMS & finish at B. Mess.	
			have transferred to Service in India DADMS visited.	
	29/12/18		BAPM visited & stayed to lunch. L. Pierrin & 44 DR 147 Sg RE arrived at 19.00 hrs and 6.12.22)	
	29/12/18		Visited 63rd F. Amb. Football match & 7th Leicesters. Revd. a dram	
	30/12/18		Major Sterling Int. proceeded on 8 days to Paris 1. Bg Gg performed athletics to the 1 North Refs	
	31/12/18			

Confidential.

MEDICAL

J 8 41

21 DIV Box 1876

WAR DIARY

OF THE

65th FIELD AMBULANCE

(3rd W. Lancs T.F.)

From 1/1/19
To 31/1/19.

Volume XL.
(3 Pages).

COMMITTEE FOR THE
MEDICAL HISTORY OF THE WAR
17 MAR 1919
Date

65 Field Ambulance
JANUARY 1919
Page 1. Volume XL

Army Form C. 2118.

MEDICAL

WAR DIARY

INTELLIGENCE SUMMARY.

(Erase heading not required.)

Place	Date	Hour	Summary of Events and Information	Remarks and references to Appendices
SAVEUSE	1/1/19	16:00 hrs	Dined with 1st Wilts on New Years Eve.	Appx 1.1.1.19.999
	2/1/19		Dues etc.	
	3/1/19	"	DDMS visited. Completed Report on all M.S. work sick.	
	4/1/19	"	Nil - furnished rain every day.	
	5/1/19		A med. wet officer detailed forward to Corps on evacuation Camp + one sick duty 2 OTO attached for duty to this Camp	
	6/1/19		DADMS visited + congratulated Horse Jumblers. Major R Taylor left force S.D. on leave 6 Explain. Visits DDMS + lunch at B. hines.	
	7/1/19	"	nil	
	8/1/19	"	nil	
	9/1/19	"	Major Sterling ind. reported for duty home.	
	10/1/19	"	DADMS visited. Divl Cross Country Race	
	11/1/19	"	Football Team Played 68" Field Amb + 1st armd Div Engrs Hn. Lost 3-1.	
	12/1/19	"	Lieut. Major Perry. Demobilized	
	13/1/19	"	2 OR Demobilized	
	14/1/19	"	nil	nil head out

65" Field Ambulance
JANUARY 1919
Page 2. Volume XL

Army Form C. 2118.

WAR DIARY
INTELLIGENCE SUMMARY
(Erase heading not required.)

Place	Date	Hour	Summary of Events and Information	Remarks and references to Appendices
AMIENS	15/1/19	18:00	Personal attended Lecture by G.O.C. 2nd Divn at BOVELLES	AMIENS 1-100,000
	16/1/19	"	Capt Ormes with 5 O.Rs proceeded on leave to England	
	17/1/19	"	nil	
	18/1/15	"	Remount Officers classified horses + mules in X, Y + Z. Football team played 14th N.F.(?) first last 2-0. Guard mtd. 6 b'nx+1 Lt	
	19/1/19		2 O.Rs proceeded for demobilisation	
	20/1/19		3 O.Rs " "	
	21/1/19		Remainder of horses + mules to X + Z lines Mulleins(?)	
	22/1/19		Major R Taylor returned from leave. 11 ORs proceeded for demobilisation	
	23/1/19		Medical Board on 2 Officers (Gas Concussion) in Ref Amns	
	24/1/15		Medical officers & one section marched to L-15 D.I.D for duty	
	25/1/15	"	Kit inspection	
	26/1/19	"	Harness " Corps pictures(?)	
	27/1/19	"	Proceeded on 5 weeks leave to Ireland. Handed over command to Major R Taylor on behalf of the same	

Army Form C. 2118.

65' Field Ambulance
JANUARY 1919
Page 3 Volume XL

WAR DIARY
INTELLIGENCE SUMMARY.
(Erase heading not required.)

Place	Date	Hour	Summary of Events and Information	Remarks and references to Appendices
Savrine	28/1/19	18 hour	Unit was paid out.	
	29/1/19	-	Nothing to Report	
	30/1/19	-	Nothing to Report	
	31/1/19	-	2 Other Ranks of the RASC attached proceeded to Corps Concentration Camp for demobilisation	

R Moy Lt
for OC 65th Field Amb

14/3524

No 65. + A.

Feb. 1919

WAR DIARY or INTELLIGENCE SUMMARY.

Army Form C. 2118.

65th Field Ambulance
February 1919
Page 1 Volume XLI

Place	Date	Hour	Summary of Events and Information	Remarks and references to Appendices
SAVEUSE	1/2/19	18.00	nil	AMIENS (1.10.000)
	2/2/19	"	CO visited Cohan to obtain money for the unit.	
	3/2/19	"	nil	
	4/2/19	"	ADMS visited. Two "Y" Army Chaplns horses procured & 2 Corps Sig Camp for demobilization	
	5/2/19	"	O.C. 163rd Field Ambulance visited, as an advance party from that unit to erect huts remained	
	6/2/19	"	Three O.R. proceeded for demobilization	
	7/2/19	"	One O.R. proceeded for demobilization	
	8/2/19	"	One O.R. " " " Capt W.H. Endean proceeded from leave	
	9/2/19	"	One Sgt. Can proceeded to Coulement under ADS's instructions	
	10/2/19	"	Two Can regmnt - demobilization Sgt "Y" Army Chapln horses proceeded to V Corps Horse Camp - for demobilization. Two must	
	11/2/19	"	One O.R. proceeded to Beauvais again under ADMS instruction	
	12/2/19	"	A big Can proceeded on Cyprus	
	13/2/19	"	Two O.R. proceeded for demobilization. One Sgt. one ORs on 14 days leave ("Y")	
	14/2/19	"	Two O.R. proceeded for Mobile Veterinary Sectn - Amny Brothers & Q Caps	
	15/2/19	"	Sgt Hughes proceeded to No. 3 CCS Cambray for duty. Two "Y" Army Chapln Horses & Capt's Horse Camp for demobilization	Morley

Army Form C. 2118.

65th Field Ambulance
February 1919
Page 2. Volume XLI

MEDICAL

WAR DIARY
or
INTELLIGENCE SUMMARY.
(Erase heading not required.)

Place	Date	Hour	Summary of Events and Information	Remarks and references to Appendices
SAVEUSE	16/2/19	16.00	OC CZ Rodie evacuated to No 5 (injuries to Jaw)	AMIENS 1-100,000 48 42
"	17/2/19		Lt Col Thompson resumed from leave	
"	18/2/19		Nil	
"	19/2/19		Visited ADMS at Div HQ	
"	20/2/19		2 OR (nursing orderlies) reported duty fr 41. Stay Hospl.	
"	21/2/19		3 OR demobilized. (Proceeded to Coy Concentration Camp) DADMS visited	
"	22/2/19		1 OR " " Unit find orders, held held Concert in evening	
"	23/2/19		2 OR proceeded on leave (to Paris & 1 to England) OC 51 San Section visited	
"	24/2/19		Nil Visited 62nd Fd Amb at MONDICOURT.	
"	25/2/19		Officers visited	
"	26/2/19		Nil	
"	27/2/19		Nil	
"	28/2/19		Nil	

K. Macgregor
Lieut Col
65 Fd Amb

Confidential

MEDICAL
43
140/3001

17 JUL 1919

WAR DIARY.

OF THE

65th FIELD AMBULANCE.

(3rd W. Lancs T.F.)

FROM 1/3/19
TO 31/3/19

VOLUME XLII

(3. Pages)

5

March

WAR DIARY

65th FIELD AMBULANCE

Army Form C. 2118.

INTELLIGENCE SUMMARY.

MARCH 1919

Page 1. Volume XLII

Place	Date	Hour	Summary of Events and Information	Remarks and references to Appendices
SAVEUSE	1/3/19	18:00	3 O.R. proceeded to demobilisation.	AMIENS (1-100,000)
"	2/3/19		3. " "	
"	3/3/19		2 Horse Ambulances + 2 G.S. waggons proceeded to Cadre Park at LONGPRÉ (sample)	
"	4/3/19		2 R.Dns. 2 H.D. horses, 6 mules proceeded to 7. Vety. Hospl. ADMS visited.	
"	5/3/19		1 G.S. waggon; 3 limbered waggons; 2 water carts; + 1 travelling cart proceeded to Cadre Park.	
"	6/3/19		One 2 mule limbered waggon + Corps stores Count et BOURDON.	
"	7/3/19		1 limber, 3 G.S. waggons + 1 ambulance and to Cadre Park.	
"	8/3/19		ADMS + DADMS visited.	
"	9/3/19		2 Riding + 3 Army Draft ... to both. hors. Cpl. SAVEUSE; arrived RILLY SUR SOMME 11.30 hrs. horses x marched approaches to PICQUIGNY. ... strength from then ...	
"	10/3/19		... ... t.63 7. A.of. 1 G.S. wag (for supply) + 1 water cart sent to Cadre Park. ADMS + DADMS visited. "Summary of Evidence" held in case of Pte. Hurtado + Pte. Grayson.	

Witho[?] Capt. hand.

WAR DIARY

65th FIELD AMBULANCE

MARCH 1919 Page 2 Volume XLII

Army Form C. 2118.

INTELLIGENCE SUMMARY

Place	Date	Hour	Summary of Events and Information	Remarks and references to Appendices
Army.S. Somme	12/3/19	18.00 hrs	MO and, nothing.	
"	13/3	"	"	
"	14/3	"	"	
"	15/3	"	2. R.A.S.C. O.R. Unrothype) + Received orders of Adams of Bart—	
"	16/3	"	8 March " O.C. Reported to Divl. HQ DISSY Chateau	
"	17/3	"	10 " " Report to 131 F.Aml. LONGEAU. (at 23.00 hrs) 16th am	
"	18/3	"	Rode to Army of Rhine	
"	19/3	"	till on agents of Ambulance. Visited 6th Lincolns HR. 164 F.Amb.	
"	20/3	"	1 Bn the attached to 27 M.A.C. for hospital duty. Cist. J.R. Cochrane US Vol.	
"	21/3	"	proceeded to own Division from which struck off. Strength of Offr 3wor—	
"	22/3	"	hund spine out. Visited 63rd Tk Bde.	
"	22/3	"	2. X. H⁰ horses sent to Corps horse camp. BOURDON.	
"	23/3	"	All Horses + Drawbridges suspended Temporarily	
"	23/3	"	Visited 63rd F. Ambt.	
"	24/3	"	" O.C. & 2 Bart instructed to report to A.D.M.S.	
"	25/3	"	Visited DDMS of Corps. Cause of Demobilization unpaying 27 hour.	W.A. Leyton Major

WAR DIARY
INTELLIGENCE SUMMARY.

65th FIELD AMBULANCE
MARCH 1919
Page 3. Volume XLII

Army Form C. 2118.

Place	Date	Hour	Summary of Events and Information	Remarks and references to Appendices
Ailly s. Somme	26/3	15.00	Order to M 64" 2nd cancelled. He will now what R.W.O. for h.b. in India.	AMIENS (1.100000)
"	27/3		Visited 64th 7 b.g. preparatory to taking over duties of DDMS. 6" R.M.C. & 1. R.A.S.C. O/Ranks transferred.	
"	28/3		12 mules transferred to 7 b.g. Home Com'd. Assumed duties of DDMS 7 b.g.	
"	29/3		Authority AG wire MD/596 & all Administrative MG's 7 Divs & Manual thus kept 1 hr Cadre 7 Field Ambulances will be struck off strength 7 their formation & units as from 29 March & will be shown on Manual strength 7 Areas — than in Petain Bro not, subject to 21 Div to be in A/DDMS. AMIENS Area (DDMS Corps Now continues to function).	
"	30/3		1. O.R. to army Laundries for transportation. One 7 DDMS at MOLLIENS VIDAME amalgamated with 65" FAml (S.M.O.) Mine at AILLY S. SOMME at 1500hrs. — Visited 6" FAml.	
"	31/3		Court Martial held at HQ. 7 65".FAml m Pt Dawson (charge 7 desertion)	

W Hornfgn Mng M
WJLS.RAml.

CONFIDENTIAL.

WW 44
Creed
140/3550

WAR DIARY

of the

65th Field Ambulance (West Lancs T.F.)

From 1st April 1919
To 30th April 1919.

Volume XLIII.
(3. Pages).

WAR DIARY

65th Field Ambulance
April 1919
Page 1. Volume XLIII

Army Form C. 2118.

INTELLIGENCE SUMMARY

Place	Date	Hour	Summary of Events and Information	Remarks and references to Appendices
Army S. SOMME	1/4/19	18:00 hrs	OC March returns at Corps HQ — afternoon marched K.R. 37th. Admin group at (VECQUEMONT) & 193 & 202 P.O.W. camps. Visited 65 F.Amb. in afternoon.	
"	2/4/19		Capt v.D.in Su Klein visited Cache Park (LONGPRÉ)	
"	3/4/19		Unit fond out — Sedan 1 2 pm. 1 HP perambulator. In case of 1st Division (Direction).	
"	4/4/19		6/DN... Billeting party proceeds to Con DIE-FOLIE OC handed over his duties to 6/DIVS. & took to F.Med. R.A. Bry.Fem.DDD (on leave then from leave)	
CONDIE. FOLIE.	5/4/19		Unit left Aux. S. Somme at 10:15 hr. & arrived at CONDIE FOLIE at 12:00 hrs. DS-AR. units from DOZIENS verse at 11:00 hrs. & Office 2 Stak.R Decd at Con DE FOZIE rendering victus DDMS & 63" & 64 F.Field Ambulances. Collin E.C.W. Stak Bac Order to help 6 F.Cop Carculation Camp & a Con attached to him from to Whirley per 27 M.A.C. W.H... kurd...	

WAR DIARY
of
INTELLIGENCE SUMMARY.
(Erase heading not required.)

Army Form C. 2118.

65th Field Ambulance
April 1919
Page 2, Volume XLIII

Place	Date	Hour	Summary of Events and Information	Remarks and references to Appendices
CONDIE FOLIE	6/4/15	18.00 hrs	4. O.R. Went [Proceeded] for Demobilization & 2. Cor. B. Infantry (6/H) A.S.C. H.T.) proceeded to 61st Divn.	
"	7/4/15		reached 63rd F.Amb.	
"	8/4/15		OTHER Office & 64th Field Amb. Inspection of Advance Depot. Infantry man proceeded to 61st Divn.	
"	9/4/15		1. Cor. B Infantryman proceeded to 61st Divn.	
"	10/4/15		Nil — Quiet Period out Captain P.M. Little proceeded to 37 Labour Front (MEAULTE) for Rudolph's kits (under instruction from GHQ)	
"	11/4/15		Visited 64th Field Ambulance.	
"	12/4/15		Captain T.H.R. Shaw proceeded on leave to England — (13th – 27th)	
"	13/4/15		2. O.R. (all Mr. Rons Men) proceeded to Cox Investment Camp at Dunkirk	
"	14/4/15		1. Ambulance attached to 51st Sanitation Section (from 64 F.Amb)	
"	15/4/15		OC 2nd Bat Train arrived	
"	16/4/15		1. O.R. (Kenn) 63rd F.Amb. posted to 2nd Divn. (DUREN).	

W.M.W
Lt. Col.

WAR DIARY

65th Field Ambulance
April 1919
Page 3, Volume XLIII

Army Form C. 2118.

INTELLIGENCE SUMMARY

(Erase heading not required.)

Place	Date	Hour	Summary of Events and Information	Remarks and references to Appendices
COND'T E- FOLIE	17/4/19	16.00	Unit hand over 1. O.R. 1st Dawson hand'g over to D.A.P.M. for commitment of prison - (2 yr. I.H.L.)	
"	18/4/19	"	Visited 64th F. Amb.	
"	19/4/19	"	1. O.R. nurse proceed'd C. 2nd Div for duty.	
"	20/4/19	"	2 O.R. R.A.S.C. (M.T. + I.M.T.) proceed't for demobilmplan. Captain R. Taylor proceed'd on leave to England. (24.4.19 - 5.5.19) Capt. Arno hill on a case of apparent encounter's wound in a P.G. blasphie to 718. A.E Coy. – Visited 64 Field Ambulance.	
"	21/4/19	"	D.M.D.M.S. to 3. Div. M., OC 64 & 2 Amb., OC. 3 Coy trans. visited.	
"	22/4/19	"	Visited 63rd Field Ambulance.	
"	23/4/19	"	Captain W.H. Sublin rejoined from leave at home.	
"	24/4/19	"	Unit hand over. OC 64th F.Amb. visited	
"	25/4/19	"	Nil	
"	26/4/19	"	3. O.R. near R.P.S.C. proceed'd for demobilisation	
"	27/4/19	"	L.C.M. in Mc.Farland + Gillgrich - 14.4.19 Wts. Promulgation	
"	28/4/19	"	Initial Road hill on patient to today.	
"	29/4/19	"	Calos of 65th F. Amb. entrained to the U.K. demob'n Catterick.	
"	30/4/19	"		

Confidential.

95/45
W/3500

WAR DIARY
OF THE
65th FIELD AMBULANCE
(2nd W. Lancs T.F.)

From 1/5/19
To 31/5/19.

VOLUME XLIV
(4 pages)

Army Form C. 2118.

WAR DIARY
INTELLIGENCE SUMMARY
(Erase heading not required.)

May 1919 Page 1 Volume XLIV

Instructions regarding War Diaries and Intelligence Summaries are contained in F. S. Regs., Part II. and the Staff Manual respectively. Title pages will be prepared in manuscript.

Place	Date	Hour	Summary of Events and Information	Remarks and references to Appendices
Conque Fra. 1.E	1/5/15	18.00 hrs	2/Lt N.S.E. BENNETT rejoins unit in France (absence in England)	
"	2/5/15		Runners of 2 Civilians taken in Town by 2/Lt BENNETT.	
"	3/5/15		1. O.R. transf. rd. R.A.S.C. (M.T.) proceeded to SAVEUSE for interval	
"	4/5/15		Unit paid out. Played Gr. 2nd Batt. fielded. Lost 1–0	
"	5/5/15		hil	
"	6/5/15		hil	
"	7/5/15		F.G.C.M. held at Staff Office to trial of 2/Lt BENNETT	
"	8/5/15		Visited Gr. 2nd Batt.; Captain W.H. Snellen presented to leave to England 10/5 – 24/5/15.	
"	9/5/15		hpm Vs. Graham 60 hrs. Rev. Capt. proceeded to England by Repatriation to Dunkerken (Inf. 45.G)	
"	10/5/15		Referral to Archival House to Repatriation. Sentence promulgated on trans. Capt. R. Taylor but beyond two leave	
"	11/5/15		2/Lt Bennett in S.E. Rep. P.P. No 2	
"	12/5/15		2/Lt Bennett sent to Prisoners Cage at FLIXECOURT. Is met by this Forces until he knows his kit met. Reassuring to service OR to the B/s/s	
"	13/5/15		Warren Officer received Pt. by 2/Lt sent to the bakery. Posted to S.S.C.C.S. 3 Crlan. Rem. Sheffield & 76. F. Ambulance.	

D. D. & L., London, E.C.
(A10256) W1. W5300/P713 750,000 2/18 Sch. 52 Forms/C2118/16.

Army Form C. 2118.

WAR DIARY
INTELLIGENCE SUMMARY
(Erase heading not required.)

May 1919 Page 2. Volume XLIV

Place	Date	Hour	Summary of Events and Information	Remarks and references to Appendices
CONDÉ FOLIE	14/5/19	15:45	Orders will Major Paton at NOUVRS.	
"	15/5/19	—	Acclimation handed to DADS. Then started "search for booties". When 2nd Lt G.R.H. Family handover.	missing column
"	16/5/19	—	Proceeded with Major Paton by car to Boulogne. Major Paton (an) Captain for Runnelington. Mangled W. Henderson back from Boulogne.	
"	17/5/19	5.230 (New Form)	Arrived AMIENS 4.45.	
"			20. OR Rank & 4 RASC (3 H.T. & 1 M.T.) attached to Corps Concentration Camp SOMEUSE. 1 OR (RASC H.T.) proceeds to 14 AUX Horse Co. & R Inf. (D. Mitchell). 31. OR Rank & 64 "Amb" reported to Capt.	
"	18/5/19	—	at SOMEUSE. Instruction received for movement. Shelters & F. report hiterits for date with Cadre 2, 59th 7 Amt. & take it to Eurflen.	
"	19/5/19	—	21 OR M.T. proceeds home via HAVRE. Cadre Shepherd order 59 7 Amb Cancelled. Proceeds them by road Cadre 2/52; 2Amb (3 Ofrs) to Gudus et LONGPRÉ. He leaves NR St. Pansa en R. at 10 et LONGPRÉ at 3 pm.	

Army Form C. 2118.

WAR DIARY
INTELLIGENCE SUMMARY.
(Erase heading not required)

May 1919 Page 3 Volume XLIV

Place	Date	Hour	Summary of Events and Information	Remarks and references to Appendices
LONGPRÉ FOL.E.	20/5/	18 hrs	Moved to ABBEVILLE & handed to O.C. Balance of 64th F.A.B. (Infant Pr.) Dest. deputation Roll 1/5 forwarded to Stf Paymaster Williams. Horse standing & vehicles & distance Inspected 7 in F.A.B. – T.C.S. LONGPRÉ Receipts Nos. 1096, ret. to D.D.O.S. to 3. Area	Lecture items received
	21/5/		Capta R. Taylor proceeded by car to BERNICOURT to report to A.P.M., Tank Corps HQ for duty.	
	22/5/		Captain + Qr.m. E.T. Grundy returned his animal to command came 2/ 64" F.A.B. He proceeded to return to join 59" Field Amb to take care 2 the wind horse S. OR. Hama 64" F.A.B. proceed to SAVEUSE for dispersal C.O.E. 10 hr H. Embleton rejoined from leave (recalled) + resumed command 2 carbine 2 65" field Amb balance	

Army Form C. 21

WAR DIARY
INTELLIGENCE SUMMARY.
(Erase heading not required.)

May 1919   page 4   Volume XLIV

Place	Date	Hour	Summary of Events and Information	Remarks and references to Appendices
CONDÉ FOLIE	23/5/19	18.00	Visited No 2. Stationary Hosp. ABBEVILLE & enquired there. Visited the DTTS hospital? (Rouen)	
"	24/5/19	"	bil - weather still fine & warm.	
"	25/5/19	"	Visited No 3. Area H.Q. Snow telp. Pki visited I.O.R. west (HT) parades to 14 ATS Cavs Hosp Cr SOESNES	
"	26/5/19	"	but paid out.	
"	27/5/19	"	Proceeded to ABBEVILLE & handed & referred to Hunt Corbie	
"	28/5/19	"	4.O.R. hand (Ge "Field Amt") proceeded for Sandringham direct with fried & Top hmp later.	
"	29/5/19	"	bil	
"	30/5/19	"	Snow. Top. pmp Pkt. Captain Alexander rocket	(Bow) =
"	31/5/19	"	bil. weather still very hot.	W Shamelevan manjor right arme Lt Col madlevan

160/3584-

28 AUG 1919

63 M + 39

O.A.

June 1919

WAR DIARY 65 Field Ambulance
June 1919
INTELLIGENCE SUMMARY.
Page 1 Volume XLV

Vol 46

Place	Date	Hour	Summary of Events and Information	Remarks
CONDÉ FOLIE	1/6/19		8 O.R. men proceed to 10 C.A. Concentration Camp for Demobilization	
	2/6/19			
	3/6/19		Orders received to hand in Surplus Medical Equipment & vehicles	
	4/6/19		Medical & Ordnance Equipment handed in to 39 D.S.S store	
			POULAINVILLE & I.C.S. LONGPRÉ respectively	
	5/6/19		5 O.R. men received liveries to T.C. Camp. Advised for demobilization. Chief Guns then finally broken up. Captain & Major 467 Surplus received instructions to report to 76 Field Ambulance.	

K. Thompson Nehow
Major
5/6/19 Cmdg 21 Divn
Field Park Unit